Journal of Biblical Literature

Monograph Series, Volume VI

TANNAITIC PARALLELS TO THE GOSPELS

by

Morton Smith, Ph.D.

Society of Biblical Literature
224 North Fifteenth Street
Philadelphia 2, Pennsylvania
1951

Copyright 1951
Society of Biblical Literature

The present monograph is the revised form of a dissertation written in Hebrew, for which the author received the degree of Doctor of Philosophy from the Hebrew University in Jerusalem.

The editors of the Journal of Biblical Literature are grateful to Professors Harry A. Wolfson and Robert H. Pfeiffer of Harvard University for their help in obtaining funds for the publication of this work from the Lucius N. Littauer Foundation, which several years ago made possible the inauguration of this monograph series. To Mr. Harry Starr, president of the foundation, and to the scholarly consultants who read and approved the manuscript we express our warm thanks.

Ralph Marcus

Editor of the Monograph Series

TO MY PARENTS

PREFACE

Apart from the debt to my parents which I have acknowledged in the dedication, I must thank, first of all, Professors H. J. Cadbury and H. A. Wolfson and Dean W. L. Sperry, whose influence obtained for me the funds necessary to go to Jerusalem and to stay there. These funds were given by the Sheldon Committee of Harvard University and by the American Schools of Oriental Research, and to these groups also I express my sincere gratitude. Since my return I have again been indebted to Professors Cadbury and Wolfson, as well as to Professor R. H. Pfeiffer for reading and recommendation of this work, and to Professor Ralph Marcus, Editor of the Monograph Series, for many helpful suggestions and, above all, for his patience. To the trustees of the Littauer Foundation I owe many thanks for their provision of the funds which have made this publication possible.

I cannot here name all the many persons to whom I am indebted for kindnesses shown me while in Jerusalem. Therefore I shall mention only Professor M. Schwabe, who directed this work and whose corrections enabled me to eliminate many mistakes. It is my duty also to state that Professor Schwabe gave me complete freedom in the composition of this work and that consequently its structure and style are by no means in perfect accord with his taste. Specifically, I have begun each chapter with a discussion of what seemed to me the most important of the previous works dealing with the subject therein to be treated, and have used such critical discussion as an introduction of whatever new things I had to say. Usually, in the course of these introductory discussions, I have found errors requiring correction, and consequently the first sections of several chapters have an acid tang of which Professor Schwabe did not always approve. However, as the chapters had been completely written before he saw them, he was content to let them stay, in main outline, as they were. For this I wish to thank him particularly, and to take this opportunity of emphasizing that I alone am responsible not only for all the statements made in this work, but also for the manner and connotations of their arrangement.

Jerusalem, 1944,   M. S.

Providence, 1950.

TABLE OF CONTENTS*

-----

*The notes are numbered consecutively within each chapter and follow the chapter.

INTRODUCTION

By the term 'Tannaitic Literature' (hereinafter TL) I mean the following works: the Mishnah, Tosefta, Mekilta, Mekilta of Rabbi Simon, Sifra, Sifre on Numbers, Sifre Zutta, Sifre on Deuteronomy, Midrash Tannaim, and certain of the oldest prayers of the Jewish liturgy, especially the Eighteen Benedictions.

The use of the term TL to refer to these works and to these alone is an arbitrary limitation made for the sake of convenience; I would not have the reader suppose that I think no sayings of the Tannaim are reported in other collections - for instance, in the Talmuds - nor that I think all the material in these works (and particularly in Midrash Tannaim) is Tannaitic. My selection of these works for comparison with the Gospels, and my selection of this term to refer to the lot of them, have been determined solely by convenience.

I do think, however, that these works chosen constitute, by representation, a literature, and in the following chapters I propose to discuss a number of parallels between them and the Gospels; again for the sake of convenience, I shall refer to the Gospels also as a 'literature.' The texts I have used are listed together with the scholarly works referred to. For the most part I have concentrated my attention on the texts as printed by the editors, and have considered variant readings only when that seemed necessary for the understanding of a passage.

The midrashim are cited according to the chapter and verse on which they comment, thus Sifra 23.12 means Sifra on Leviticus 23.12. When tractates of Tosefta are cited, the name of the tractate is followed by T; when no T follows, the tractate is from the Mishnah.

In translation I have often preferred idiomatic English to word-for-word accuracy. Transliteration I have simplified for typographical convenience: A simplified system adequately indicates, to those who know the original languages, the words transliterated; those who do not know the original languages would not be helped by greater accuracy. Familiar names have been left in their familiar forms. What is familiar? I don't quite know, but the line falls somewhere between Eliezer and Elazar. Paul's teacher is Gamaliel and his descendants of the same name are Gamliel.

In discussion of the parallels I have attempted to classify them according to their various natures and have begun each chapter with an effort to define the nature of the parallels therein to be discussed. This classification seems to me one of the most important respects in which this work differs from its predecessors. Those who previously wrote on such parallels made no attempt to classify them by nature; therefore they either produced lists in which all sorts were strung together indiscriminately - as in Strack-Billerbeck - or they divided the material according to the various academic interests of the previous students, as did, for example, G. Kittel in <u>Die Probleme des palästinischen Spätjudentums u. das Urchristentum</u> (Stuttgart, 1926), which takes up, in order, problems of archaeology, linguistics, form-criticism, literary history, the history of religion, and comparative religions - clearly a division of the subject matter according to external criteria, without consideration of its natural divisions. Incidentally, the effort to work out a more natural classification has called to my attention several types of parallel which hitherto have been practically unnoticed.

In the following chapters I have tried, also, to emphasize the difference between the facts actually revealed by the comparison of the texts, and the explanations of these facts current in the form of historical theories. However, the primary concern of this book is rather philological than philosophical, therefore, as directly concerned with fact, it could give only occasional and passing notice to theory. For the same reason, I have not attempted a complete classification of all the possible forms of literary parallelism, which would be rather a philosophical than a philological exercise. The following chapters list only some of the more important classes, illustrating each by a number of examples.

Chapter 1

VERBAL PARALLELS

Of the sorts of parallels hereinafter to be discussed, the simplest is the verbal. One word may resemble another in one or more of several ways: semantically (λέγω — אומרני), or grammatically (εἶπαν – שלחו), or etymologically. In this chapter I shall discuss only etymological parallels, and of these only one group - for it is necessary to distinguish, for example, between parallels like שולחני[1]- τραπεζίτης, [2], אשמורה[3]- φυλακή, [4], and between parallels like משיח[5] - Μεσσίας [6], ליסטיס[7] – ληστής[8]. Words of the first group are parallel in respect of formation - τραπεζίτης being formed from τράπεζα as שולחני from שולחן, and שולחן corresponds in meaning to τράπεζα as שולחני does to τραπεζίτης, so that the two latter terms are etymologically similar.[9] But the two words משיח and Μεσσίας are similar by reason of their derivation from a single root, and it is only such parallels, that is to say, the Semitic words in the Greek of the Gospels, and the Greek and Latin words in TL, which are here to be considered.

The difficulty of determining the roots of these foreign terms is illustrated by the differences of opinion between the experts in the two fields. So, for example, in the criticism of the Gospels, Grätz[10] thought that the word καναναῖος found in Mat 10.4 was correctly translated by ζηλοτής in Lk 6.15. Strack-Billerbeck concurred in this opinion.[11] But Torrey[12] thinks that it is impossible to get καναγαῖος from קנאי and therefore supposes for its source קנני , a word of his own formation which he explains as 'a man from the village of Cana in Galilee.' (How far, in the literature of this period, it is possible to rely on such distinctions of one or two letters, will appear in the course of this chapter. Here it is sufficient to cite only one example of variations of spelling found in a single passage of one MS. In Shabbat T, 10.1-2(123) the word strata is written: אסטרא , סרטא, א׳סרטא, and in 10.13 (124), א׳סטרט׳א.

Yet another example of differences of opinion: Fiebig[13] thought Ἰσκαριώθ [14] (and its variants) derived from א׳ש־קריות, and Strack-Billerbeck[15] agreed with him. But Wellhausen[16] had previously written that in the days of Jesus the word א׳ש was no longer used, and this in spite of the fact that names compounded with א׳ש are found about twenty-five times in the Mishnah alone.[17] Now Torrey,[18] relying on the opinion of Wellhausen, has gone on to derive the name from the root שקר . It is interesting to note that we know of one man whose name was certainly compounded with א׳ש and who may very

well have been a disciple of Jesus, to wit, יעקב איש כפר סמא, concerning whom we are told in <u>Hullin T</u> 2.22 (503) that he came to cure
R. Elazar ben Dama in the name of Yeshua ben Pantera.

Many such contradictions are found in the criticism of the Gospels.
The single question: From what Semitic word is Ναζωραῖos [19] (and
its variants) derived? has called forth a small literature;[20] and there
are even some words which are thought Greek by some critics and
Semitic by others, for example μωρέ in Mat 5.22, which is generally
thought a form of μωρόs, but which Schulthess[21] has explained as a
Greek transliteration of מורה.[22]

In the criticism of TL, questions of the latter class, to wit, whether
a given word be Greek or Semitic, are more customary and more important than those of the former - From <u>which</u> Greek word is derived
the form found in the text? However, examples of this sort, too, are
not hard to find, and there is even one passage (<u>Abodah Zarah T</u> 2.5-7
(462)) in which three successive verses admit of completely different
interpretations according to the different interpretations given the
Greek or Latin words they contain. I translate the text as printed in
Zuckermandel's edition, leaving the dubious words untranslated:

' "He who goes up to the תרטיאות of the gentiles (is doing a thing)
prohibited on the ground that it is an occasion of idolatry." - the words
of R. Meir. But the majority say, "When they are sacrificing it is
prohibited on the ground that it is an occasion of idolatry, and if they
are not sacrificing it is prohibited on the ground (that the place is a)
'seat of the scornful.' " He who goes to   איצטרטיונין and to
כרקומין and sees the serpents and the charmers [or: the sleight-
of-hand tricks and the crowds. The Hebrew is ambiguous.]   בוקיון
and   סגלריא , סגלריון , מוליין , מוקיון - behold, this is a
'seat of the scornful,' for it is said, 'nor sitteth in the seat of the
scornful, but in the Law of the Lord is his delight.' (Ps. 1.1-2) See,
you have learned that these bring a man to neglect the Law. He who
goes up to תרטייאות (and) cheers [so the Vienna MS and the printed
eds.] because of the need of his city - this is permitted; if he calculate (to benefit himself by so doing) - this is forbidden. He who sits
[or: dwells] in איסטרטון is (guilty as if he were) shedding blood.
R. Nathan permits (it) for two reasons: Because he cheers and (so)
saves lives, and (because, if he see a man killed, he can) bear witness
concerning the widow (that she is surely a widow) so that she can
(re)marry. Men may walk to   איצטריונין because (there one)
cheers and (so) saves lives, and to כרקום because of the population
of the city, and if one calculate (to benefit himself by so doing) - this
is forbidden.'

The basis of the difficulty here is the confusion of the Hebrew
words corresponding to στρατ(ε)ία , θέατρον, and perhaps also
to στάδιον and <u>castra</u>.[23] For the first of the untranslated words
Jastrow - with specific references to this passage - proposes, s.v.

2

סרטיא, the equivalent στρατεία, and s.v. תיאטרון, the equivalent θέατρον . His subsequent interpretation fluctuates between the meanings required by <u>army</u> and <u>theatre</u>. איצטרטיונין he thinks a corruption of אצטדין which he derives from סרר and believes a scornful paradoy of θέατρον , meaning a place of corrupt pleasures; but it could equally well have come from στάδιον or either στρατεία(ν) or στρατιά(ν) . כרקומין he takes as equivalent to כרכומין , and כרכום he thinks a fortified city; but it could just as well be derived from <u>circus</u>. בוקיון and the following words he refers to the theatre and gives as equivalents βουκκίων, <u>Maccus</u>, <u>mulio, saeculares</u> and <u>sigillaria</u> (of which the first three are characters in Latin comedy, the last are the final days of the Saturnalia); had he referred them to the army he could have found equally plausible equivalents in <u>buccina</u>, <u>machina</u>, <u>molis</u>, <u>singulares</u>, and <u>sagittarii</u>. תרטיאות he takes as from στρατεία, but it could have come from θέατρον ; אסטרטון (as above) from סרר and θέατρον , but it could have come from στρατ(ε)ία ; and so on. He does not refer any of these forms etymologically to στάδιον, nor to <u>castra</u>, and I am by no means sure whether <u>castra</u> be involved or not, whether or not one should consider the possibility that some influence has been exerted by yet other words, like <u>strata</u>, and whether or not one should suppose, with Jastrow, that for reasons of ridicule the word θέατρον appears in Hebrew not only in the form תיאטרון and its variants (טיאטרון , תרטיאות, etc.), but also in forms like אצטדיא and אצטדין (according to Jastrow from the root צד) and אצטריא and אצטרין (according to Jastrow from the root סרר) and their variants (אסטריא etc.) and the variants of their variants (אסטרטיאות and the like).[24] Since στρατ(ε)ία also appears in the forms אסטרטיא and סרטיא and their descendants, it is quite impossible to know which Greek words were originally referred to in the first part of this section, and quite possible to pardon Jastrow for having translated the passage in one place according to one interpretation, in another place according to another.

No doubt the scribes who copied the MSS of Tosefta were similarly confused, and from their confusion the section emerged thus consistently ambiguous. But it would seem desirable at least to interpret the ambiguity consistently. Thus if one goes to the theatre or the stadium and sees Maccus and his ilk, then כרקום in the immediate context is probably <u>circus</u>. Or if one does go to the כרכום in what Jastrow believed to be its Hebrew meaning[25] - then he must also go to the army and see the weapons and soldiers listed above.[26] However, Jastrow's interpretation of the last section of the passage is more plausible: R. Nathan permitted two different things - to sit in the (audience of the) stadium because by appropriate outcry one helps to save the gladiator who asks for mercy,[27] and to go to camp or take part in military expeditions because one is thus enabled as a witness

3

to prove the widowhood of a woman whose husband was killed in the military operations. Nevertheless, even here it is possible to understand the text according to the alternate meaning.

As this example has shown, the question: From <u>which</u> foreign word comes the form found in the text? is by no means strange to the criticism of TL, nor to that of the Gospels. But more important and more frequent in the criticism of TL is the question whether a given word be foreign or not. This question is important because efforts have been made to gauge from the Greek and Latin words in TL the extent of the influence exercized on this literature by the Greco-Roman culture and to determine in which fields this influence was greater, in which less. Thus Jastrow in the preface to his dictionary[28] (in which he began from the supposition that the Greek influence on TL was very small and <u>thence</u> concluded that dubious words must be explained from Semitic roots) was actually begging the question, for his task should have been, first of all, to show, from examination of the vocabulary, how great the Greek influence on TL actually was. And there is no question that his supposition led him into many errors. He erred, for instance, in attempting to explain: איסתניס [29] (i.e. ἀσθενής) from נ״ס, אסטלית [30] (i.e. στολή) from טלל, אוכלוס [31] (i.e. ὄχλος) from כלי, איסטמא [32] (i.e. στέμμα) from צם, and טפוס [33] (i.e. τύπος) from טפף. Admittedly, not all his explanations were of this sort, but how far he succeeded in reducing the number of foreign words in TL, and how much further yet he wished to reduce it, is easily seen from a comparison of his explanations of the suspect words in <u>Shabbat</u> with the explanations given by Fiebig in his article <u>Das Griechisch der Mischna</u>.[34] Fiebig gave an almost complete list of the Greek and Latin words in <u>Shabbat</u> (of the certain examples he skipped only האספני in 22.2 and לובדקי in 5.1, and in place of קורדי״מא in 22.6 he cited פ״לומה - i.e. πήλωμα - which is found there in the <u>Yerushalmi</u>). From his list I have excluded: דוכסוסטוס (i.e. δίξεστος (sic)[35] which is suspect by reason of the readings in the better MSS, ס״קרא and פקס for which Fiebig himself thought Semitic derivation likely, סנבטי׳ן of the source of which he professed himself ignorant, and ק״ק (i.e. κίκι) and אספור (i.e. ψάλιον) which are no less foreign to Greek and Latin than to Hebrew. The remaining words of his list (with the three mentioned above, which he omitted)[36] are as follows:

(I have added the derivations given by Krauss[37] and by Jastrow when one or the other differed substantially from those given by Fiebig.)

Word	Cited from	Fiebig	Jastrow		Krauss
אויר	11.3	ἀήρ		אור	ἀήρ (sic)
אובזין	1.6	ἶνες		אובזא	ἶνες (sic)
גילפקס	3.5; 8.5	λοπάς		למפס	λοπάς
גיספלנית	19.2	σπλήνιον		בלע	σπλήνιον (sic)
ונדרוגינוס	19.3	ἀνδρόγυνος			
אלונטמת	22.5 (twice)	λέντιον		לוטי	λέντιον
אנדיפי	8.4	νετώπιον	בשיפות		νετώπιον
אנומלין	20.2	οἰνόμελι	οἰνόμελι		οἰνόμηλον
אנטכי	3.4	ἀγγοθήκη	ἀγγοθήκη		ἀνθράκιον
אבקטמין	6.8	ὄνος κατ' ὤμον		אנק קסמין	ὄνος κατ' ὤμον
אסטיס	7.5	ἰσάτις			
אספני	22.2	F. omits	hispanus		Ἱσπανία
אסקופה	10.2 (twice)	σκόπος (sic)		סקף	σκοπός
אפקרטיזין	22.6	ἀποκοτταβισμός	ἀποκοτταβίζειν		ἀπέκπτυσις
בולסי	1.2	βυρσική			
ביברי	13.5	βιβάριον			
גווטורא	11.2	ξυστός		גזר	ἐξώστρα
גמון	5.4	κημός		גמם	K. lacks
דיגמא	10.1	δεῖγμα			
דיוטא	11.2	δίαιτα			
הילמי	14.2 (twice)	ἅλμη			
טבלא A	21.3	τάβλα			
כובלת B	6.3 (twice)	κοχλίας		כלכל	K. lacks
כוליאר	6.3	κοχλιάριον			
כרוב C	8.5	κράμβη		כרב	κράμβη
כרכר	8.6; 17.2	κερκίς		כרר	κερκίς
לבלר	1.3	λιβελλάριος	librarius		libellarius
לגין	20.2	λάγυνος		לגג	lagena
לודקי	5.1	F. omits	Libycus		Laodiceus
לסטיס	2.5	λῃστής			
מוליר	3.4	μιλιάριον			
מרצופין	8.5	μαρσύπιον		רצף [38]	marsupium
בוטריקון	12.5	νοταρικόν			
סודרין	3.3; 20.2	σουδάριον		סדר [39]	σουδάριον
סיבר	10.4	ζωνάριον		סור	K. lacks
סלון	3.4	σωλήν		סלן	σωλήν
סם	12.4	σῆμα		סמם	σῆμα D
סממניות E	12.3	σημεῖον			K. lacks
סנדל	6.2,5; 10.3; 15.2	σάνδαλον	Persian		σάνδαλον
ספוג	21.3	σπόγγος		ספג [40]	σπόγγος
ספסל	23.5	συμψέλλιον		ספל	συμψέλλιον
פונדא	10.3 (twice)	φούνδα			
פלייטון	6.3; 8.2	φολᾶτον (sic)			
פנקס	12.4,5	πίναξ			
פסקיא	15.2 (twice)	φασκία			
פרומביא	5.1	φορβεία (sic)			
פרף F	6.6,7 (twice)	πόρπη			
פתקין	10.4	πιττάκιον		פתק	πιττάκιον
קובא	23.2	κυβεία			
קוליס	22.2	κολίας			
קולמוס	1.3; 8.5	κάλαμος			
קומוס	12.4	κόμμι			
קופה	4.2; 8.2; 9.7; 10.2(twice) 18.1	κύπη		קפף	κύπη
קורדיימה	22.6	F. read פילומה	κήρωμα		K. read פילומא
קורנס	12.1; 17.2	κορύνη		קרן	κέαρνος [42]
קטלא	6.1	κατέλλα			
קילור	8.1	κολλύριον			
קירוס	13.2	καῖρος	καῖρος		καιρός (sic)
קיתון	4.2	κώθων			
קמוליא G	9.5	κιμωλία (γῆ)			
קנקנתום	12.4	χάλκανθος			
קסא	6.2	κάσσις			
תורמוס	18.1	θέρμος			
תיק	16.1 (twice)	θήκη			
תריס	6.4	θυρεός		הרס	θυρεός

A: F. & J. write סובלת. C: F. & K. write כרכר. E: F. writes סמיון G: F., J. & K. all write קלקנתום
B: F., כובלת; J., כוליאר. D: but v. note to p. 398. F: F, פרוק, K., פרוס

From the number of Hebrew roots here given by Jastrow, it can be seen how greatly, in the matter of derivation, the opinions of experts differ. In terms of numbers: There are, in the list, 65 words, occurring in all 89 times. According to Jastrow only 38 of these words came from Greek or Latin, and these 38 words are found only 46 times. It can be seen, also, that neither side is entirely in the right. On the one hand, there is no cause to think סנדל a sign of specifically Greek influence, and סמניות - certainly a more difficult form than סמין - cannot easily be explained by reference to σημεῖον. On the other hand, to derive איספלנית from בלע and אלונטית from לוט is impossible.

The importance of this discussion becomes yet clearer when we compare the above list with the list of the Semitic words found in the Gospels. But here also there is no certain list. That given at the end of Thayer's dictionary[43] is by no means complete and includes or excludes words in a fashion completely arbitrary. For example: Ἰουδαῖος (although found twice as an adjective) is not included, but Ἰουδαϊκός is; βεελζεβούλ is, but Γαβριήλ is not; and so on. The following list contains all the Semitic words in the Gospels - to the best of my knowledge - except proper nouns, and all instances of their occurrence except those of Ἰουδαῖος - Ἰουδαία used as a noun, and of ἀμήν. I have included nicknames and also adjectives formed from proper nouns (even when, like Μαγδαληνή, they almost constituted proper nouns themselves) and also two doubtful cases, σατᾶν and γέεννα. In questions of spelling I have always followed the usage of Nestle, and so in questions of reading, but I have included in parentheses several words not found in his text. The sign Δ indicates words not in Thayer's list; the sign (?), words of which the root may not have been Semitic.[44]

ἀββά	Mk 14.36[45]
Δ ἀλόη	Jn 19.39
ἀμήν	Mat 30 plus two dubious; Mk 13 plus two dubious; Lk 6; Jn 50.
(βάρ	Mat 16.17)
βάτος	Lk 16.6
βοανηργές	Mk 3.17
γαββαθά	Jn 19.13
Δ γαδαρηνός	Mat 8.28
Δ γαλιλαῖος	Mat 26.69; Mk 14.70; Lk 13.1,2 (twice); 22.59; 23.6; Jn 4.45
γέεννα	Mat 5.22,29,30; 10.28; 18.9; 23.15,33; Mk 9.43, 45,47; Lk 12.5
Δ γερασηνός	(?) Mk 5.1; Lk 8.26,37
γολγοθά	Mat 27.33; Mk 15.22; Jn 19.17
(ἑβραϊκός	Lk 23.38)

ἑβραϊστί	Jn 5.2; 19.13,17,20; 20.16
ἐλωΐ	Mk 15.34 (twice)
ἐμμανουήλ	Mat 1.23
ἐφφαθά	Mk 7.34
ζιζάνιον	Mat 13.25,26,27,29,30,36,38,40
ἠλί	Mat 24.46 (twice)
Δ ἱεροσολυμίτης	Mk 1.5; Jn 7.25
Δ Ἰουδαῖος	(adjective) Jn 3.22, Mk 1.5
	(noun) (Ἰουδαῖος) Mat 5, Mk 6, Lk 5,
	Jn 68 plus 2 dubious (Ἰουδαία) Mat 8,
	Mk 3 plus 1 dubious. Lk 9 plus 1 dubious,
	Jn 6
Δ Ἰσραηλίτης	Jn 1.47
Δ κάμηλος	Mat 3.4; 19.24; 23.24; Mk 1.6; 10.25; Lk 18.25
καναναῖος	Mat 10.4; Mk 3.18
Δ κηφᾶς	Jn 1.42
κορβᾶν	Mk 7.11
κορβανᾶς	Mat 27.6[46]
κόρος	Lk 16.7
κοῦμ	Mk 5.41
Δ κύμινον	Mat 23.23
Δ λευΐτης	Lk 10.32; Jn 1.19
λαμά	Mk 15.34
λεμά	Mat 27.46
Δ λίβανος	Mat 2.11
Δ μαγδαληνή	Mat 27.56,61; 28.1; Mk 15.40,47; 16.1,9;
	Lk 8.2; 24.10; Jn 19.25; 20.1,18
Δ μάγος	(?) Mat 2.1,7,16 (twice)
μαμωνᾶς	Mat 6.24; Lk 16.9,11,13
μάννα	Jn 6.31,49
μεσσίας	Jn 1.41; 4.25
Δ μύρον	Mat 26.7, (9),12; Mk 14.3,4,5; Lk 7.37,38,46;
	23.56; Jn 11.2; 12.3 (twice), 5
μωρέ	(?) Mat 5.22
Δ ναζαρηνός	Mk 1.24; 10.47; 14.67; 16.6; Lk 4.34; 24.19
Δ ναζωραῖος	Mat 2.23; 26.71; Lk 18.37; Jn 18.5,7; 19.19
Δ νάρδος	(?) Mk 14.3, Jn 12.3
Δ νινευίτης	Mat 12.41; Lk 11.30,32
Δ οὐά	Mk 15.29
Δ οὐαί	Mat 11.21; 18.7 (twice); 23.13,(14),15,16,23,25,
	27,29; 24.19; 26.24; Mk 13.17; 14.21; Lk 6.24,
	25 (twice), 26; 10.13; 11.42,43,44,46,47,52;
	17.1; 21.23; 22.22
πάσχα	Mat 26.2,17,18,19; Mk 14.1,12 (twice), 14,16;
	Lk 2.41; 22.1,7,8,11,13,15; Jn 2.13,23; 6.4;
	11.55 (twice); 12.1; 18.28,39; 19.14

προσάββατον	Mk 15.42
ραββί	Mat 23.7,8; 26.25,49; Mk 9.5; 11.21; 14.45; Jn 1.38,49; 3.2,26; 4.31; 6.25; 9.2; 11.8
ραββουνί	Mk 10.51; Jn 20.16
ρακά	Mat 5.22
σαβαχθάνι	Mat 27.46; Mk 15.34
σάββατον	Mat 12.1,2,5 (twice), 8,10,11,12; 24.20; 28.1 (twice); Mk 1.21; 2.23,24,27 (twice),28; 3.2, 4; 6.2; 16.1,2,9; Lk 4.16,31; 6.1,2,5,6,7,9; 13.10,14 (twice), 15,16; 14.1,3,5; 18.12; 23.54,56; 24.1; Jn 5.9,10,16,18; (6.59); 7.22, 23 (twice); 9.14,16; 19.31 (twice); 20.1,19
σαδδουκαῖος	Mat 3.7; 16.1,6,11,12; 22.23,34; Mk 12.18, Lk 20.27
Δ σαμαρίτης	Mat 10.5; Lk 9.52; 10.33; 17.16; Jn 4.9,39,40; 8.48
Δ σαμαρῖτις	Jn 4.9 (twice)
σατανᾶς	Mat 4.10; 12.26 (twice); 16.23; Mk 1.13; 3.23 (twice), 26; 4.15; 8.33; Lk 10.18; 11.18; 13.16; 22.3,31; Jn 13.27
σάτον	Mat 13.33; Lk 13.21
Δ σιδώνιος	Lk 4.26
σίκερα	Lk 1.15
Δ σμύρνα	Mat 2.11; Jn 19.39
Δ συκάμινος	Lk 17.6
Δ σύρος	Lk 4.27
Δ συροφοινίκισσα	Mk 7.26
ταλιθά	Mk 5.41
ὕσσωπος	Jn 19.29
φαρισαῖος	Mat 3.7; 5.20; 9.11,14,34; 12.2,14,24,38; 15.1, 12; 16.1,6,11,12; 19.3; 21,45; 22.15,34,41; 23.2.13,(14),15,23,25,26,27,29; 27.62; Mk 2.16,18 (twice), 24; 3.6; 7.1,3,5; 8.11,15; (9.11); 10.2; 12.13,(14); Lk 5.17,21,30,33; 6.2,7; 7.30,36 (twice), 37,39; 11.37,38,39,42,43,53; 12.1; 13.31; 14.1,3; 15.2; 16.14; 17.20; 18.10,11; 19.39; Jn 1.24; 3.1; 4.1; 7.32 (twice), 45,47,48; 8.(3), 13; 9.13,15,16,40; 11.46,47,57; 12.19,42; 18.3;
χαναναῖος	Mat 15.22
ὡσαννά	Mat 21.9 (twice),15; Mk 11.9,10; Jn 12.13.

In all, this list contains 70 words. Of these, two (βάρ and ἑβραϊκάς) are not found in our text. Another four (γερασηνός , μάγος, μωρέ and νάρδος) may perhaps be derived from nonsemitic roots. If so, 64 words would remain, and of these there are still a number (ἐλωΐ – ἠλί , λεμά - λαμά, κορβᾶν – κορβανᾶς σαμαρῖτις - σαμαρίτης)[47] which make the sum dubious. Of all the 70 words there are 627 occurrences. Of these the first six words listed above as dubious account for 12. 15 more are uncertain by reason of variants in the MSS. That leaves 600. Of these, 112 are accounted for by Ἰουδαῖος – Ἰουδαία, 99 by ἀμήν, 87 by φαρισαῖος and 56 by σάββατον; in all, 354 instances, constituting 3/5 of the total. Of the total 600, 161 are in Mat, 101 in Mk, 126 in Lk and 212 in Jn.

In order to compare these numbers - as related to the total number of words in the Gospels - to the numbers of the Greek and Latin words in Shabbath - as related to the total number of words in the tractate - it is necessary to define the term word. One cannot say 'a group of letters written together,' since the oldest MSS do not usually show separation of words. Yet to define a word as any letter adding meaning to the original root would require that even the n of the niphal be considered a word. Without further insistence on such difficulties of definition, it is possible to state as a general rule that, according to the division of letters now customary, Hebrew is written with far fewer 'words' than Greek. The definite article, the commonest conjunction, the commonest adverb of comparison, most prepositions, many pronouns - appear in Greek as individual words and in Hebrew as letters attached to other words. However, if each of these were to be counted as an individual word, and the Greek words were to be counted as commonly divided, it would appear that Hebrew is written with far more words than Greek. For Greek also combines prepositions with verbs (e.g. ἀφαιρέω) and with nouns (e.g. ἔξοδος); it has the genitive instead of שׁל , the dative instead of ל , and the accusative instead of את ; it frequently uses one word where Hebrew requires a phrase (αὐτῷ - בּ־יד, ἑαυτῷ - לעצמו), and customarily makes names of places, composed of several Hebrew words, into single words, for example: βηθφαγή [48] (and all compounds of ב־ת: βηθλεέμ, βηθσαϊδά, and so on), γέεννα,[49] γεθσημανί ,[50] γεννησαρέ ,[51] and the like, and a similar unification is effected in nouns and adjectives which in Hebrew are formed of several words, as ἀρχιερεύς - כהן גדול, ἀρχισυνάγωγος — ראש הכנסת, αὐτόπτης - ראה בעיניו,[52] δυσβάστακτος·לסבול קשה,[53] ἀχρεῖος —— אין בו מועיל.[54]

It would be easy to multiply examples, but the upshot is clear: That any method of counting the words in the Gospels and Mishnah is open to criticism as producing a disproportionately high count for the one or the other. Further, the lack of ancient translations makes it impossible to determine accurately how large the Gospels or the Mishnah would have been in the Hebrew or the Greek of their own times. As an arbitrary method of procedure, in spite of these difficulties, I have

decided, in counting the words of <u>Shabbath</u>, to skip all signs of the
binyanim, שֶׁל , אֶת, and prepositions written together with other words,
but to count the definite article, the conjunction וֹ , the comparative
adverb כְּ , all pronouns, and all prepositions written separately.
This method also yields a number of strange results, e.g. כָּל שֶׁהוּא
(3 words), וְאֵינוֹ (3), וְאֶעְפִּ"י שֶׁ־ (5), and compounds like these must
be taken into account. According to this method the number of words
in <u>Shabbath</u> is 6,775.[55] As against this, the number of 'words' (most
likely of groups of letters, according to the customary division) in the
Synoptic Gospels is given by Hawkins[56] as: Mat 18,222, Mk 11,158,
Lk 19,209. Accepting these figures, the number in Jn should be about[57]
13,700, and in all four, 62,289. If so, the Gospels are about 9 or 10
times the size of <u>Shabbat</u>; Mk being a little less and Jn a little more
than twice the size of the tractate. When we recall that in Mk only 30
Semitic words are found, and these, in all, only 101 times, and that in
<u>Shabbat</u> are found (according to Fiebig's reckoning as I have corrected
it) 65 Greek or Latin words occurring 89 times, it will be clear that
the vocabulary of <u>Shabbat</u> shows a Greco-Latin influence far stronger
than the Semitic influence shown by the vocabulary of Mk. And even if
one accept the reckoning of Jastrow, which would allow in <u>Shabbat</u>
only 38 Greco-Latin words, occurring only 46 times, yet the frequency
of occurrence would be almost the same as in Mk, and the number of
words occurring would be twice as great as in Mk - in proportion, of
course, to the size of the works.

The truth, certainly, lies somewhere between the two reckonings;
I should say, rather on the side of Fiebig than on that of Jastrow. My
opinion in this matter is determined by two considerations: 1. In going
over the list of words from <u>Shabbat</u>, I find only three or perhaps four
of Fiebig's etymologies (σάνδαλον, σημεῖον, ὄνος κατ' ὦμον ,
and perhaps λοπάς) which do not seem plausible, whereas the etymologies peculiar to Jastrow are almost always more difficult, and
are generally suspect because of his apologetic bias. 2. The Greco-
Roman words in the list from <u>Shabbat</u> bear evidence to a <u>linguistic</u> influence, the words in the list from the Gospels do not do this to anything like the same degree. The words from <u>Shabbat</u> are most of them
names of common objects or utensils, and these are not explained in
the text; but of the words from the Gospels, 19, almost a third, are
explained in the text itself,[58] i.e., they were felt to be foreign words
and consequently are not good evidence of Semitic influence on the
Greek language. Another 17 are adjectives derived from proper
nouns,[59] generally from names of places, and used to describe men as
coming from those places. These again are not good evidence of
<u>linguistic</u> influence, for in no language whatever is it possible to say
that a man comes from Nineveh without using a word somehow derived from Nineveh. If one add to these the technical terms which
practically defy translation (such as μάννα , πάσχα , σάββατον,

σατανᾶς, φαρισαῖος, and so on) it will be seen at once how far the Semitic influence on the vocabulary of the Gospels dwindles, and we shall apparently be justified in reiterating our conclusion: That in respect of vocabulary Shabbat[60] shows a Greco-Roman influence far stronger than the Semitic influence shown by Mk.[61]

NOTES

1. Baba Mezia 2.4; 3.11; 4.6; 9.12; Shebuot 7.6; Kelim 12.5; Eduyot 3.8; Meilah 6.5; Maaser Sheni 4.2.

2. Mat 25.27.

3. Berakot 1.1; Yoma 1.8.

4. Mat 14.25; 24.43; Mk 6.48; Lk 12.38.

5. Berakot 1.5; Horayot 2.3 etc.(The same word, in spite of the different meaning.)

6. Jn 1.42; 4.25.

7. Peah 2.7,8; Shabbat 2.5; Nazir 6.3; Kiddushin 4.14; Baba Kamma 6.1; 10.2; Baba Mezia 7.9; Berakot 1.3.

8. Mat 21.13; 26.55; 27.38,44; Mk 11.17; 14.48; 15.27; Lk 10.30,36; 19.46; 22.52; Jn 10.1,8; 18.40.

9. Further parallels of this sort: ἀπόστολος – שליח
   μαθητής —— תלמיד
   συναγωγή —— כנסית

The last of these is mentioned in L. Blau's article, Observations sur l'histoire du culte juif, REJ 73.138 ff., pp. 154 f. B. cites כנסית from Abot 4.11, where its use is not such as to assure the equivalence of its meaning to the common meaning of συναγωγή. Note B's curious supposition that 'Le latin Ecclesia...est une survivance de l'hébreu כנסית et de l'équivalent grec συναγωγή.'

10. H. Grätz, Geschichte der Juden, 5 ed., ed. M. Brann. Leipzig 1905, v. 3, pt. 1, p. 297, n. 1.

11. Citations from Strack-Billerbeck, unless otherwise specified, come from their commentary on the verse under discussion.

12. C. Torrey, The Four Gospels, N.Y., 1933 p. 307.

13. P. Fiebig, Pirque 'aboth, Tübingen, 1906, p. 2.

14. Ἰσκαριώθ : Mk 3.19; 14.10; Lk 6.16
    Ἰσκαριώτης: Mat 10.4; 26.14; Mk 14.43 (A(D)θetc.);Lk 22.3; Jn 6.71; 12.4; 13.2,26; 14.22.

15. In their commentary on Mat 10.4.

16. J. Wellhausen, Einleitung in die drei ersten Evangelien, 2 ed., Berlin, 1911, p. 28, 'es zu Jesu Zeit kein isch mehr gab.'

17. According to Kassowski, Ozar, s.v. איש , which lists 26 instances.

18. C. Torrey, The Name 'Iscariot,' HTR 36.51 ff. The explanation is found on pp. 60-61.

19. Ναζωραῖος : Mat 2.23; 26.71; Lk 18,37; Jn 18.5,7; 19.19

Ναζαρηνός : Mk 1.24; 10.47; 14.67; 16.6; Lk 4.34; 24.19.

20. C. Guignebert, La vie cachée de Jésus, Paris, 1921, pp. 190 f., cites in his notes a number of the more important articles. He himself, in the body of the book - pp. 68-76 - inclines to the opinion that the root was נזר , but many well-known scholars hold other opinions, e.g., Strack-Billerbeck on Mat 2.23 (נזרי). Yet other explanations are given in W. Caspari's article Ναζωραῖος , ZNW 21.122 ff. With these compare the explanations of the word βοανηργές (Mk 3.17): Torrey, Four Gospels, p. 298, בני רגש ; Chajes, Markus-Studien, ad loc., בני רעש ; Strack-Billerbeck, ad loc., בני רגשא or בני רגיז ; D. Völter, ZNW 17.212, בני עיש . בני עיש is found in Job and is thought to be the name of one of the signs of the zodiac. Völter supposes that it would therefore have occurred to Jesus as an appropriate name for the two disciples because 'Niemand kann sie voneinander scheiden, so wenig als man dies bei den Sternen einer Sterngruppe zu tun vermag.'

21. F. Schulthess, Zur Sprache der Evangelien, Anhang, ZNW, 21.241 ff. (The vocalization מָרָה actually found in S.'s text is presumably a typographical error.) S. expresses himself as in agreement with the opinions of F. Field and A. Merx. Torrey (The Four Gospels, p. 291) agrees with them, and the position seems, in fact, a strong one, for after ῥακά (Mat 5.22) one expects another, and a stronger, Semitic word, i.e., מורה and not μωρέ.

22. Prof. Schwabe called to my attention the opinion of S. Krauss, Griechische u. lateinische Lehnwörter, Berlin, 1898-9, v. II, p. 328, that מורה for μωρέ is found in Sifre on Dt. 21.18 as the Greek translation of שוטה. The text there reads וטורד שוטה תורמין , which Finkelstein corrects to ד״א סורד מן , and Jastrow to שוטה ל״י מידון , taking ל״י to have been the abbreviation of לשון יון . But see Lieberman's note in his review of Finkelstein's Siphre zu Deuteronomium in קרית ספר , 14.335.

23. The greater part of the material in Jastrow will be found in his explanations of the words: אצטריא, אסטרטיא, אסטרין, אסטריא, תיאטרון, טרטיאות, אצטרין See also s.v.: קסטרא, אסטרא, אסטרטא. I think forms like אבטדרין almost certainly come from στάδιον.

24. Compare אסטריא, אסטרא, אסטרטיא. It is almost impossible to distinguish the plurals of these.

25. viz., siege or camp of the besiegers. Krauss, Lehnwörter, II.300, thinks both כרקום and כרכום forms of χαράκωμα , and with this opinion Prof. Schwabe concurs. Krauss, loc. cit. gives also the meaning circus.

26. I am by no means satisfied with these suggestions. Of my own, sagittaria is not sufficiently close to סגלריא, and I am not sure there were enough singulares in Palestine for the Rabbis immediately

to think of them on attempting to list the things seen in a camp. But it seems to me yet more doubtful that the Rabbis knew the minor figures of Latin comedy; and yet more that the saeculares, which took place rarely and at Rome and not in a theatre, were so important to the Jews of Palestine as to be thus specified. It is interesting to note that none of the words found in this list appears in the list of theatrical personages found in Dura Europus. See The Excavations at Dura-Europos, Preliminary Report of the Ninth Season, Part I, New Haven, 1944, Appendis II, pp. 203 ff.

27. Jastrow so explains the parallel passage in the Yerushalmi; see his dictionary s.v. תִיאַטרוֹן .

28. p. VI: 'The Jewish literature here spoken of is specifically indigenous, in which respect it is unlike the Syriac literature contemporary with it, which is mainly Christian, and as such was influenced, not only in thought but also in language, by the Greek and Latin tongues .... Foreign influences came to Jewish literature merely through the ordinary channel of international intercourse.... Hence it is natural to expect that, in extending the horizon of thought, it also extended its vocabulary on its own basis, employing the elements contained in its own treasury.'

29. Berakot 2.6; Yoma 3.5. For all Jastrow's explanations see his dictionary. The words are here given his spelling rather than that of the passages of the Mishnah from which they are cited in the notes (except אוכלוס , v.i. n. 31.)

30. Gittin 7.5; Yoma 7.1.

31. In Jastrow v. s. אוכלוזא . Menahot T 10.23 (528); Berakot T 7.2 (14) (twice); Pesahim T 4.3 (163) (Here the reference is clearly to the ὄχλοι coming to sacrifice, each man, his passover; the meaning proposed by Jastrow - 'levy of troops' - is quite impossible.) Makkot T 3.8 (441) (twice).

32. Shabbat T 4.6,7 (115).

33. Demai 5.3,4 (twice).

34. P. Fiebig, Das Griechisch der Mischna, ZNW 9.297 ff.

35. Prof. Schwabe reminds me that only δίξεστον is known to Liddell-Scott.

36. I follow the spelling of my edition of Mishnah for the Hebrew words, and have given Fiebig's proposed Greek equivalents as he wrote them, in spite of the fact that some - e.g. νοταρικόν - are unknown to Liddell-Scott.

37. Jastrow on Krauss (Preface, p. 12): 'It is to be regretted that the proclivity to find Latin and Greek in words indisputably Semitic has led the author into a labyrinth of fatal errors.'

38. Jastrow thinks μάροιπος (sic) borrowed from the Semitic.

39. In the words of Jastrow, 'The Latin sudarium is a phonetic coincidence with our word.'

40. Jastrow derives the noun from the verb and the verb from the noun.

41. Fiebig, by error, 22.1, where the verb is found.

42. Sic. Only κέαρνον and κέαρος are known to Liddell-Scott.

43. J. Thayer, A Greek-English Lexicon of the New Testament... corr. ed., N.Y., 1896.

44. To one of these (νάρδος) there is, almost certainly, an Indo-European root, but I think that the word, as found in the Gospels was taken from the Old Testament.

45. The references are given according to Moulton & Geden, but I have verified all except those for Ἰουδαῖος – Ἰουδαία and ἀμήν.

46. According to G. Dalman, Gramm. d. jüd. -pal. Aramäisch. 2. ed., Leipzig, 1905, p. 174, n. 3, κορβανᾶς is formed from the Aramaic, κορβᾶν from the Hebrew. This seems probable. According to Strack-Billerbeck (in Mat 12.1) there is a similar distinction in source between σάββατον (from the Hebrew) and σάββατα (from the Aramaic). If so, this distinction does not seem to have been felt by the collectors or copyists of the Gospels, since these forms alternate from verse to verse; see, for example, Mk 2.23-3.3.

47. ἐλωΐ - ἠλί are certainly two different words; λεμά - λαμά may be, the textual tradition is very bad; κορβανᾶς – κορβᾶν are also dubious; σαμαρῖτις – σαμαρίτης I have listed as two words only because of the change in the declension.

48. Mat 21.1; Mk 11.1; Lk 19.29.

49. See the list.

50. Mat 26.36; Mk 14.32.

51. Mat 14.34; Mk 6.53; Lk 5.1.

52. So F. Delitzsch (in Sifre Habberit Hehadashah, Berlin, 1877) translates the word in Lk 1.2.

53. Mat 23.4; Lk 11.46.

54. Lk 17,10. I again follow the translation of Delitzsch.

55. I counted only once and may well have erred by two or three hundred words.

56. J. Hawkins, Horae Synopticae, 2 ed., Oxford, 1909, p. 2, n. 1. H. cites Nestle, Textual Criticism of the N. T., p. 48, and N. gives the figure on the authority of 'American scholars.'

57. In my ed. of the Gospels (Nestle & Nestle, ed. 14, Stuttgart, 1930) Mk fills 57 columns, Jn 70. Therefore 70 is to 57 as x is to 11-158; 57x equals 781,060; x equals approx. 13,702.

58. To wit: ἀββά, βοανηργές, γαββαθά, ἐλωΐ, ἐμμανουήλ, ἐφφαθά, ἠλί, κηφᾶς, κορβᾶν, κούμ, λαμά, λεμά, μεσσίας, ναζωραῖος (explained in Mat 2.23), ῥαββί, ῥαββουνί, σαβαχθανί, ταλιθά, γολγοθά.

59. To wit: γαδαρηνός, γαλιλαῖος, γερασηνός, ἱεροσολυμίτης, Ἰουδαῖος, ἰσραηλίτης, λευΐτης, μαγδαληνή, ναζαρηνός, νινευΐτης, σαδδουκαῖος, σαμαρίτης, σαμαρῖτις, σιδώνιος, σύρος, συρο—φοινίκισσα, χαναναῖος.

In the list from Shabbat there are only three of this sort, and of those
two serve as names for common objects (לובדקי and קמוליא) -
clear proof that they have already been taken into the language.

60) For convenience' sake I have discussed only tractate Shabbat,
but the Greek influence is clearly perceptible in almost all the tractates. In only one - Kinnim - have I failed to notice Greek words in
the course of my reading; and from many - Abodah Zarah, Middot,
Demai, Yoma, Sotah, Gittin - I have lists as long in relation to the
length of the tractate as that given from Shabbat. Indeed I should suppose, without having counted, that in Kelim the proportion of Greco-
Latin words is even greater than in Shabbat. And Tosefta and the
Midrashim are even richer in such words than is the Mishnah.

61. In this chapter the discussion has been deliberately limited to
matters statistical and philological and to the influence of one group
of languages on another - an influence which can be gauged pretty well
by the number of foreign words in typical documents. I have not
wished to discuss the influence of one culture on another - an influence
which can be estimated from a consideration of the meanings of such
words. It does happen, however, that in this instance the difference
of meaning between the words of the two lists is particularly striking
and shows as clearly as such evidence can a Greco-Roman influence
on all the aspects of Palestinian economic and social life, and a
Semitic influence on one single aspect of Greco-Roman culture - the
religious. However, in this instance it is also possible to prove that
such evidence is unreliable, for almost every verse of the Gospels
shows traces of a more far reaching Semitic influence, which is revealed in the sentence-structure and sequence of thought, although it
had little effect on the vocabulary. Prof. H. J. Cadbury remarked,
on reading this chapter, that the Latin words in the Gospels belong to
the governmental control of Palestine, by Roman military and fiscal
agencies, more often than do the Latin words in Shabbat.

Chapter 2

PARALLELS OF IDIOM

An idiom is essentially a conventional way of grouping words.
Parallels of idiom therefore come next in degree of complexity after
the parallels of single words discussed in the chapter above. But here
the problem of definition is much more complex. For if it proved difficult to define the term <u>word</u>, it will, a fortiori, prove more so to define the concept <u>a group of words</u> and to determine which groups are
idiomatic. Fortunately, this problem can be avoided, for this chapter
will discuss only a few of the simpler and better-recognized forms of
idiom - those generally dealt with by grammar or singled out as
'idiomatic expressions,' for example,[1] euphemisms, such as δύναμις
-גבורה,[2] forms of citation, such as γέγραπται – כתוב, oaths,
such as קורבן,[3] and blessings, such as εἰρήνη – שלום. And even
of these I shall not attempt to cite every example. On the contrary, I
wish to pass over without comment most of the previous work in this
field and to discuss only certain questions in reference to which I can
make corrections or point out new material. This course is recom-
mended by the fact that these parallels have already been the subject
of three controversies: that between the Hellenists and the Hebraists
of the eighteenth century, that concerning the mother-tongue of
Jesus, and that concerning the original language of the Gospels.[4] In
the course of these controversies, many parallels of idiom between
the Gospels and TL have been cited. The number might be estimated
from the 61 page list found in the back of Moulton's grammar,[5] a list
derived from a selection only of the books concerned with these problems.

As remarked in the introduction, there is occasion to distinguish
between the parallels, which actually exist, and the influences, which
certain scholars have inferred from a study of the parallels they
happened to know. If a given expression be found in the Gospels, in
TL, and in the papyri, good. Let it be included both in the list of the
parallels between the Gospels and TL, and in the list of the parallels
between the Gospels and the papyri. For only after complete lists of
all the parallels between the Gospels and all the other literatures of
their time and region have been drawn up, will it be possible to decide
accurately the relationship between the Gospels and those literatures.
At present, there are no such lists and there is not even the possibility of making them. Therefore the controversies mentioned above
have succeeded only in raising interesting questions as to the nature
of history, and in broadening the concept of parallelism. For example,

16

Torrey remarked early in his studies of the language of the authors of
the Gospels, that, apart from the grammatical parallels themselves, it
is possible to consider the frequency of their occurrence. In his article <u>The Translations Made from the Original Aramaic Gospels</u>[6] he
wished to base his proof of the Aramaic source primarily on this frequency. But, according to him, there was no proof of this frequency
apart from the impression received by the expert while reading.[7]
Therefore he himself later abandoned the question of the frequency of
grammatical parallels and devoted his efforts to the discovery of
errors of translation. And so, previously, did Wellhausen, who emphasized the Semitic elements in the style of the Gospels,[8] but remarked only that <u>generally</u> the predicate is found before the subject,
<u>generally</u> the subject when emphasized or following ἰδού is found be-
fore the predicate, and so on, without citing evidence sufficient for his
judgments and without remarking the difference between isolated
parallels and <u>the parallelism to be found in the frequency of parallels</u>.

Burney was the first[9] who attempted to express this parallelism of
frequency in accurate numerical terms, supported by references. So,
for example, in discussing asyndeton he remarks[10] that in Daniel 1.1-
2.4, which is written in Hebrew, every sentence but the first begins
with a conjunction, whereas in Dan. 2.5-2.49, which is written in Aramaic, 22 out of 44 sentences begin without connective particles. So,
too, in Jn 1, of 62 sentences 34 begin without connectives, in Jn 11, of
59, 17, in Jn 18, of 52, 20, and on the contrary, in Mat 3, of 13 sentences not even one begins without a conjunction, in Mk 1, of 38, only
2, in Lk 8, of 60, only 2. But here Burney's interest in history led
him over from the collection of parallels to the collection of differences. He wished to prove that there was an Aramaic source (written
or otherwise here makes no difference) for Jn, and for the sake of the
argument supposed the other Gospels to be products of the typical
koine; he therefore endeavored to show that in Jn are found many
more examples of Aramaic idiom than appear in the other Gospels.[11]
Consequently he most often remarked only that a given form of expression was typically Aramaic, and therefore compared the number
of its occurrences in Jn with that in the Synoptics.[12] In the examples
which he chose the number in Jn was always higher. Thus he succeeded in showing that Jn was written in a style more similar to Aramaic than that of the other Gospels, but in order to prove that Jn was
translated from the Aramaic it is necessary to show something more:
It is necessary to show not only that typically Aramaic expressions
are found in Jn, and not only that they are found in Jn more often than
in the other Gospels, but also that they are found in Jn <u>with about the</u>
<u>same frequency as that with which they are found in Aramaic works</u>.
The proof of translation must be built not on the <u>difference</u> between
Jn and the other Gospels, but on the <u>parallelism</u> between Jn and Aramaic works, and specifically on the <u>parallelism to be found in the fre-</u>
<u>quency of parallels</u>.[13]

Here research is brought up short by the fact that there are no Aramaic works from the period of the Gospels (except, perhaps, for Megillat Taanit). Consequently, if for no other reasons,[14] there is some historical interest in the grammatical parallels and parallels of 'idiomatic expressions' to be found between the Gospels and TL of which the language is so close to Aramaic. This is so especially because TL began to be written fairly soon after the composition of the Gospels. I have therefore chosen five words of which the usage is particularly typical of the grammar or idiomatic expression of TL, have counted the times they are cited in Kassowski's concordance to the Mishnah (having revised the text according to the corrigenda), and have compared the number of citations in Moulton & Geden. It is possible that owing to errors in the concordances or in my counting the numbers given below may not be perfectly accurate, but in any event they will give an adequate impression of the difference between the use of these words in the Mishnah (M) and their use in the Gospels (G).

אב - πατήρ

The customary meaning	M 272	G 60
בית אב[15]	M 12	_____
אב מלאכה	M 3	_____
אב בית דין	M 3	_____
אב הטומאה	M 26	_____
אבי אביו (או אמו)	M 11	_____
אבות נזיקין	M 1	_____
אבות העולם	M 1	_____
אבות (A part of the Eighteen Benedictions	M 2	_____
אב (Of animals or plants) . . .	M 6	_____
אב (Auctor generis[16])	M 42	G 22
אב שבשמים	M 7	G 14 and 1 dubious
πατήρ ὁ οὐράνιος [17]	_____	G 6
πατήρ ὁ ἐπουράνιος	_____	G 1
πατήρ ὁ ἐξ οὐρανοῦ	_____	G 1
πατήρ (i.e. God)[18]	_____	G 159 and 3 dubious
πατήρ (i.e. the devil)	_____	G 5
πατήρ (As a title)[19]	_____	G 3 (M has not אב but אבא 28 times)
In all	M 386	G 271 and 4 dubious

בן - υἱός

The customary meaning	M 290	G 48 and 1 dubious
In names and titles	M 693[20]	G 10[21]
בן (א"ש) פלוני	M 7	_____

18

בן (i.e. prognatus)

	M	G	
בן אברהם	2	2	
בן ישראל	1	2	
בן לוי	13		
בן דוד		17	
בני טובים	2		
בני כהנים גדולים	2		
בני מלכם [22]	4	2	
Other combinations	23	3	
בבי אדם	18	1	(τοὶς υἱοὶς τῶν ἀνθρώπων)
ὁ υἱὸς τοῦ ἀνθρώπου		81	and 3 dubious
בן (Of animals or birds)	36	1	(In a citation from the Old Testament)[23]
בן בנו (בתו)	2		
בני (i.e. my grandson)	1		
בן אחיו (אחותו)	3		
בני (In conversation)[24]	2		
υἱός (i.e. one who will serve as a son(?))[25]		1	
Children of God[26]	4	4	
ὁ υἱὸς τοῦ θεοῦ		26	and 2 dubious
ὁ υἱός alone, meaning 'The Son of God'		24	and 2 dubious
ὁ υἱός μου (Spoken by God)		7	
υἱὸς τοῦ πονηροῦ		1	
υἱὸς φωτός		1	
υἱὸς εἰρήνης		1	
υἱὸς τῆς βασιλείας		2	
υἱὸς γεέννης		1	
υἱὸς τῆς ἀπολείας		1	
υἱὸς τοῦ αἰῶνος τούτο		2	
υἱοὶ τοῦ νυμφῶνος		3	
בן (With the name of a place)[27]	28		
בן בית	10		
בן משפחה	1		
בני חבורה	2		
בני הכנסת	2		
בני הגדולה	1		
בני ברית	1		
בני תרבות	1		
בן סורר ומורה	10		
בן חורין	29		
בן (With a period of time, to express age)	65		

19

	M	G
בן קיימא	6	
בן יוג	1	
בן (Meaning a small)[28]	4	
בני מעים	10	
In all	**1274**	**241 and 8 dubious**

יד – χείρ

	M	G
The customary meaning	373	62 and 3 dubious
יד לשלוח	3	6 (ἐπιβάλλω)
יד (Of God)[29]	6	3
יד (Of an angel)		2 (Both from the OT)
יד (i.e. physical power)[30] . . .	43	9
יד (i.e. legal power)[31]	104	3
(חובה או כדומה) לצת ידי . .	20	
ידן כידו/ה	1	
יד (Of animals)	15	
יד (Of vessels, tools etc.) . .	26	
יד (Descriptive, of instru-		
ments used by hand)[32]	11	
יד (Of fruits)	7	
יד (A measure)	4	
אחזת יד	2	
בית יד[33]	2	
השג יד	2	
תפיסת יד	5	
תשומת יד	4	
ביד : (1) An adverb[34]	4	
(2) מצוה ביד sense a[35] .	4	
(3) מצוה ביד sense b . .	6	
יד (i.e. with)[36]	112	
מיד (i.e. at once)	51	
על יד על יד	1	
על יד [37]: i.e. with	2	
After מעט	12	
i.e. על	12	
i.e. בעד	20	
i.e. על אודות	12	
i.e. למען	2	
i.e. ומשתמש ב	2	
i.e. דרך	20	G 1
i.e. אל	3	
i.e. אצל	3	
In all	**894**	**86 and 3 dubious**

פה - στόμα

	M	G	
The customary meaning	36	11	
στόμα (Of God)		1	
פה (Of animals)[38]	16		
פה (Of vessels, tools etc.)	38	1	(στόματι μαχαίρης Lk 21.24)[39]
פה (Of the earth)	1		
פה (i.e. a man)	16		
פה (i.e. speech)	7	2	(Both in Lk)
פה (An adverb)[40]	6		
לפי [41]	107		
לפי ש	26		
מפי (Figuratively)	25	4	and one dubious (4 in Lk and in Mat from the OT)
על פי : i.e. על	38		
i.e. בפני	1		
i.e. להנאת	10		
i.e. על דברי	85	1	(From the OT)
אף על פי ש	234		
אף על פי כן	5		
פי שנים	7		
In all	658	20 and 1 dubious	

ראש - κεφαλή

	M	G	
The customary meaning[42]	92	29	
ראש (Of God)	1		
ראש (Of animals and birds)	48		
ראש (Of vessels, tools etc.)	79	3	(All from the OT)[43]
ראש (Of mountains, etc.)	38		
ראש השנה	41		
ראש חדש	24		
ראש (Of social groups):			
בית אב	3		
בית דין	2		
הכנסת	4		
המעמד	1		
Without determinant	1		
ראשי בשמים	1		
ראשי דברים	1		
ראש תור	3		
כובד (קלות) ראש	3		
חיי הראש	1		
חלק בראש	3		
עון תלוי בראש	1		
In all	347	32	

I have not attempted any fine distinctions of meaning, and have deliberately omitted several obscure passages,[44] because it was my
purpose to show the great difference between the common, well-known
and customary usage of the language of the Mishnah and that of the
language of the Gospels. How great this difference is can be seen
from this fact, that from 113 usages cited from the Mishnah, only 25
are found in the Gospels.[45] Of course, these figures can be whittled
down. The Gospels had no occasion to use בן סורר , אב הטומאה ,
ומורה , תפיסת יד and חשומת יד and the like. But on the other
hand a number of the usages found in the Gospels are found there only
in citations from the Old Testament, so, for example, υἱός used to
refer to the offspring of an animal, which is found only in the citation
in Mat 21.5, ἐπὶ πῶλον υἱὸν ὑποζυγίου , where the text before
and after the citation (21. 2 and 7) has only πῶλον . So, too, κεφαλή
used to refer to part of an inanimate object, found only in the citation
from Ps. 118.22, ἐγενήθη εἰς κεφαλὴν γωνίας .[46] Moreover,
as before remarked, the frequency of usage is also to be noted. Now,
taking the sums of all the instances of all the words discussed, the
relation between their usage in the Gospels and their usage in the
Mishnah is a bit under 1 to 12.[47] But:

The use of בן in names, found in   M 693, in G 28[48] times,
    of יד to mean legal power, found in M 104, in G 3   times,
    of על יד to mean through, found in   M 20, in G 1   time,

these show very small percentages, even if the instances in the Gospels be not citations from the Old Testament nor imitations of its
style. Further, the question arises, How many of these expressions
which are rarely or never found in the Gospels could have been translated word for word into Greek? Here the answer may be indicated
by the usage of the Septuagint (LXX):

בי״ת אב	M 12	G --	LXX customarily οἶκος πάτριος
אב הטומאה	M 26	G --	Not found in the OT
אבי אביו (ו אמו)	M 11	G --	LXX, Judges 9.1: πατρὸς μητρός (Text B)
בן In names and titles	M 693	G 28	LXX customarily υἱός
בני לוי	M 13	G --	LXX customarily υἱοί [49]
בן Of animals or birds	M 36	G 1	The instance in G is a cit. of LXX.[50]
בן With place-names	M 28	G --	LXX customarily υἱός [51]
בן חורין	M 29	G --	LXX, Ecclesiastes 10.17: υἱὸς ἐλευθέρων
בן In expression of age	M 65	G --	LXX customarily υἱός [52]
יד i.e. legal power	M 104	G 3	LXX Lev. 5.7; 25.35; Est. 2.8[53]

22

לצאת ידי		M 20	G -- Not found in the OT
יד Of animals		M 15	G -- LXX, I Sam (I Kgs) 17.37[54]
יד Of vessels, tools etc..		M 26	G -- LXX, 3 Kings 7.18,19,21; 10.19
יד i.e. with		M 112	G -- LXX customarily χείρ [55]
מיד i.e. at once		M 51	G -- Not found in the OT
פה Of animals		M 16	G -- LXX customarily στόμα[56]
פה Of vessels, tools etc..		M 38	G 1 The instance in G is a cit. of LXX[57]
לפי		M 107	G -- LXX, 3 Kings 17.1; Prov. 27.21
לפיש		M 26	G -- Not found in the OT
על פי i.e. על		M 38	G -- LXX, Gen. 29.2,3,8,10
על פי i.e. על דברי		M 85	G 1 The instance in G is a cit. of LXX[58]
אף על פי ש		M 234	G -- Not found in the OT
ראש Of animals		M 48	G -- LXX customarily κεφαλή[59]
ראש Of vessels etc.		M 79	G 3 The instances in G are cits. of LXX[60]
ראש Of mountains etc..		M 38	G -- LXX, Gen. 8.5; 11.4; 2 Sam (2 Kgs) 2.25
ראש השנה		M 41	G -- In the OT only in Ezek. 40.1, where LXX reads ἐν τῷ πρώτῳ μηνί
ראש חדש		M 24	G -- LXX customarily νεομηνία
ראש Of social groups		M 11	G -- LXX, Judges 10.18; 11.9,11; 2 Sam (2 Kgs) 22.44; Ps. 18 (LXX 17).44

Here also it must be remarked that the lack of certain of these from the Gospels is the result of pure chance. There is no doubt that had the authors of the Gospels had occasion to mention the head or mouth of an animal they would, had they been writing in Greek, have written κεφαλή or στόμα. But nevertheless, the upshot of the evidence is clear. In the above list are found 28 expressions, of which 5 are not found in the Old Testament, but of the 23 which are found in the Old Testament, 20 were translated word for word by the Septuagint, i.e., translated according to the Hebrew of the Mishnah and not according to the Greek of the Gospels. These 28 expressions are found 1,925 times in the Mishnah. They include more than a third of the 3,559 instances in which the words we have discussed are found in the Mishnah; and if from those 3,559 be subtracted the 1,063 instances in which the words appeared in their literal meanings, then the 1,925 instances of the usages given above constitute more than three-quarters of the remainder, more than three-quarters, that is, of all the instances in which the language of the Mishnah has used these words idiomatically. And of these 28 expressions, three-quarters were known in Greek from the Septuagint. Nevertheless, against their 1,925 occurrences in the Mishnah, they are found only 37 times in the Gospels. Consequently it is impossible to speak - as Torrey spoke[61] - of the language of the Gospels as a word-for-word translation of a Hebrew or Aramaic text, for it does not contain the expressions which any such translation would necessarily contain. On the other hand it is possible to think that in the Gospels we have a free or partially free translation. But this theory does not admit of factual demonstration and such evidence as may be found for it is particularly weak because the dialects of first-century Palestine are known almost exclusively by remote inference, i.e., the theory goes over from the domain of philology to that of history, and there I shall leave it.

To return to the factual basis of such theories, i.e., to the observable parallels of idiom between the Gospels and TL: These were divided, at the beginning of the chapter, into grammatical parallels, on the one hand, and, on the other, parallels of 'idiomatic expression.' Actually, however, sharp distinction of these groups is impossible and in what follows examples from either will be discussed indiscriminately. Their common characteristic, which makes them noticeable, is that the expression paralleled is unusual in one or the other language, or in both languages. Of course, the languages also afford many examples of parallelism between uses of words which are quite customary in both tongues - so, for example, the parallel uses of יד-χείρ , פה-στόμα, ראש - κεφαλή in their usual meanings. But these are normally explained as the results of independent development (and it is not implausible that Greek and Hebrew should independently have words of these meanings and should use them similarly), and parallels of idiom are usually studied not for their own sake but as indicative of the 'influences' to be inferred from them; now outside influence can be inferred only when the object studied - in this case, the language - does something unusual, therefore I shall discuss here only those parallels of which one or the other or both the parallel expressions are unusual.

Of these, the last sort (i.e., unusual uses of Hebrew words parallel to unusual uses of Greek words) has not yet attracted scientific attention, and I have noted only a few examples, of which perhaps the most interesting is that afforded by the use of χορτάζω in Mat 5.6: 'Blessed are they that hunger and thirst after righteousness, for they shall be stall-fed,' parallel to the use of הדביע in Midrash Tannaim 32.6 (end): 'He established you on your basis, fattened you on the spoil* of peoples and gave you what he promised you.' For the commonest meaning, both of χορτάζω and of הדביע [62] is, 'to stall-feed an animal in order to fatten it.' But here, both in Mat and in Midrash

---

*Reading בְּזַיִת for בבת.

Tannaim, God is feeding the righteous metaphorical food. Moreover, it is interesting to note that the 'righteousness' (צדק - justice - and not צדקה - works of charity) which God is expected to perform for Israel is: to exalt his chosen people and to humble before them the gentiles who persecuted them.[63] It is possible, therefore, that the food of the elect (δικαιοσύνη in Mat and בז״ת עמים in Midrash Tannaim) was once, in both traditions, the same. I question whether this meaning of 'righteousness' was known to the final editor of Mat, but it may well have been known to the author of the source from which the final editor took this saying; certainly among the various sources of the Gospels there were some which envisaged Jesus as the Messianic King destined to feed his people the spoil of the gentiles, and other blessings from the same list in Mat can be understood in the same sense, for example, 'Blessed are the meek, for they shall inherit the earth.'[64]

But parallels of this sort are few in comparison with the large number of instances in which a usage extraordinary in the one language is found parallel to a usage customary in the other. Typical are these examples taken at random from the hundreds in Strack-Billerbeck:

Mat 18.6 μύλος ὀνικός , Kelim Baba Mezia T 2.14 (580) and Baba Batra T 1.3 (398) רח״ים של חמור

Mat 18.7 σκάνδαλον , Berakot 4.2, Sanhedrin 7.4 (end) מכשול תקלה

Mat 19.29 ζωὴν αἰώνιον κληρονομήσει, Abot 5.19 נוחלין בעולם הבא

Mat 20.14 ἆρον τὸ σόν , Baba Mezia 6.6 טול את שלך

Mat 22.40 ὁ νόμος κρέμαται, Hagigah 1.8 הלכות כהררים....התלוין בשערה

Most often the peculiarity which makes the parallelism remarkable depends on a single word, so that these might be considered the simplest sort of parallels of meaning. But even this sort provides sufficient opportunity for error,[65] and this opportunity increases as does the complexity of the parallels. In particular it proves difficult to determine, when discussing parallel idiomatic expressions, whether a group of words is in fact an idiomatic expression or whether it is merely an accidental and occasional formation. For example, Schlatter[66] and Fiebig[67] both thought they saw in the 'Come and see.' of Jn (ἔρχεσθε καὶ ὄψεσθε   Jn 1.39, ἔρχου καὶ ἴδε   Jn 1.46; 11.34) a parallel to the rabbinical expression 'Come and see.' which they found in Mekilta 12.1 (end); 15.25; 20.12 and 21.6 (end). But it is enough to look at these instances in context[68] to see that in Jn the words have their common meaning and are brought together only by

the accidents of conversation, whereas in Mekilta they do not have
their literal meaning but constitute a fixed expression, part of the
technical terminology of rabbinical exegesis.*   Another example:
Schlatter[69] cites three instances from Jn[70] in which a singular speaker uses the plural. He says, 'Ein solches "Wir" war bei den Paläs-
tinensern sehr verbreitet.' As examples he cites, from TL, Mekilta
12.10 (end) לעבֿין שאמרנו - an editorial cliché[71] utterly irrelevant
to the question - and from Mekilta 17.9 the following passage, ' "To-
morrow I will stand" (etc.) To-morrow we shall be with you, ready
and standing on the top of the hill. "This means just what it says"
(i.e., is to be understood literally), - the words of R. Joshua; R. Elazar
of Modiïm says, "To-morrow we shall decree a fast and shall rely
upon the works of the patriarchs." ' But here it is at once clear from
the words 'we shall decree a fast' that Moses (the speaker in the passage)[72] was thought of as referring not to himself alone, but to all the
elders of Israel; and if further proof were needed it could be found
nearby in the immediately preceding exposition of Mekilta to the same
verse: ' "And Moses said to Joshua, 'Choose us men.' " Hence we
learn that he was accustomed to treat him as his equal. Let every
man learn courtesy from Moses, who did not say to Joshua, "Choose
me men," but, "Choose us men." ' If the source of Mekilta thought
that, when the Old Testament represented Moses as using the plural
in place of the singular, it was best to suppose that Moses associated
Joshua with himself to make a plural subject, then it follows <u>a fortiori</u>
that when, immediately afterwards, they put the plural in the mouth of
Moses, <u>they</u> also associated with him, to form the subject, either the
companions who would stand with him on the mountain or the elders of
Israel with whom he would decree the fast.

    It would be easy to add other examples of this sort: באמת אמרו in
the Mishnah is not (as Danby[73] thought) a form of intensified assertion,
and still less (as Schlatter thought)[74] a parallel to Jn 4.18 τοῦτο
ἀληθὲς εἴρηκας , but is a concessive expression, meaning, 'I, indeed, say otherwise, but I must admit that they (my elders) did say....'
λύσῃ in Mat 5.19 ('Whoever, then, relax one of the least of these
commandments.') is not (as Fiebig[75] thought) a parallel to התיר (<u>per-
mit</u>). Commandments are not 'permitted,' nor 'adjudged permissible.'
It must be said, also, that there are many instances when it is dubious
whether or not two expressions are parallel. A famous example is the
question whether אמרת in <u>Kelim T</u>, Baba Kamma 1.6 (569) is really
parallel to σὺ εἶπας (and the corresponding expressions) in the Gospels,[76] as an affirmative answer at a moment when such an answer
would be disadvantageous. Here Abrahams[77] well remarked that the
passage in <u>Kelim T</u>, 'is cited by two competent authorities (Dalman
and Chwolson), who both regard it as practically decisive, but

---

*As such, partially paralleled by Jn 7.52: ἐρεύνησον καὶ ἴδε

curiously enough in opposite senses.' To add another pair to the tradition I may remark that Abrahams himself inclines to the negative,
Klausner,[78] to the affirmative. Another example: Schlatter[79] thought
that the command not to wonder, found twice in Jn,[80] is prallel to the
expression אל תתמה, which is found many times in the Midrashim.[81]
But in Jn the expression introduces only propositions which Jn thought
true, whereas in the Midrashim it generally[82] introduces propositions
which are afterwards to be proved false. Consequently there is some
reason to doubt that the expression was known to Jn <u>as a technical
term</u> with the meaning it has in the Midrashim.

But after the elimination of all such erroneous and dubious instances, there remain many indubitable parallels between the every-
day expressions found in TL and those found in the Gospels. For example καλῶς εἶπες in Jn 4.17 parallel to יפה אמרת in Mekilta
19.24,[83] ὁ κύριος μετὰ σοῦ in Lk 1.28[84] parallel to ה' עמכם in
Berakot 9 (end), and so on. It is not my intention to list all these, but
only to add to their number one as yet unnoticed: the use of the expression ἐγὼ δὲ λέγω , parallel to ואני אומר to introduce a contradictory halakic (i.e. legal) opinion.[85] The most famous passage in
which this expression is found is the fifth chapter of Mat, where it occurs in vss. 22, 28, 32, 34, 39, and 44, always introducing a contradiction to a teaching derivable from the Old Testament, in the form of a
legal requirement more stringent than that made by the Old Testament.
Many Christian exegetes have claimed, therefore, that in these words,
ἐγὼ δὲ λέγω, is expressed an important aspect of the peculiar personality or teaching of Jesus. Strack-Billerbeck pass over the expression in complete silence, as if nothing like it were to be found in
all TL. The usual opinion is stated by Travers Herford:[86] 'Jesus...
by his declaration, "But I say unto you"...virtually repudiated the
principle of the Halachah.' And the same notion is found even in W.
Kümmel's article Jesus u. der jüd. Traditionsgedanke:[87] 'Und darin
liegt nun eben das Erschreckende für den Pharisäer: mag Jesus auch
in Gesetz u. Tradition Gottes Willen finden, dieses "ich sage euch"
beseitigt mit einem Strich den ganzen jüd. Traditionsgedanken.' Yet
stronger is the article of E. Stauffer in Theol. Wörterbuch[88] s.v. ἐγώ:
'Fünfmal[89] steht in Mt 5.22 ff das scharfe Ἐγὼ δὲ λέγω ὑμῖν ....
Dies λέγω ὑμῖν schliesst eine Epoche ab in der Geschichte der Religion und Ethik, es schafft eine neue Situation.' u.s.w.

But as a matter of fact, things are quite different. A little later I
shall cite evidence for the use of ואני אומר. Here I must first emphasize that the question depends altogether on the use of these words
ἐγὼ δὲ λέγω . For their context is invariably, 'You have heard that
it was said to the men of old.' and it has long been known that this expression is composed of rabbinical material. Both Kümmel[90] and
Strack-Billerbeck[91] demonstrate that such use of 'You have heard' and
'It was said' is typical of the rabbinical tradition. And similarly it is

27

well known that the Rabbis claimed the right to lay down laws more
severe than those of the Old Testament. Nor can it be maintained that
Jesus went beyond the limits of their practise in wholly forbidding divorce and so completely abolishing a liberty which the Old Testament
had provided, for Strack-Billerbeck in their exposition of Mat 15.6
('And you have made the word of God void for the sake of your tradition.') collects other instances[92] in which the Old Testament's provisions were completely abolished by the Rabbis. Moreover, it has long
been known that the severities advocated by Jesus in Mat 5 were also
advocated by the Rabbis themselves, and in particular Jesus' ruling
on divorce, <u>as given in Mat</u>, is exactly that of the House of Shammai
(see Strack-Billerbeck on Mat 5.32 and the other vss. introduced by
'But I say unto you'). As for 'the men of old,' G. Delling in <u>Theo-
logisches Worterbuch</u>[93] thought that these were הראשונים [הזקנים]
or [אבות] הראשונים, an explanation possible, but somewhat difficult, since of these worthies TL always declares that <u>they</u> said or did
something, and not that something was said <u>to them</u>. I prefer to suppose that the words in Mat are parallel to the expression בראשונה
(At first), often found in the Mishnah and Tosefta in the context
בראשונה היו אומרים....חזרו לומר ('At first they used to say....They
came round to saying') (and its variants).[94]   At any event there is no
doubt that the corresponding words in Mat are related to the rabbinical
tradition. Therefore the words ἐγὼ δὲ λέγω are found in a context
of which every word has its parallel in the technical terminology of
TL, and therefore it would be no wonder were a parallel to be found
there also for them, and for the peculiar use which they have in this
chapter of Mat, i.e. to introduce a legal opinion contradicting that
generally accepted.

In point of fact there are several such parallels:

Sifre on Numbers 11.21-2: ' "And Moses said, 'Six hundred thousand footmen.' " R. Simon b. Yohai (who was of a generation later
than that of R. Akiba) says, "R. Akiba used to draw one lesson from
this text, and I draw two lessons from it, and my words are preferable
to those of my teacher. Behold, he says, ' "Shall the flocks and the
herds be slain for them, to suffice them?" - even should you collect
for them all flocks and herds would they suffice them?' <u>And I say</u>
(ואני אומר), Was it because they had no flesh to eat that they were
tumultuous?" '

Sifre on Dt. 6.4: 'R. Simon b. Yohai says, "There are four passages which R. Akiba used to expound, and I also expound them, and
my words are preferable to his words. Behold, he says, 'And Sarah
saw the son of Hagar the Egyptian' - (she saw) that he committed
idolatry.' <u>And I say</u> (ואני אומר), They quarreled only about a question of fields....And I prefer my exposition rather than his. Likewise,
you say, 'Shall the flocks and the herds be slain for them?' (etc. as
above)....(These are) the words of R. Akiba. And I say, Even should

you collect for them all the flocks and the herds of the world, they would find fault with you in the end....And I prefer my words to his. Likewise, you say....And I say....." ' (And so so, several times more in the following passage.)[95] However, these are aggadic innovations, rather than halakic (i.e. they concern biblical history rather than law), and one might suppose that such contradiction as this was permitted in historical but not in legal exegesis. But it happens that in Tosefta the same expression is found in discussions of the law. For example:

Bikkurim T 1.2 (100): 'R. Jose says, "R. Meir used to say, 'The priests bring (offerings of first-fruits), but do not read (when they offer them, the passage in the Old Testament commanding such offerings to be brought), because they did not receive a share of the land (and the Old Testament passage relates the offering to land-holding).' But I say (וַאֲנִי אוֹמֵר), In the same way as the Levites received (a share of the land) so did the priests." '

Mikwaot T 3.4 (655): 'R. Jose says, "R. Meir used to say, 'They immerse themselves in the upper one.' But I say, 'In the lower.' And the sages say, 'Whether in the upper, so and so (כן וכן , Zuckermandel corrects to בֵּין כָּךְ וכָךְ , meaning, in either case), they should immerse themselves only in the middle.' " ' It seems to me possible to doubt, here, whether the words 'And the sages say' (and what follows) belong, or not, to the opinion of R. Jose. In any event, the most customary form of introduction to an opinion contradicting that generally accepted is not And (or But) I say (וַאֲנִי אוֹמֵר) but simply I say (אוֹמֵר אֲנִי) which is found often, especially in Tosefta, but also in other books of TL, for example: Sifra 14.21: ' "And if he be poor"...He, and not those who vowed on his behalf. (For one might argue that) as, in the evaluations (of vows), a poor man who vowed the worth of a rich one (nevertheless) gives the worth of a poor one, it is also possible that should he say, "I shall undertake to provide the sacrifice of this leper.", and the leper were a rich man, he should (nevertheless) bring the sacrifice (which the leper would have brought had he been) a poor man. The Sacred Text says He, and not those who vowed on his behalf. Rabbi says, "I say this is so even in the evaluations (of vows)." ' Bekorot T 6.15 (541): 'The first-born (son) does not receive a double share of the increment which has accrued to the property after the death of their father. Rabbi says, "I say that the first-born (son) does receive a double share of the increment which has accrued to the property after the death of their father." '

In conclusion, as a note to all the learned material written on the Selbstbewusstsein Jesu and on the basis of his moral teaching in his peculiar awareness of 'die Zuständigkeit seiner Person...die Rechtmässigkeit seiner Sendung,'[96] I shall cite a passage from Eduyot T 3.1 (459): 'Menahem ben Sungai testified that the finger-like projection (reading הָאַצְבַּע for הָצֹבַּע) on the lip of the pot in which olive-soakings are kept is unclean, and that of (the pot in which) dyes (are kept) is clean, whereas at first they used to say the opposite; and when they installed him in the academy they all marvelled at him.[97] He said to them, "So and so if I am not the first of all those who come after me." ' I grant, of course, that Jesus possessed a peculiar awareness and evaluation of himself - so peculiar, in fact, that students of the New Testament cannot accurately describe them. But I should not agree that it is possible to find evidence of this peculiarity in the fact that Jesus used an expression customary in Jewish legal argumentation.[98] Nor should I agree that Jesus was the only self-confident Rabbi, or the only one to rely on his self-confidence in his legal teaching.

I think these sufficient as examples of the sort of parallels to be found in the use of every-day expressions, but there is another group of parallels in idiom which requires special examination because of its historical importance - those which serve as the basis for many theories about mistakes of translation.

How can a mistake of translation be recognized when the text translated is not available? Only by means of something unusual in the translation. An expression, the use of a word, is felt to be 'not Greek,' or is not understandable - i.e. the word or expression is not one of those we have been accustomed to find in contexts like that in which it is now found. This sense of difficulty, this awareness of the unusual, is the necessary sign which enables us to suspect the existence of a mistake in translation.[99] But more is needed. Our suspicion can be confirmed only if the words which are difficult - unusual or incomprehensible - in Greek - yield a text which is easy - comprehensible and customary - in Semitic. For example (to introduce a new theory) Mk 8.32 f. reads: 'And Peter took him (Jesus), and began to rebuke him. But turning and seeing his disciples, he rebuked Peter, and said, "Get behind me, Satan! For you are not on the side of God, but of men." ' (Almost the same words are found in Mat 16.22-3.) Now:

1. 'Get behind me' does not match 'rebuked'; the expression is not generally known as a rebuke.[100]

2. Peter already was behind Jesus. This was the customary place of a disciple,[101] and that Peter occupied it at this moment is proved by the word 'turning.'

3. Immediately following (Mk 8.34, Mat 16.24) the text goes on: 'And, calling near the crowd with his disciples, he said to them, "If any man would come after me, let him deny himself and take up his cross and follow me." ' (So Mk. The differences in Mat are minor and irrelevant to the point under discussion.) Here it is almost certain that 'follow me' (ὀπίσω μου ἐλθεῖν) means 'be my disciple,[102] and this is evidently the opposite of the rebuke to Peter.

If so, in 8.32 the rebuke should have been, not 'Get behind me,' but 'Get from behind me.' (ὕπαγε ἐξ ὀπίσω μου), i.e. 'Cease to be my disciple! '

4. 'Get from behind me.' could have been, in Hebrew, סור מאחרי
and one who was translating rapidly and who knew that, generally,
את = מאת, תחת = מתחת, על = מעל, and מאחרי = אחרי could
have easily skipped the מ and translated, by mistake, 'Get behind
me.' (ὕπαγε ὀπίσω μου where the text required ὕπαγε ἐξ ὀπίσω
μου).

But here there is reason to doubt point 1 of the proof, for, although
hitherto unnoticed, an expression like 'Get behind me.' is found as a
sort of rebuke in <u>Shabbat T</u> 6.6 (117): 'If a crow cawed (at a man) and
(the man) said to him, "Go back where you came from." (חזור
לאחורך) this would be a superstitious act.' (<u>Lit.</u> 'from the ways of the
Amorite.') There is no recorded variant which would authorize a correction of the text to read חזור ל אחורי. (Get behind me.) Consequently the parallel is not sufficiently close to settle the question.
But, as it is, it suffices to prevent the above argument from quite con-
vincing, and the question remains open.

I hope this example has illustrated not only the sort of evidence
necessary for the discovery of mistakes in translation, but also the
sort of proof by which it can be shown that in spite of such evidence
the translation may be after all correct. In order to demonstrate the
existence of a mistake in a translation it is necessary, logically, to
prove two things as regards the expression suspect: 1. that it is difficult in Greek; 2. that it is easy in Semitic. Therefore any such
demonstration may be refuted by refutation of either one of its two
necessary parts. So, for example, when Strack-Billerbeck attempt to
find an error of translation in Mat 16.18 'And I say to you, you are
Peter.' (κἀγὼ δέ σοι λέγω ὅτι σὺ εἶ Πέτρος = אמר אנא ואף
לך את פטרוס = κἀγὼ δέ σοι λέγω (σοί, Πέτρε) it is sufficient
to remark either that the Greek they correct is not difficult, or that
the Aramaic they propose is difficult. Another example: When Moore
declares that the words ὀψὲ δὲ σαββάτων in Mat 28.1 'are a literal reproduction of בהפוק' שבת'[103] it is enough to say that the expression which he found difficult in Greek is not equivalent to that
which he found easy in Aramaic. 'A literal reproduction of'
שבת בהפוק' would have been τοῦ δὲ σαββάτου ἐκπορευομένου
or (in Lk) ἐν δὲ τῷ ἐκπορεύεσθαι τὸ σάββατον, but certainly
not ὀψὲ δὲ σαββάτων. I grant that the meaning required here is
that of שבת בהפוק' , but I cannot understand how any translator,
and above all one who translated literally, could make בהפוק' שבת
into ὀψὲ δὲ σαββάτων . Moreover, Prof. Schwabe has pointed out
to me that ὀψὲ δὲ σαββάτων is not difficult in Greek, for the same
use of the genitive with ὀψὲ is found in Thucydides 4.93.1 (ἤδη γὰρ
καὶ τῆς ἡμέρας ὀψὲ ἦν .) Another example: What seems, of all
passages in the Gospels to be most assuredly the result of a mistake
in translation, is the use of κοιναῖς in Mk 7.2-5: 'And (the Pharisees) seeing some of his disciples eating with common, that is,

unwashed, hands' etc. Of this Wellhausen said,[104] 'Jüdisch ist κοινός unrein, es muss den griechischen Lesern des Markus erklärt werden.' But, of course, the fact of the matter seems to be quite otherwise. To quote Levertoff,[105] 'From the point of view of contemporary Judaism, the expression in Mk 7.2,5 κοιναῖς (χέρσιν) (sic) is impossible. For κοινός (sic) corresponds to Hebrew "holl" (sic) which qualifies things (vessels and food) that have not been <u>consecrated</u>, but which are not <u>impure</u>; it is used also of weekdays in contrast to the Sabbath....LXX always has βέβηλος for holl.' It was not Levertoff's wish to deny that things which are common (חולין) may also be impure (טמאים), but to state that they are not impure of necessity; so understood, his statement is - for the usual usage of κοινός - substantially correct. Accordingly it would appear that this verse in Mk contains one of the clearest instances of mistranslation to be found in all the Gospels. And it is interesting to note that the explanation of the word κοινός here seems not to correspond to the word itself, but to explain the word which should have been written in its place, i.e. ἀκάθαρτος viz. טמא. Therefore this explanation seems to be, according to its content, a correction, and only according to its form (τοῦτ' ἔστιν) an explanation. On these facts it should be possible to build all sorts of historical theories concerning the translation of the Gospels, but here it is necessary to add yet another fact which would annihilate most of them - κοινός apparently meaning טמא is found not only in Mk 7.2,5 but also in Rom. 14.14, Heb. 10.29 (?) and Rev. 21.27 and in three particularly interesting verses of Acts (10.14, 28; 11.8) in which occurs the expression κοινὸν καὶ (ἢ) ἀκάθαρτον From these passages I was led to conjecture that in the New Testament literature κοινός (apart from its customary Greek meaning) served as an abbreviation for עשוי לטהרת חולין .[106] Prof. Lieberman, however, has since shown me that κοιναῖς χερσίν is equivalent to סתם ידים , an expression which, although not found in the Mishnah, appears frequently in the Talmuds. Therefore τι κοινόν must stand for סתם אוכלין , in spite of the fact that this expression is not frequent (though analogous expressions are fairly common, e.g. סתם יין in the Babylonian Talmud, <u>Abodah Zarah</u> 74.1). These expressions with סתם refer to objects of which the cleanness or uncleanness is uncertain, and which are therefore a sort of third class, apart from the clean (certainly so) and the (certainly) unclean. טהרת חולין, on the other hand, refers to food certainly clean, but of a low degree of cleanness. From all of this it appears that the passage in Mark illustrates, not the ignorance of the translator, but the author's technical accuracy in preserving the nice distinctions of Pharisaic rules about the cleanness of food - an accuracy which reflects the peculiar importance such rules acquired in primitive Christianity.

The historical questions raised by this interpretation[107] cannot here be discussed, for here I wish only to show how easily it is possible for

a passage, which seems most certainly to be the result of an error in
translation, to prove, in fact, the result of a usage peculiar to the
language of the Gospels.[108] Thus students who investigate these questions find themselves between Scylla and Charybdis: On the one hand
questions as to possible errors in translation - whether from a text
or from thought - are so numerous and so important that they cannot
be passed over in silence. (For, to cite a famous example, the essential point in the discussion as to the meaning of 'the son of man' is
the question, whether this be an error of translation - the result of a
literal translation where the meaning would have been rendered correctly by the single word 'man' - or whether this be a correct translation of a peculiar title.) On the other hand, any one who undertakes
to point out 'errors of translation' is likely at any moment to fall into
a trap. Torrey has very well said:[109] 'It happens in nine cases out of
ten, that renewed study of the "mistranslations" which we have discovered shows us either that there was no translation at all, or else
that it was quite correct.' So, to round off this chapter and to illustrate a little further the nature of errors of translation, I shall add to
these words of Torrey's a few examples taken from his works.

In the errors discovered by Torrey the thing generally lacking (of
the two signs of an error in translation, which were discussed above)
is the first indication, to wit, the difficulty of the Greek. Therefore
their correction would not be in place here, for it requires only the
demonstration that the suspect expression is found elsewhere in the
New Testament. For example, Jn 5.36 reads ἐγὼ δὲ ἔχω τὴν
μαρτυρίαν μείζω τοῦ Ἰωάννου (so ℵΘ syrᶜ, B and A read
μείζων) and Torrey[110] thinks μείζων τοῦ an error in translation
of מן דרב which should have been rendered μείζονος τοῦ. But
this is the meaning of the Greek text as it stands. μείζων and similar adjectives are sometimes, in the Greek of this period, not fully
declined.[111] Deissmann has already remarked[112] the similar use of
πλήρης in Jn 1.14. Another example: Mk 10.17-18 tells of one who
asked Jesus, ' "Good teacher, what shall I do that I may inherit eternal
life?" But Jesus said to him, "Why do you call me good? No one is
good but only God." ' Almost the same words are found in Lk 18.18-19,
but in Mat 19.16-17 is written, ' "Teacher, what good thing shall I do
that I may have eternal life?" But he said to him, "Why do you ask
me about the good? One is good." ' (εἷς ἐστιν ὁ ἀγαθός) It
seems to me that the apologetic purpose of the change made by Mat -
or by Mat's source - is sufficiently clear. But according to Torrey[113]
the original form was חד הוא טבא - which should have been translated εἷς ἐστιν τὸ ἀγαθόν . Mat erred in his translation of this
philosophical material, and as for the other texts, Torrey explains,[114]
'The interpretation which appears in Mk 10:18 and Lk 18:19 took the
field at once.'

However, it is impossible that all instances should be as clear as

33

these, and often a consideration of the general usage of the Gospels leaves a clash of theories undecided. When this happens, the usage of TL is sometimes sufficient to decide the question. For example: Lk 21.5 reads 'And when some said of the Temple that it was adorned λίθοις καλοῖς καὶ ἀναθήμασιν .' Torrey[115] wants to take ἀναθήμασιν as a translation of קורבנין, and קורבנין as a scribal error for רורבנין , meaning 'large stones.' But ἀνάθημα in the Septuagint is not the translation of קרבן but of חרם. And Sifra 27.28 (On the vs., 'Notwithstanding, no devoted thing that a man shall devote unto the Lord' -אך כל חרם אשר יחרם איש - in the Septuagint πᾶν δὲ ἀνάθημα ὃ ἂν ἀναθῇ ἄνθρωπος) declares explicitly,' R. Judah ben Beterah says, "Whence do we learn that all things which are simply 'devoted to the Lord' (סתם חרמים) are used for the repair of the Temple?"' So there is no cause to correct the technically accurate language of Lk.

Another instance is furnished by Jn 6.32: 'Amen, amen I tell you, Moses did not give you the bread from heaven, but my Father gives you the true bread from heaven.' Torrey would translate, 'Did not Moses give you the bread from heaven?' But the following facts tell against his interpretation:

1. Of 25 instances in Jn, there is no other in which 'Amen, amen' introduces a question.

2. It is not plausible that 'Amen, amen' ever should introduce a question.

3. Were this a question, it would expect an affirmative answer, and therefore would presuppose a Jewish tradition to the effect that Moses gave the manna to the Children of Israel. But as a matter of fact Mekilta speaks of the manna as a gift of the Lord and not a gift of Moses.[116]

4. To the antithesis: Not Moses but God did the miracle, there is a parallel in Mekilta 17.9: 'And so you find in (the case of) Gehazi, when Elisha said to him, "Gird up your loins and take my staff in your hand and go" (2 Kings 4.29); he went, putting his reliance on the cane.* People said to him, "Where are you going, Gehazi?" He said to them, "To raise a dead man." They said to him, "And are you able to raise a dead man? Is it not (written), 'The Lord killeth and maketh alive.'"'

Another example: Mk 14.68: 'But he denied, saying, "I neither know nor understand what you say."' The parallel in Mat 26.70 reads, 'I do not know what you say.' So does that in Lk 22.60, though the Greek differs. Torrey[117] thinks that these represent erroneous translations of Aramaic of which the meaning must have been, 'I am neither a companion of, nor do I know at all, him of whom you speak.' In justification of this opinion he says,[118] 'Are we not led by the narrative to

---

*The Hebrew might also mean, 'He began to put more and more reliance on his cane.' The context has determined my preference.

expect Peter to <u>deny Jesus</u> at this point? He does not do so, according to our Greek.' On the contrary, our Greek translates, in Mat and Lk literally and in Mk with slight emphasis, the form common in rabbinical law for formal, legal denial, e.g., <u>Shebuot</u> 8.3, ' "Where is my ox?" He said to him, "I do not know what you say." ' (So again in 8.6.)[119] Torrey concludes his remarks on these vss. by saying,[120] 'These three passages are capital examples of mistranslation.'

NOTES

1. For brevity's sake, in order not to interrupt the flow of the thought, I have here cited as examples single words, which, as their peculiar meanings are known only from their use in contexts, serve well enough, without citation of the context, to illustrate parallelism of idiom.

2. δύναμις - Jehovah: Mat 26.64; Mk 14.62 (citations from the Old Testament, but the use of δύναμις for <u>Jehovah</u> is added by the Gospels); גבורה - Jehovah: Mekilta of Rabbi Simon 14.21; Sifre on Numbers 15.31; Mekilta 15.24; 16,9,10; 17.13 etc.

3. For κορβᾶν in Mk 7.11; v.s. in the list of foreign words in the Gospels.

4. From the first controversy it is customary to refer to:

D. Diodati, <u>De Christo Graece loquente</u>, Naples, 1767.

G. de-Rossi, <u>Della lingua propria di Cristo</u>, Parma, 1772.

From the second, the most important books are:

G. Dalman, <u>Die Worte Jesu</u>, I, 2 ed. Leipzig, 1930.

idem, <u>Jesus-Jeschua</u>, Leipzig, 1922.

F. Schulthess, <u>Das Problem der Sprache Jesu</u>, Zürich, 1917.

From the last:

C. Burney, <u>The Aramaic Origin of the Fourth Gospel</u>, Oxford, 1922.

C. Torrey, <u>Our Translated Gospels</u>, N.Y., 1936.

idem, <u>The Four Gospels</u>, N.Y., 1933.

A. Schlatter, <u>Die Sprache u. Heimat des vierten Evangelisten</u>, Gütersloh, 1902.

E. Colwell, <u>The Greek of the Fourth Gospel</u>, Chicago, N.D. (c. 1931).

Of books published since the completion of this study, should be mentioned M. Black, <u>An Aramaic Approach to the Gospels and Acts</u>, Oxford, 1946.

5. Moulton and Howard, <u>A Grammar of N.T. Greek</u>, vol. II, Edinburgh 1929, pp. 412-485 (Appendix). The list of Semitic expressions, pp. 416-77, was made by Howard and comes mostly from the words of Wellhausen (especially the <u>Einleitung</u>) and Burney (<u>Aramaic Origin</u>),

though he also used the earliest articles of Torrey, Charles' Studies in the Apocalypse, Allen's commentaries on Mat (International Critical Commentary) and Mk, the commentaries of Lagrange on all the Gospels, and a number of less important works. Schlatter's Sprache und Heimat (the most important work in the field after that of Burney) is not mentioned. Chajes is not mentioned; there is no reference to Strack-Billerbeck, and so on.

6. C. Torrey, The Translations Made from the Original Aramaic Gospels, in 'Studies in the History of Religions pres. to C. H. Toy,' N.Y., 1912, pp. 269 ff., p. 273. And on p. 284 he says explicitly that the most important thing in testing a text is, not to parallel one expression to another, and not to find evidence of errors in translation (which are generally errors of the critic's), but to show that every verse contains evidence of underlying Semitic expressions.

7. id. p. 284.

8. J. Wellhausen, Einleitung in die drei ersten Evangelien, ed. 2, Berlin, 1911, pp. 10-15.

9. C. Burney, The Aramaic Origin of the Fourth Gospel, Oxford, 1922.

10. id. pp. 49-52. His remarks are accurate in substance rather than in detail, e.g., in Mat 3, unless the sentences in the question be counted it is difficult to find 13 sentences, and if they be counted, several begin without connectives.

11. For example, he shows (p. 57) that the use of a participle in place of a second verb (καὶ ἐμβλέψας .... λέγει etc.) is found only once in Jn for every 5 times in the Synoptics, and that, instead of it, Jn usually uses parataxis with καί. Then he asks, if parataxis was the customary usage of the koiné, why did the synoptists use it so little? 'The answer has been supplied elsewhere by Dr. Moulton.... "The over use of locutions which can be defended as good koiné Greek" is a test of "Greek which is virtually or actually translated." ' And so (p. 65) the casus pendens is found in Jn 27 times, in Lk, 6; if Lk wrote typical koiné, why did Jn use this locution so much more often?

12. So in the instances mentioned in the previous note, and often after.

13. Of course, if the translation were free, it would not contain the same proportion of expressions typical of the language from which it was made, as did the text translated. But if the translation were free we should not be able to prove from its style that it was a translation. The possibility of philological proof that a given book is a translation from a given language, depends on the supposition that the translation was not free.

14. I think it quite possible that Jesus spoke Hebrew, at least in his discussions with the Pharisees. It is also possible that passages in the Gospels describing these discussions go back to documents originally written in Hebrew. Considerable material for the support of

these opinions will be found in M. Segal, A Grammar of Mishnaic Hebrew, Oxford, 1927 and in the introductory volume of E. ben Iehuda's dictionary. Section IV, ch. 11. See also H. Chajes, Markus-Studien, Berlin, 1899, esp. the introduction and the note on Mk 11.5.

15. Meaning, family. Never with a personal name except in Sotah 1.4. (Bezah 2.6 and Eduyot 3.10 are examples of a different usage.)

16. i.e. Abraham, Mishnah 13, Gospels 6.

17. There is no doubt that these three expressions are merely variations of the Hebrew form (ὁ πατὴρ ὁ ἐν τοῖς οὐρανοῖς), but since this analysis depends on verbal peculiarities they must appear individually, and instances like this must be allowed for throughout all the coming calculations.

18. The instance in Taanit 3.8 is found in an illustrative story and I have therefore taken it as evidence of the customary meaning (as I have all usages within parables in the Gospels).

19. The use in direct address to God is not listed here, but under the heading πατήρ (i.e. God). As opposed to that, this heading is based on instances when the term is used as a title for men who are not themselves fathers of those using it. This includes also Mat 23.9 'Call no man father.'

20. Kassowski, Ozar Leshon Hammishnah, cites, s.v. בֵּן, one nick-name, 3 instances in which the word is found as part of a typical name Joseph ben Simon (equivalent to 'Robert Roe'), 59 instances in which a man is referred to only as the son of his father (e.g. ben Azzai) and 126 names which include ben; I have reckoned that these names, in their forms including ben, appear on an average of 5 times each in the Mishnah.

21. To these are to be added: βοανηργές (Mk 3.17), βαραββᾶς (11 times), βαρθολομαῖος (4 times), βαριωνᾶς (Mat 16.17), βαρτιμαῖος (Mk 10.46.)

22. In Mat 17.25: 'From whom do the kings of the earth receive toll or tribute, from their sons or from aliens?' The words their sons almost certainly mean, 'their subjects,' whereas in the Mishnah בְּנֵי מְלָכִים mean 'the king's own sons.' Nevertheless, because of the verbal congruence, I have listed the two terms together.

23. Citations from the Old Testament are noted only when they constitute all the instances from the Gospels to be found for a given heading.

24. To one who is not the son of the speaker.

25. Jn 19.26: 'Jesus, then, seeing his mother and the disciple whom he loved standing near-by, says to his mother, "Woman, behold your son."'

26. Sometimes children of God, sometimes 'children' in speech with God, but always - in the Mishnah - with the meaning 'the children of Israel.' In Greek, υἱοὶ τοῦ ὑψίστου, υἱοὶ τοῦ πατρός, υἱοὶ θεοῦ.

27. בֶּן עִיר 18 times, בֶּן כְּרָךְ 3 times, בֶּן מְבוֹי twice, בֶּן חָצֵר once, בֶּן מְדִינָה thrice, בֶּן כְּפָר once.

28. בֶּן הַפְּטִישׁ once, בֶּן חֲרִיץ twice, בְּנֵי בְצָלִים once.

29. In the Gospels χεὶρ κυρίου, χεὶρ τοῦ πατρός, χεὶρ σου. In the Mishnah יַד שָׁמַיִם, יַד כּוֹתֵב (לְמַעֲלָה)

30. In the Gospels χεῖρας ἀνθρώπων (3), - ἁμαρτωλῶν (2), χεῖρας ἀνθρώπων καὶ ἁμαρτωλῶν (1), - αὐτῶν (1), - τῶν μισούντων ἡμᾶς (1), - ἐχθρῶν (1). In the Mishnah there are very many expressions of this sort, e.g.: מֵת תַּחַת יָדוֹ, יָדוֹ לְחַזֵּק בְּיָדֵי אָדָם, לִיפּוֹל בְּיַד מַעֲשֵׂה יָד (never בִּידֵי אֲנָשִׁים).

31. Under this heading I have collected all Mishnaic uses of יָד as meaning authority, legal right, legal class (e.g. יָד כְּלִי חֶרֶס (Kelim 8.2) מַעֲשֶׂה מְבַטֵּל מִיַּד מַעֲשֶׂה (Kelim 25.9), possession, possibility, condition (so מֵבִיא לִידֵי and מִידֵי) and the like. In the Gospels this meaning is found only in Jn, and the 'hand' is always that of the Son, but a similar usage was listed above under the heading Of God. (χεὶρ τοῦ πατρός)

32. e.g. מִטְפַּחַת שֶׁל יָד, מַגַּל יָד, etc.

33. Meaning, once, hand-hold and once margin, border.

34. Only with the meaning by hand; not as a phrase meaning literally in the hand.

35. a : with the meaning devolves on. With this I have included instances of רָשׁוּת בְּיַד. b: with the meaning has been performed by. With this I have included instances of עֲבֵירָה בְּיַד.

36. תַּחַת יַד = עִם, בְּיַד also מֵעָם = מִיַּד and the like.

37. Following the analysis in Kassowski, Ozar Leshon Hammishnah.

38. In 6 of these 16 instances is found the measure כְּמְלֹא פֶה.

39. פִּי חֶרֶב is not found in the Mishnah.

40. מַפִּיו, בְּפֶה, עַל פֶה, all in contrast to reading from a book.

41. Including the instances of לְפִיכָךְ.

42. Including both the part of the body and the hair of the head, for in many passages it is impossible to decide which is meant.

43. In the Gospels only κεφαλὴ γωνίας (3 times); in the Mishnah many expressions.

44. e.g., רֹאשׁ וּפָתִיךְ (Negaim 13.2), בְּנֵי מָרוֹן (Rosh Hashshanah 1.2).

45. It is interesting to note that the uses in the Gospels which are not found in the Mishnah are most of them typically Semitic. Such are certainly: πατὴρ ὁ οὐράνιος

_____ ὁ ἐπουράνιος

_____ ὁ ἐξ οὐρανοῦ

_____ = ὁ θεός

_____ as a title

υἱὸς Δαυείδ

ὁ υἱός μου (spoken by God)

υἱὸς εἰρήνης

υἱὸς τῆς βασιλείας
υἱὸς γεέννης
υἱὸς τῆς ἀπολείας
υἱὸς τοῦ νυμφῶνος
χείρ (of God)
στόμα (of God)

With these compare: πατήρ = ὁ διάβολος, ὁ υἱὸς τοῦ ἀνθρώπου ὁ υἱός (= ὁ υἱὸς τοῦ θεοῦ), ὁ υἱὸς τοῦ πονηροῦ, – τοῦ φωτός, – τοῦ αἰῶνος τούτου. In any discussion of these last it would be necessary to distinguish sharply between the questions of the source of the ideas, on the one hand, and on the other, the mere linguistic usage illustrated.

46. Apart from the citations of the Old Testament, it must be remembered that many passages of the New Testament imitate the Old Testament without citing it. I have chosen not to place any weight of argument on such passages, because their discovery and determination is necessarily subjective, but I think it undeniable that they do exist and that, had account been taken of them, the following figures would have been somewhat modified, for, e.g., in the case of פה – στόμα, all usages found in the Gospels, except the customary usage, are found either in citations from the Old Testament or in Lk, in which they are certainly imitations of the Old Testament style. (See M. Johannessohn, Der Gebrauch der Präpositionen in der Septuaginta, Berlin, 1926, pp. 352-62.

47. More accurately:

אב	M	386	G 275	= 1-1/3 to 1.
בן	M	1274	G 249	= 5 to 1.
יד	M	894	G 89	= 10 to 1.
פה	M	658	G 21	= 31 to 1.
ראש	M	347	G 32	= 11 to 1.

58-1/3 to 5 - 12 to 1.

48. See n. 21 to this chapter.

49. For example: Ex. 32.26,28; Nos. 3.15,17; 4.1; 16.7,8,10; Deut. 31.9; Joshua 21.10; Chron. I.9.18; 23.24,27; Malachi 3.3, Nehemiah 12. 23. (i.e., II Esdras 22.23).

50. Mat 21.5.

51. For example: Ps. 149.2; Ezra 2.1 (i.e. II Esdras 2.1).

52. For example: Gen 11.10; Judges 2.8; II Sam 4.4; 5.4; 19.33,36. I Kings 14.21; 22.42; II Kings 8.17,26; 14.2; 15.2,32; 16.2; 21.1; 23.36; 24.8.

53. The usage is not frequent in the Old Testament, where יד generally means rather physical than legal power. Of the three examples I have cited, two (in Lev.) use יד to mean money, and one (in Esther) to mean custody.

54. And a number of other instances in which יד means physical power. Here and hereafter in this list unexplained cits. from LXX

indicate that in the vss. cited the Hebrew expression is found translated literally.

55. Many instances, e.g.: Gen. 38.20; 39.6; Lev. 16.21; I Sam. 13.22; 16.20.

56. For example: Gen. 8.11; Ps. 21 (LXX numeration).14, 12; Job 41.11.

57. Lk 21.24 (στόματι μαχαίρης), certainly an imitation of the style of the Old Testament. The expression is found some 27 times in LXX in the Law and the Prior Prophets. στόμα of other utensils: Gen. 42.27; 44.1; Zach. 5.8.

58. Mat 18.16 - Deut. 19.15. Other uses in the Old Testament translated by פה in LXX: II Sam. 13.32 etc.

59. For example: Ex. 29.10,15,19; Lev. 1.12; 4.4; 8.14.

60. εἰσ κεφαλὴν γωνίας Mat 21.42; Mk 12.10; Lk 20.17, all from Ps. 118 (LXX 117).22. Other uses in the Old Testament translated by κεφαλή in LXX: Gen. 28.12; I Kings (LXX III Kings) 7.4, 8 etc.

61. Of the translators of the Gospels he writes in The Four Gospels (N.Y., 1933, p. 245) that their purpose was like that of the translators of the LXX, viz: 'To produce something which could be understood by Greek readers, while remaining faithful to every word and idiom of the original.' On Mk see The Four Gospels pp. 242-3. On Lk he wrote in Our Translated Gospels (N.Y., 1936, p. lix), 'His habit as a translator resembles that of Aquila.'

62. The solitary use of הלעיט meaning to feed a man found in Gen. 25.30 will not serve as evidence here where the discussion is limited to the usage in TL.

63. However, I do not recall any passage in TL where divine justice is explicitly thus described, not, at least, in a manner sufficiently clear for me to use the passage as a proof text.

64. Mat 5.5.

65. For example: A. Schlatter, Sprache u. Heimat des vierten Evangelisten (Beitr. z. Förd. christl. Theol. 6.4) Gütersloh, 1902, p. 31 (On Jn 1.46, 'Can any good come out of Nazareth?'): 'Josephs Sarg u. Gottes Lade zogen miteinander, u. es sagten die Leute, "Was Gutes ist an diesen beiden Laden?" מה טיבן של שני ארונות הללו "Was Gutes ist am Toten, dass er gehe mit der Lade des ewig Lebendigen?" מה טיבו של מת להלוך עם ארון זי העולמים.' And so on. The citation is from Mekilta 13.19. Unfortunately מה טיב is a well-known idiom meaning 'What is the nature of?' In spite of this passage and a few others cited below, Schlatter's book is the best of those on the subject of this thesis, and just for that reason I have made a point of correcting the few mistakes I found in it.

66. id. p. 30.

67. P. Fiebig, Altjüdische Gleichnisse, Tübingen, 1904, p. 56, idem, Jesu Bergpredigt, Göttingen, 1924, pt. I, p. 27. In his Pirque 'aboth

(Tübingen, 1906, p. 9) F. finds a parallel to Jn 1.46 (ἔρχου καὶ ἴδε) in Abot 2.9 where also the expression has a figurative meaning, as opposed to the literal meaning of the expression in Jn.

68. Jn 1.38-9: '(Jesus) says to them (the disciples), "What are you looking for?" They said to him, "Rabbi...where are you staying?" He says to them, "Come and see." So they came and saw.'

Jn 1.45-47: 'Philip finds Nathanael and says to him, "We have found him of whom Moses...wrote, Jesus...the man from Nazareth." And Nathanael said to him, "Can anything from Nazareth be good?" Philip says to him, "Come and see." Jesus saw Nathanael coming to him' etc.

Jn 11.34: '(Jesus) said, "Where have you put him (Lazarus)?" They tell him, "Sir, come and see." '

As against these:

Mekilta 12.1 (end): 'Come and see how the Lord answers him'...

Mekilta 15.25 'Rabbi Simon ben Gamliel says, "Come and see how far the ways of the Holy One, Blessed be He, differ from the ways of flesh and blood." '

Mekilta 20.12: 'Come and see how they were paid off. It is said'...

Mekilta 21.6: 'Rabbi says, "Come and see that (the expression) the world (הָעוֹלָם) (means) only 50 years, for it is said" '...

69. Sprache u. Heimat, p. 39.

70. Jn 3.2: 'This man (Nicodemus) came to him by night and said to him, "Rabbi, we know you are a teacher come from God." '

Jn 9.4: (Jesus is speaking to his disciples) 'We must do the works of him who sent me, while it is day...(5) When I am in the world, I am the light of the world.' (And thereupon he heals the blind man.)

Jn 20.2 (Mary Magdalene) 'runs and comes to Simon Peter and to the other disciple whom Jesus loved and says to them, "They have taken the Lord out of the tomb and we don't know where they've put him." '

71. So, for example, all the instances recorded in Kasowski, Thesaurus Thosephthae, s.v. אמרנו.

72. In the opinion of the source of Mekilta.

73. H. Danby, tr., The Mishnah, Oxford, 1933. D. translates, 'Rightly have they said,' but the correct translation would be 'However, they did say.' Kassowski, Ozar, cites the expression from Kilayim 2.2; Terumot 2.1; Shabbat 1.3; 10.4; Nazir 7.3. The reading in the last of these passages is dubious.

74. Sprache u. Heimat, p. 58.

75. Jesu Bergpredigt, Göttingen, 1924, pt. I, p. 27, note on nos. 78-9.

76. σὺ εἶπας : Mat 26.25,64. σὺ λέγεις Mat 27.11 // Mk 15.2 // Lk 23.3 // (?) Jn 18.37. ὑμεῖς λέγετε Lk 22.70.

77. I. Abrahams, Studies in Pharisaism and the Gospels, II, Cambridge, 1924, p. 2.

78. J. Klausner, Jesus of Nazareth, tr. Danby, N. Y., 1925, p. 346 and n. 48.

79. Sprache u. Heimat, p. 41.

80. Jn 3.7: (Jesus speaks to Nicodemus) 'Do not marvel that I said to you, "You must be born again." '

Jn 5.28: (Jesus speaks to the Jews) 'Do not marvel at this, that (as I said to you) the hour is coming in which all those in the tombs shall hear his voice (viz. the Son of Man's).'

81. Schlatter cites as evidence Sifre on Deut. 12.23 and 24 (twice); Sifre on Numbers 5.3; 6.10,29; Mekilta 12.37; 14. (should be 13) 19, 24. (6.29 does not exist. 14.24 lacks אל תתמה).

82. So, for example, in all but three of the instances cited above, and in these in Sifra 1.2 (twice); 2.1 (beginning and end); 4.22 (end); 5.1 (beginning), 23; 14.3 (end); 15.2 (end), 3 (beginning), 10 (middle), 13 (beginning); 22.27 (beginning).

As against these there is only one, of all the instances I noticed in Sifra, in which אל תתמה introduces an opinion which is finally adjudged correct, and in this (Sifra 4.4) the opinion - although finally approved - appears at first to contradict the text of the Old Testament, and therefore has this introduction.

83. So Schlatter, S. u. H. p. 57. Prof. Lieberman, in a conversation to which I shall several times refer, told me that in the Babylonian Talmud, Shabbat 108.1 (bottom) in a baraita from the second century, καλῶς is found written in Hebrew letters.

84. Strack-Billerbeck on the verse in question.

85. Cf. M. Dibelius, From Tradition to Gospel, tr. B. L. Wolf, London, 1934, p. 28, 'The sayings of Jesus were handed down within the framework of a Christian Halakha.'

86. R. T. Herford, The Pharisees, London, N. D. (c. 1924), p. 115, n. 1.

87. ZNW 33.105 ff. The citation is from p. 126.

88. Theologisches Wörterbuch zum Neuen Testament, ed. G. Kittel, vol. II, Stuttgart, 1935. p. 345.

89. A slip. 6 times.

90. op. cit., n. 76.

91. On Mat 5.21.

92. To wit: Sotah 9.9: 'After murderers became numerous the law about the heifer of which the neck is to be broken was allowed to fall into abeyance (cf. Deut. 21)....After adulterers became numerous the ordeal of the bitter water (cf. Num. 5.11 ff.) was stopped, and Rabbi Johanan ben Zakkai put an end to it.' (cp. Sotah T 14.1-2 (320))

Shebiit 10.3: '(A debt for which) a prosbol (has been drawn) does not lapse (at the seventh year). This is one of the reforms instituted by Hillel the Elder.' (cf. Gittin 4.3).

93. v. I, Stuttgart, 1933, s.v. ἀρχαῖος. The explanation given by Strack-Billerbeck in Mat. 5.21 (דורות הראשונים) is even less satisfactory.

94. בראשונה Nedarim 11.12; Gittin 6.5; Niddah 10.6; Tebul Yom 4.5 (twice); Demai T 3.4 (49); Gittin T 1.1 (323); 4.5 (327); Abodah Zarah T 7.2 (471). Variant expressions which I find interesting in relation to Mat are: Nedarim 9.6: בראשונה היו אומרים... עד שבא ר"ע ולימד ש.....; Sifra 15.33: זקנים הראשונים היו אומרים... עד שבא ר"ע ולימד....

95. The same controversy is found in clearer form in Sotah T 6.6-11 (304-6) and there the expression ואני אומר appears 5 times.

96. E. Stauffer, ἐγώ in Theologisches Wörterbuch z. N. T. ed. G. Kittel, II. Stuttgart, 1935, pp. 345-6. (What makes such criticism particularly tiring is the fact that ἐγὼ δὲ λέγω in Mat 5 is almost certainly an editorial device, and cannot be referred even to Mat's sources, much less to Jesus himself.) Additional material of the same sort in G. Kittel, Die Probleme des palästinischen Spätjudentums u. das Urchristentum, Stuttgart, 1926, the sections (III and IV) on αὐτοβασιλεία at the end of Das religionsvergleichende Problem. In contrast see the excellent article of D. Daube, ἐξουσία in Mk 1.22 and 27 in The Journal of Theological Studies, 39.45 ff.

97. Cp. Mat 7.28 and its parallels. "And it came to pass that when Jesus finished these words the crowds were astonished at his teaching." These verses also are usually taken as proof of the difference between Jesus and the Rabbis.

98. In discussing the use of אני in TL it is necessary to distinguish between אני אומר used in contradiction, and שאני אומר used to introduce a reason for an opinion. The second of these is not relevant here. (It is found, e.g. in Kinnim 3.3; Demai 5.3; Teharot 3.7; Maaser Sheni T 4.12 (94); 5.1 (95); Gittin T 6.9 (329); Oholot T 16.1 (613); 16.10 (614); and many other places.) In it the אני has no reference to any particular person. Nor does it in the similar expressions הריני אומר (Terumot T 8.17 (40)); מה אני מקיים (Sifra 26.3); אני יודע (Sifra 25.9, where the text reads איני); אדון אני (Sifra 22.27 (end)) etc. But even here generalization is misleading, for these expressions are sometimes used to introduce contradictions and then the pronoun they contain is emphasized. For example: שאני אומר in Mikwaot T 6.3 (658) and again in 1.2 (652). See also Niddah T 1.6 (641) where the expression may be from the hand of the editor. Prof. Lieberman tells me that Solomon Adani, in his book Meleket Shelomoh, tractate Arakin, ch. 4, mishnah 2, lists the rabbinical uses of אומר אני. See also the article of Prof. Lieberman in Tarbiz 2.110.

99. If this be so it follows that, supposing the Gospels were, in fact, translated, most of the errors which occurred in their translation will never be discoverable, for most such errors, like most errors by

copyists, result in easier readings. The passages which would cause errors of translation would be the difficult ones, and the translator would always attempt to make them comprehensible, i.e., easy. Therefore, if the gospels were translated it is probable that the passages which we now find difficult are those in which the translator was most accurate.

100. Not to Strack-Billerbeck, not to W. Allen in his commentaries on Mk (The Gospel according to St. Mark, N. Y., 1915) and on Mat (ICC), not to Lagrange in his commentaries on Mk (Évangile selon St. Marc, 4e ed. Paris, 1929) and on Mat (Évangile selon St. Matthieu, 3e ed., Paris 1927), and, according to Cornelius a Lapide (Commentaria in quatuor evangelia, ed. A. Padovani, 2 ed. Augustae Taurinorum) on Mat 16.23, also not to such ancient commentators as Jerome and Chrysostom, who understand here only φύγε.

101. e.g. Sifre on Deut. 29.9 (end). 'It happened that R. Johanan b. Zakkai was riding on his donkey and his disciples were walking after him'...See also Sifra 14.4 (end), Mekilta 31.13 etc. Also Mekilta 13.2 where the expression ר׳ רבי׳ תירינן appears with the meaning We are your disciples. (It is so explained in the parallel passages). This last instance was called to my attention by Prof. Lieberman, who contradicted the explanation given in Horovitz' note ad loc.

102. According to A. Plummer, An Exegetical Commentary on... Matthew, London, 1909, on 16.23, Origen felt that ὕπαγε ὀπίσω μου should normally mean Be my disciple. The figurative use of ὀπίσω is noted by M. Johannessohn (Der Gebrauch der Präpositionen i.d. LXX, Berlin, 1925, pp. 215-6): It is frequently found in the LXX with πορεύομαι and the name of some alien god.

103. G. F. Moore, Conjectanea Talmudica, JAOS 26.315 ff.,cit. from p. 324.

104. Einleitung in die drei ersten Evangelien, 2 ed., Berlin, 1911, p. 20.

105. P. Levertoff, Midrash Sifre on Numbers, London, N.D. (1926), p. 116, n. 6.

106. For which see Hagigah T 3.2-3 (236).

107. For example: a: Just what was the point at issue in Mk 7 - did it concern a prohibition thought to be based directly on the text of the Old Testament, or merely a rabbinical ruling? And how would the answer to this question, if it could be discovered, change the answer to the general question of the relation of Jesus to the Judaism of his day?

b: What was the history of that part of the early church in which such rules were preserved?

108. And the Greek and Semitic worlds were so close that it is now possible, as was seen above and will be seen again below, to prove from Semitic parallels that dubious Greek usages were actually customary.

109. C. Torrey, The Translations Made from the Original Aramaic Gospels, in 'Studies in the Hist. of Rel. pres. to C. H. Toy,' N.Y., 1912, p. 284.

110. Our Translated Gospels, N.Y., 1936, p. 39.

111. Moulton and Howard, A Grammar of NT Greek, II, Edinburgh, 1929, p. 161 (and the notes there): 'The form in –ω has in Hellenistic an indeclinable (sic) use, of which there are two or three traces in N.T.....Mt 26.53 חפס...23.19D....P. Leid C verso ii,17...P. Oxy vii. 1029.24.' Prof. Schwabe reminded me that 'indeclinable' is not the mot juste for an accusative form. In Moulton and Howard see also I, p. 50.

112. A. Deissmann, Licht vom Osten, 4 ed., Tübingen, 1923, pp. 99 f.

113. Our Translated Gospels, p. 16.

114. id. p. 20.

115. id. p. 134.

116. Manna is mentioned as a gift of God in Ex. 16.4,6,8; Mekilta 16.4,5,7,8,12,13,28,29,33 and 35; Mekilta of Rabbi Simon to the same vss., except 33 and 35, and also to 16.15; Sifre on Numbers and Sifre Zutta 11.19. As against these, I have not noticed any place in which it is mentioned as a gift of Moses. (It is, however, given because of Moses' virtue (בזכות משה): Mekilta and Mekilta of R. Simon 16.33. And Moses is said to have brought it down, in Sifre on Deut. 1.9; 32.48 and 32.50 (?), but it is one thing to bring it down, another to give it, as shown by the adjacent words in 32.48 and 32.50, where Moses is said to have 'brought down' the Law. Certainly these words were not intended to imply that he gave it.)

117. Our Translated Gospels, p. 16.

118. id. p. 17.

119. The same idiom is found in The Testaments of the Twelve Patriarchs (Joseph 13.2).

120. Our Translated Gospels, p. 18.

Chapter 3

PARALLELS OF MEANING

Of all the parallels between the Gospels and TL, those of which most has hitherto been written have been the parallels of meaning. In the notes I have listed some of the most important books which deal with them.[1] Here I want, first of all, briefly to define the concept, parallel of meaning.

In the parallelism of single words, discussed above, the essential relationship lay in the form of the words, the parallelism of their meanings was merely a conditio sine qua non, i.e., it would have been out of place there to discuss pairs of words which were parallel in meaning alone, as ὕδωρ - מים , and equally out of place to discuss words parallel only in external form, as שפט and τόπος ; as opposed to both these groups, we were there concerned only with pairs of words parallel both in meaning and in external form, as סימן - σημεῖον , but, given such pairs, we then concerned ourselves only with the parallelism of external form, and thought of the parallelism in meaning only as of a condition necessary to make the parallelism of form significant. The same was true in the discussion of parallels of idiom. In noticing, for instance, the fact that the expression οὐκ οἶδα τί λέγεις [2] (and its variants) closely paralleled the Hebrew expression איני יודע מה אתה סח we were primarily concerned, not with the meaning of the two expressions, but rather with their external form. Their meaning - simple denial of a proposition - is found frequently in every language; what made the pair interesting was the coincidence of the somewhat unusual external form in which this meaning was conveyed, yet this coincidence of form would not itself have been interesting had not the meanings also coincided.

Now, as against these previous examples, the pairs of passages to be discussed in this chapter are of interest primarily because of the parallelism of their meanings, and the external form in which these meanings are expressed is of no essential importance.

The concept 'meaning' I shall not attempt to define. Anyone who wants to enter on the question, 'How can two sentences, having no word in common, yet have the same meaning?,' can turn to Bertrand Russell's book An Inquiry into Meaning and Truth[3] and get from it whatever meaning he is able. Russell himself says[4] 'The net result is to substitute articulate hesitation for inarticulate certainty.' So, from here on, I shall write as if I knew both, in general, the meaning of 'meaning' and, in particular, the meanings of those sentences I shall have to discuss.

Again, I shall not attempt to list all the parallels of meaning between the Gospels and TL which have hitherto been noted. The subject is too wide. Every word, from the name of the simplest thing to the name of God himself, can serve as the basis for a parallel of meaning, and on many of these parallels, of which the number is at least equal to the number of nouns and verbs in the Gospels, the standard commentators have already written. In general there are to be distinguished parallels between words referring to concrete objects (utensils, garments, drugs, countries, etc.), parallels between words referring to social phenomena (customs, social groups and classes, laws, etc.) and parallels between words referring to intellectual and psychological entities, the concepts of philosophy and religion. Of these groups I shall discuss only the last, which has hitherto been considered the most important. The interest which has hitherto motivated the study both of TL and of the Gospels has been basically and principally religious, and although both these literatures may serve as important sources for knowledge of the archaeological bric-a-brac and sociological curiosities of their times, yet most students have approached them as religious literatures. It is necessary to emphasize this fact for only it explains why so many of these students have fallen into error.

Sometimes, indeed, the error resulted from ignorance of the sources,[5] but most often it resulted from the desire to apologize for one religion at the expense of the other. A clear case of such apology is found, for example, in I. Abrahams, Studies in Pharisaism and the Gospels, First Series,[6] pp. 142-3. It happens that two theories - a. that there is an unforgiveable sin; b. that some men will have no part in the world to come - are found both in the Gospels and in TL. Nevertheless, Abrahams attempts to contrast the two literatures in respect of their theories concerning these matters (or, as he thought, this matter, for he confuses the two theories and talks about them as if they were one). According to his opinion, but in the words of Mat,[7] the synoptic Gospels shut the kingdom of Heaven against men, whereas TL left it open. As a proof of this he refers to several passages from the Gospels.

(1) The parables of the wheat and the tares (Mat. 13.24-30, 37-42) and of the sheep and the goats (Mat 25.31-46). These parables teach that at the last judgment some men will be condemned to punishment, but they do not suffice to prove what Abrahams wants, viz., that these men are conceived as evil by their very nature, for no parable goes on all four legs, and from a comparison made to illustrate one point it is not legitimate to draw conclusions concerning another. This should have been clear from the parable of the sheep and the goats, where the good men and the bad are compared to the two groups of animals differing by nature, and yet it is explicitly said that the bad are found guilty because they did not practise charity:[8] 'Depart from

47

me, ye accursed, into the everlasting fire....For I hungered and ye gave me no food.'

(2) The expression found 6 times in Mat[9] and once in Lk:[10] 'There shall be weeping and gnashing of teeth.' This is completely irrelevant. Of course the wicked are not expected to enjoy themselves in Gehenna, but the question in point here is not, How will they like it?; it is, Why will they go there?

(3) Jesus' words as reported in Mat 11.24 and Lk 10.12, that in the day of judgment the men of Sodom will be better off than those who did not receive the Gospel. This will serve as a proof for theory b - that some men have no part in the world to come - but not for theory a - that there is an unforgiveable sin - for in both passages Jesus speaks against the inhabitants of certain cities of Galilee because they did not repent at his preaching, from which it is a reasonable inference that he thought them capable of repentance and wished to occasion their repentance by his warning.

(4) The parable of the two ways, found once in the Gospels (Mat 7.13-4) and often in TL (e.g., Abot 2.9; Sifre on Deut. 11.16, 22 (middle), 26, 28; Mekilta 14.29 (end); Mekilta of R. Simon ib.; Midrash Tannaïm 11.26, 28; 13.16; Mekilta to Deut. (printed in Midrash Tannaïm) 11.28 and 13.17, all of them apparently based on Jeremiah 21.8). As a matter of fact the use of this figure in Mat is one of the most striking and best known signs of the Jewish influence on this 'Jewish' Gospel, and I cannot understand how it was possible for Abrahams to suppose it evidence of a difference between G and TL.

(5) 'The invariable intolerance and lack of sympathy when addressing opponents, and the obvious expectation that they will be excluded from the Kingdom.' If Abrahams thought these evidence for theory a - that there is an unforgiveable sin - he was wrong, for Mat - the Gospel which is hardest on the Pharisees - 3.7-8 represents John the Baptist as saying, when the Pharisees and Sadducees came to be baptized, 'Who taught you to flee from the wrath to come? Produce fruit worthy of repentance.' etc., and almost the same words are found in Lk 3.7-8. If, however, he thought that according to the sources of the Gospels there would be no part in the world to come for most of those who opposed Jesus, he was doubtless correct, but this opinion furnishes no ground for distinction between the Gospels and TL, for it is also the opinion of TL that heretics (מינים) have no part in the world to come (for example: Sanhedrin T 13.5(434); Sifre Zutta 15.30-31; Sifre on Numbers 15.31;[11] Sifre on Deut. 32.36). As for 'lack of sympathy,' I can recall no place in TL in which any sympathy whatsoever is shown for heretics.

(6) Finally, he brings one adequate proof text for theory a - that there is an unforgiveable sin: Mk 3.29: 'One who blasphemes against the holy spirit has no forgiveness forever, but is guilty of an eternal sin.' As against all these proofs, adequate and otherwise, he cites

from TL only one piece of evidence for theory a: Abot 5.18: 'One
who causes many to sin is not given the opportunity to repent;' and
one for theory b: Sanhedrin 10.1: 'And these are they who have no
part in the world to come: He who says that the Law does not teach
the resurrection of the dead, and (he who says that) the Law is not of
God (lit. from the heavens), and the Epicurean. R. 'Akiba says, "Also
he who reads heretical books and he who says spells over wounds"...
Abba Saul says, "Also he who pronounces the Tetragrammaton according to its letters."' And of these passages Abraham says, 'Such
views, however, were theoretical metaphysics (sic) rather than practical religious teaching.' Now in the first place, these views in no
way concern 'theoretical metaphysics.' (And what, by the way, are
practical metaphysics?) In the second place, the expression 'He has
no part (in the world to come - or its equivalent).' is frequent in TL,
being found, for example, in Sanhedrin T 12.9 ff. (433); Mekilta 22.24
(end) and Mekilta of R. Simon ib.; Abot 3.11; and the passages in
which this expression is found are only a few of those in which a given
man or group of men is denied a part in the world to come. It would
be too much trouble to make a complete list of such places, which
would have to contain not only the passages on the heretics, like those
cited above, but also such passages as Sifre on Numbers 18.20 (on
money); Sifre on Deut. 11.22 (end) (on the use of the Law), and so on,
and it is already clear from those cited above that in TL it was nothing strange to deny to a given man or group of men a part in the world
to come; therefore I go on to the question of the unforgiveable sin.
Beside the above-cited passage in Abot I have noted only Yom Hakkippurim T 5.11 (191) which is parallel to the passage in Abot; Shebuot T
3.4 (449) (the opinion of R. Ishmael contradicting ben Dama): 'The
(Sacred) Text made forgiveness of sin depend on confession (lit. on
those who confess). To this, (false) witnesses (against the defendant)
in capital trials are an exception; whether or not they confess, God
does not pardon them (lit. They do not pardon them from the Heavens.);'
and Sifre on Deut. 32.38 (end): 'The Holy One, Blessed be He, pardons
everything (else, but) on profanation of the Name He takes vengeance
immediately.' These are, admittedly, few, but I think them sufficient,
with the one passage cited from the Gospels by Abrahams, to show
that the theory was common to the Gospels and to TL.

One more example, and one more striking, of the way apologetic
motives have led students into error, is the article of Strack-Billerbeck on the Jewish theory of rewards for virtue.[12] Here there is no
need even to review the opinions found in TL, for Strack-Billerbeck
in their commentary misunderstood the meaning of the Gospels. The
text on which they comment is Mat 20.1-15: 'For the kingdom of
Heaven is like a householder who went out early to hire laborers for
his vineyard. Having settled with the laborers for a dinar the day, he
sent them into his vineyard....And, going out about the eleventh hour,

he found others standing (idle) and says to them, "Why have you stood here all day idle?" ' (Strack-Billerbeck: 'Die Frage....lässt erkennen, dass zur Mitarbeit im Reiche Gottes jeder ohne Ausnahme verpflichtet ist.'[13]) 'They say to him, "Because no one has hired us." ' (The answer shows that Strack-Billerbeck's explanation of the question is false.) 'He says to them, "You go into the vineyard, too." When it gets late, the owner of the vineyard says to his steward, "Call the laborers and give (them their) pay, beginning with the last, up to the first. And those (hired) about the eleventh hour, coming, got a dinar each, and the first, coming, thought that they would get more, and they also got a dinar each. But, taking it, they grumbled against the householder....But he answered one of them and said, "Fellow, I'm not wronging you. Didn't you agree with me for a dinar? Take yours and get out. I want to give this last (man the same as) I gave you. Can't I manage my own affairs to suit myself? Or is your nose out of joint because I am generous?" ' (οὐκ ἔξεστίν μοι ὃ θέλω ποιῆσαι ἐν τοῖς ἐμοῖς; ἢ ὁ ὀφθαλμός σου πονηρός ἐστιν ὅτι ἐγὼ ἀγαθός εἰμι;)

Strack-Billerbeck:[14] 'Die Frage des Hausherrn an einen der Murrenden: "Steht es mir nicht frei..." ..stellt fest, dass der Lohn für die Arbeit im Reiche Gottes völlig vom freien Belieben Gottes abhängt. <u>Die Arbeit für Gottes Reich vollzieht sich nicht auf Grund eines Rechtsvertrages zwischen Gott und Mensch, so dass der göttliche Lohn der menschlichen Leistung entspräche,</u> sondern die Arbeit ist einfach des Menschen Pflicht, die zu leisten ist ohne jede Rücksicht auf Lohn; wird trotzdem von Gottes Güte Lohn gewährt, so ist und bleibt dieser ein reiner Gnadenlohn. Das ist der Grund- und Eckstein der neutestamentlichen Lohnlehre.' (my underlining.)

I have cited the text and the beginning of the commentary at length, fearing that a mere summary might seem a misrepresentation. In commenting on the commentary I have only to say that the underlined words contradict the plain sense of the text of Mat. According to the plain sense of Mat: (1) The householder <u>settled</u> with the laborers that they were to work for a dinar a day. (2) At the end of the day he paid them what he owed them, a dinar each for the work they had done, and when the payment was contested he reminded them that that was the rate on which they had <u>settled.</u> (3) The first workers had a legal claim to their pay, and this claim was admitted by the householder when he said, 'Take yours' (ἆρον τὸ σόν). (4) The last workers did not receive a bit more than the first. (5) Whatever the last workers did receive they received only <u>because</u> they went and worked in the vineyard. (6) In fine, the important difference between the first and the last workers is merely this, that the last received <u>the same pay</u> as the first <u>in return for less work.</u>

If so, the question arises, What was the purpose of the parable? Strack-Billerbeck attempted to understand it as teaching the theory of

salvation found in or read into the letters of Paul, i.e., in looking for
parallels of meaning between it and other texts of the same period,
they decided to think it similar to certain passages of Paul's letters.
In that, as we have seen, they erred. So the question remains, To
what other texts of the period is it truly similar.

I think it most similar to the <u>mashal</u> found in Sifra 26.9 - so similar, in fact, that I think the teaching of the parable in Mat intended to
contradict the teaching of which the <u>mashal</u> in Sifra is a later expression. Sifra reads: ' "And I shall be free for you." (ופניתי אליכם)
To make a comparison, what is this like? It is like a king who hired
many laborers, and there was there one laborer who worked for him
a long while. The laborers came in to get their pay, and that laborer
came in with them. The king said to him, "My son, I shall be free for
you (in a moment). (בני אפנה לך) These many (laborers) are those
who did little work for me, and I am giving them little pay, but as for
you, I have a large account to settle with you." So Israel were asking
their pay of God and the gentiles also were asking their pay of God.
And God says to Israel, "My children, I shall be free for you (in a
moment). These gentiles did little work for me, and I am giving them
little pay, but as for you, I have a large account to settle with you."
Therefore it is said, "And I shall be free for you." '

I am not sure of the correct translation of פנה in this passage.
Strack-Billerbeck, who cited the passage[15] without seeing its relation
to the story in Mat, translated according to the meaning given the
verb by its Biblical context, 'zu dir wenden (dich besonders berück-
sichtigen).' But it seems to me more probable that the meaning given
it in Sifra, here, is like that given it in <u>Parah T</u>. 3.8 (632) where Jastrow[16] translates it by the words 'be free, be at leisure.'[17] If this be
the correct translation, then the meaning of the passage in Sifra is that
God is now giving the gentiles their little pay, and when he will be free
to settle with Israel (i.e., in the world to come) he will give them their
great pay. And if this interpretation be correct, then there is yet
another relationship between this story and that in Mat, of which the
last words[18] (not cited above) are, 'Thus the last shall be first and the
first last.' These words caused Strack-Billerbeck considerable difficulty, and their explanation of them contradicts not only the plain
meaning of the story, but also their own exposition cited above, for
they say,[19] 'Darum müssen sie (the laborers first hired) es sich gefal-
len lassen, dass ihnen nach dem kalten Buchstaben des Lohnvertrags
das gegeben wird, was mit ihnen vereinbart war.' If man have no legal
claim against God, why was anything given them? If all pay is pure
'Gnadenlohn,' what is the force of the agreement to pay? But inasmuch as they did get exactly the same as those hired last, what advantage is there to trust in the mercy of God (along with a little work)
as over against 'dem kalten Buchstaben des Lohnvertrags'?

As against this interpretation, it seems to me certain that the texts in Mat and in Sifra contradict each other. The gist of the story in Sifra is that the amount of the pay varies according to the amount of the labor; the gist of that in Mat is that the same pay is given to all the laborers, without relation to the amount of the labor. Moreover, it seems to me probable that the story in Mat deliberately contradicts another form (older than that before us)[20] of the story in Sifra, i.e., that the story in Mat presupposes the other as already known to the audience. For of the two stories, that most plausible, that true to the way of the world, and, therefore, that better adapted to a parable, is the story in Sifra. And from many passages, such as 'You have heard that it was said to those of old...but I tell you.'[21] it is known that Mat liked to present the words of Jesus as contradicting those of the Rabbis. This hypothesis already verges on historical theory, nevertheless I note further that if it be correct, then the last words of the story in Mat can be explained easily. For these - 'The last shall be first and the first last' - are not only the conclusion of the story, but also its introduction,[22] connecting it with the previous saying, which is:[23] 'Amen I tell you that...everyone who leaves houses or brothers ...for my name's sake, will receive manifold and will inherit eternal life.' And this saying, in Mat (as in Mk and Lk[24]) comes as an answer to Peter. For when Jesus said (of the 'rich, young ruler') that it is hard for a rich man to enter the kingdom of Heaven, Peter asked, 'What then shall we have, we, who have left everything and followed you?' And Jesus answered him that everyone who had lost anything for the Gospel's sake would be paid for it both in this world and in the world to come. This last point, that they both 'eat in this world and inherit in the world to come' (like the disciples of Abraham in Abot 5.19) appears yet more clearly from the texts in Mk and Lk.[25] So the sequence of thought is clear, and the words to be emphasized in the saying as reported by Mat are everyone and eternal life. The story which was current before the Christian one, taught that the gentiles receive a little pay for their little work, and Israel great pay for their work; but that the gentiles get theirs in this world, not in the world to come, and Israel in the world to come, not in this world.[26] Thus the first are last, and the last first. As against this, the Christian story teaches that everyone who works in the vineyard gets paid both in this world and in the world to come, everyone gets the same pay, but this pay is given first to those who began their work last, and last to those who began first, and only thus are the last first and the first last. The reason for this order of payment could be found in the fact that the gentiles (who had not been previously working for God) soon outnumbered the Jews (who had been employed for a long time) in their reception of the Gospel. This representation of Israel as working in the vineyard of God, and of the converted gentiles as called to the same work, agrees with the general description of Mat as a 'Jewish-Christian' Gospel. Moreover, the parable thus interpreted agrees

especially with Mat 21.31-2: 'Amen I tell you that the tax collectors
and the prostitutes precede you into the kingdom of God. For John
came to you in the way of righteousness and you did not believe him,
but the tax collectors and the prostitutes believed him.' It must be
noted that this concerns individuals (tax collectors, etc.) whereas the
story in Sifra deals with the gentiles generally. What the laborers of
Mat 20 were I shall not venture to guess. In order to emphasize the
parallel with Sifra I have written as if they were also the gentiles
generally, but I think it quite possible that they were now one, now the
other, according to the different periods and environments in which
the story was handed down. However, the discussion of such questions
would lead far from the subject of this chapter, to which I now return.

   This passage from Strack-Billerbeck was introduced to show how
apologetic motives have led students into error, and it is clear that in
this instance such motives led them to 'understand' Mat according to
Paul, and Paul according to Luther. Another example of the same
sort of 'understanding' is their notion that the Gospels contained one
theory of pay and that this theory could be demonstrated from one
parable. And just as they wrote of 'die neutestamentliche Lohnlehre,'
when as a matter of fact this is a question on which some passages of
the Gospels flatly contradict some of Paul, so they wrote of the Gospels
as if they had been written complete, by one man, at one time, to teach
one theory, when as a matter of fact every one of them is a collection
of texts differing widely from each other.[27] They erred again, in the
same way, when (as opposed to 'die neutestamentliche Lohnlehre')
they attempted to describe 'die altsynagogale Lohnlehre,' for the texts
of TL are also collections, written by no one man, and, on questions
like this, to hunt through them for the Jewish doctrine is like hunting
the chimaera. However, Strack-Billerbeck succeeded in finding the
Jewish doctrine which they were looking for. How did they do it?
They decided a priori that, according to TL, salvation is given only as
pay and never as grace,[28] they collected a great many passages which
could serve to prove that salvation was given as pay, and finally they
quoted a few of the passages contradicting these - quoted them as[29]
'Korrektive, die die ofizielle (!) Lohnlehre selbst herausforderte.'
Students too often use historical concepts like 'cause,' 'development,'
'correction' and 'demand,' in order to extract from texts disorderly
and contradictory as life itself, the simple and beautiful truth of the
ideal world.

   I indulge in this rhetoric not only for its own sake, but also because
it serves as a transition to another cause (or, to another aspect of the
same cause) of this sort of error, which has been illustrated above by
one example, but which could easily be illustrated by many examples
from the works of most of the scholars who have hitherto treated
these subjects.[30] This other cause is: That scholars have come to
these questions of parallels of meaning, from the side of ideas and not

from the side of texts, from the side of concepts and not from the side of words. For in spite of the fact that a concept may seem to be definite and clear in the mind of the student, yet when he comes to look through the text for sentences which express or imply it, he will find it involved in so much of the material that to treat the evidence fully he will have either to write a commentary on the whole text, or to chose certain passages which are (he thinks) more important and to write of the concept as it is expressed in these passages, and these only. And, of those who resign themselves to the second of these alternatives, every one will choose his own passages, according to his own theories.

Thus Strack-Billerbeck, to illustrate the concept Gnadenlohn, chose one passage from all the Gospels, and thus G. F. Moore, in order to refute the theory advanced by Strack-Billerbeck, chose one passage from all TL, viz. Sanhedrin 10.1 ('Everyone of Israel has a share in the world to come.') and wrote, on the basis of it and of two citations from the later literature,[31]: 'These facts are ignored when Judaism is set in antithesis to Christianity, a "Lohnordnung" over against a "Gnadenordnung." "A lot in the World to Come" is not wages earned by works, but is bestowed by God in pure goodness upon the members of his chosen people, as "eternal life" in Christianity is bestowed on the individuals whom he has chosen, or on the members of the church. If the one is grace, so is the other.' But Moore cited only the beginning of the passage in Sanhedrin. The second half ('And these are they (of Israel) who do not have a part in the world to come') would suggest to the reader a different conclusion. As a matter of fact, one who thinks of the religion of the Tannaim as a Lohnordnung, has one important piece of evidence on his size, viz., the opinion of Paul, who, as a pupil of R. Gamaliel the Elder,[32] certainly knew the Judaism of his time, and who nevertheless wrote of it as of a Lohnordnung. But one who thinks of the religion of the Tannaim as a Gnadenordnung has on his side no important evidence at all, for the religion, as described in TL, is not an Ordnung. The Ordnung, in all the theories, has been added by men who wanted to write about religious concepts and to find one concept expressed by the whole literature.

To the question of Paul's opinion, I shall return at the end of this chapter. First I have to discuss the words for 'pay,' שכר in TL and μισθός in the Gospels, and the other words derived from these two roots. I presuppose a knowledge of their customary social meanings, and I shall try to determine all the other meanings found in the two literatures, by means of an examination of all the passages in which they are found.

The word μισθός is found 15 times in the Gospels.[33] To these must be added μίσθιος (thrice in Lk 15),[34] μισθόομαι (twice in Mat 20),[35] and μισθωτός (Mk 1.20, Jn 10.12, 13). All in all, 23 words.

Of these only two are used quite simply: Mk 1.20: 'And thereupon he (Jesus) called them (James and John); and, leaving their father Zebedee in the boat with the hired men (μετὰ τῶν μισθωτῶν), they went away after him.' Lk 10.7 (The words of Jesus to his 70 messengers): 'Remain in the same house, eating and drinking what they provide, for the workman deserves his pay.' To these may be added the instances in which the word is found in a parable, where, according to the literal sense of the parable, it has its customary meaning. So in Lk 15.17-19, the prodigal son says to himself: 'How many of my father's hired men have more food than they can eat, and here I am dying with hunger! I shall get up and go* to my father and say to him, "Father, I have sinned against Heaven, and in your eyes I am no longer worthy to be called your son, make me as one of your hired men."' (In vs. 21 (according to some of the older MSS)[36] he repeats what he resolved to say.) Here I think the hired men (μίσθιοι) are mentioned only for the sake of contrasting the condition of the son before he left his father with that after his leaving. This interpretation is supported by the opinion of Fiebig,[37] that the essential of parables, as of meshalim, is the similarity of situation, and that therefore many details may appear which admit of no interpretation corresponding to the interpretation of the parable as a whole. (See the comments above on Abrahams' misinterpretation of the difference between the sheep and the goats.) It is demonstrable that such details are found in this parable of the prodigal son, for the son says, 'I have sinned against Heaven,' and 'Heaven' is certainly 'God.' But according to the interpretation of the parable the father is God. What, then, is 'Heaven' according to the interpretation? From the impossibility of finding a satisfactory significance, it follows that the parable contains details which cannot be interpreted according to the general interpretation of the whole; and I think that the hired men, too, are details of this sort. So also in Jn 10.11-13, the words of Jesus to the Pharisees: 'I am the good shepherd. The good shepherd gives his life for the sheep. The hired man, who is not a shepherd and doesn't own the sheep, sees the wolf coming and leaves the sheep and runs away...because he is a hired man and the sheep are no concern of his.' It is not necessary here to discuss in detail, Who is the hired man? Suffice it for the argument that he is typical of the men of this world and that his hire is the customary pay which men receive for labor; such is the opinion of most of the commentators.[38]

As opposed to these there are four passages in which μισθός (or μισθόομαι) is found in parables in which it has (apart from its customary meaning, which gives it its place in the story) a special meaning given it by the interpretation, viz: reward given to a man by God. Three of these places are found in Mat 20[39] and have already been

_____
* Or,'I shall go at once,' if ἀναστὰς πορεύσομαι is here equivalent to וקמתי והלכתי.

55

discussed. The fourth is found in Jn 4.36.[40] (See Appendix A.) Here a number of commentators have found the word ἤδη difficult, and Torrey[41] suspects an error of translation - In Aramaic the word belonged to the preceding sentence, for 'It was not at all true that the reapers were "already receiving their wage." '[42] This is another example of correction without need, for, as was said above, passages both in the Gospels[43] and in TL[44] teach that the righteous receive their reward both in this world and in the world to come.

In the remaining passages, of which there are 12, the text deals not with pay for work, but with pay for good deeds. In three of these,[45] however, there is room to doubt whether this be pay given by God, or not, for in these three instances Jesus speaks of the pay given hypocrites, and it is customarily supposed that this consists of being seen and being thought righteous and so getting honor and money. If that supposition be correct, then this pay is given by men and not by God. But here it is necessary to recall the theory (already referred to)[46] found in Sifre on Numbers, Sifre on Dt., and Midrash Tannaim, that all the reward of the righteous and all the punishment of the wicked is laid up for them in the world to come, and that the righteous receive their little punishment, and the wicked their little reward, in this world. The words in Mat can be interpreted according to this theory, and it can be maintained that when Jesus said of the hypocrites, 'They have their pay.' he was thinking of the pay given by God to the evil for what little, or apparent, good they do.

Having thus outlined the uses of these words in the Gospels, it remains to review those uses which are other than the customary and to extract from them answers to the following questions: (1) Just what is the 'pay'? (2) To whom, (3) by whom, (4) when, and (5) why is it given?

(1) Just what is the pay? Mat 5.12 and Lk 6.23 put pay last in a list of blessings. In Lk there are only three other blessings in the list, and each is the opposite of some unpleasant condition which the righteous formerly endured: Blessed are the poor, for theirs is the kingdom of Heaven; blessed are the hungry, for they shall be fed;[47] blessed are those that weep, for they shall laugh. Consequently, since pay is here promised those who suffer from slander, it is plausible to suppose that pay here stands for good repute, which, in Hebrew, is also glory (כבוד) - the opposite of the effect of slander. But this conclusion does not follow so clearly from the list in Mat, which has been expanded and now includes other blessings not simply the opposites of the sorrows with which they are linked. It is worth noting, though, that the interpretation based on Lk agrees with that customarily given the three passages in Mat 6 discussed above - the reward of hypocrites is good repute.

In Mat 5.12 and Lk 6.23 it is also said explicitly that the pay is in

56

heaven, and this thought is found also in Mat 6.1 where the text has: παρὰ τῷ πατρὶ ὑμῶν.

Further, in Mat 5.12 and Lk 6.23 it is said that the pay will be great (πολύς), and in Mat 10.41 a distinction is made between the pay of a prophet and the pay of a just man. On the contrary, as remarked above, the parable in Mat 20 insists that all the workers receive the same pay. From the expression 'his pay' (τὸν μισθὸν αὐτοῦ) found in Mat 10.42 and Mk 9.41 it might be thought that the source of these passages conceived of pay as differing according to men and to their labor, but this is by no means certain from the texts as they are now.

One passage (Lk 6.32) uses the word 'grace' (χάρις) where the word 'pay' (μισθός) is found in the parallel in Mat 5.46. In the context (6.35) Lk repeats the saying and there uses μισθός, as Mat did the first time. (The repetition in Lk is not paralleled in Mat.) Therefore it seems likely that in this passage Lk thought pay meant grace.[48] This would explain why Lk wrote, 'And your pay will be great and you will be the children ("sons") of the Highest,' for the notion that a man is made a son of God by grace is of great importance in the letters preserved in the NT, e.g., Ephesians 2.1-6.[49] In Mat 5.42-6, are found the same ideas as in Lk 6.32-5, but in reverse order: 'Love your enemies...in order that you may become children of the Father...for if you love those who love you, what pay do you have?' In Jn 4.36 pay is linked to fruit, but it is uncertain whether they are meant to be distinguished or identified, and it is yet more uncertain what is meant there by fruit, so the passage throws little light on the nature of the pay, except incidentally by its declaration that he who gets paid will rejoice.

In this discussion it is dangerous to try to find a sort of sum or average of all the teaching about the nature of pay, something which could be read into all passages of all the Gospels. As a matter of fact it is impossible to know how far one opinion expressed in one passage coincided with another opinion expressed in another, and how far we are right in finding parallelism, or contradiction, between different passages. Therefore it is impossible to give here a general outline of the theory as to the nature of pay, held by the Gospels, and the best substitute must be a brief summary of the different opinions detailed above. It seems likely that in Mat 5.12 and Lk 6.23 pay is good repute or glory, and so also in Mat 6.2, 5, 16. But in Mat 5.46 and Lk 6.32 it is probably grace, by which the recipient becomes a son of God. In Mat 5.12 and 10.41-2, and Mk 9.41 and Lk 6.23 pay is spoken of as if it admitted differences of degree or kind, but Mat 20 explicitly contradicts this. In Mat 5.12 and Lk 6.23 pay is said to be in heaven, but Mat 6.2, 5, 16 speak of pay given the wicked in this world, and Jn 4.36 (according to the present text) speaks of pay given the good in this world - but on this point see below, under the heading 'When is the pay given?' How far these contradictions were felt as such at the time when the Gospels were composed, and how far, if they were felt, the men of that time believed they had succeeded, or did succeed, in explaining them away, are unanswerable questions.

(2) To whom is the pay given? Pay is promised to the disciples of Jesus in Lk 6.23 and 35, and in Mat 5.2; to those who receive or assist the disciples of Jesus in Mat 10.42-2 and Mk 9.41; and again to the disciples in Jn 4.36. Mat 6.2, 5, 16 declares that the hypocrites have their pay. Mat 20 promises pay to all who work in the vineyard of God (cp. Jn 4.36 'He who reaps gets pay.' But in Jn the expression appears in a saying applicable to the disciples of Jesus.) All these are, apparently, human beings. On their personal peculiarities, see 'Why is the pay given?'

(3) By whom is the pay given? In Mat 6.2, 5, 16, according to the customary interpretation, it is given by the men who are taken in by hypocrites. The contrast between these passages (so interpreted) and Mat 6.1 leads to the supposition that in the latter, speaking of pay παρὰ τῷ πατρί, the meaning is, 'pay which remains in the hands of God and which He Himself will give.' That this is correct appears from the context, 6.4, 6, 18: 'And your Father...will reward you.' As against these, Mat 20.8 represents the pay as given by a servant of God (His steward, i.e., either an angel or the Messiah). But apparently the householder himself was present at the paying, for he himself answered the grumbling laborers, and it may be that the steward of vs. 8 is only another of those details added to make the story plausible, and has no meaning for the interpretation.

(4) When is the pay given? The workers of Mat 20 receive their pay at the end of the day, according to Biblical law and contemporary custom.[50] Whether this detail was determined by the story or by the interpretation or by both together, there is no knowing. Similarly it is impossible to rely on the use of the tenses in the passages quoted in Appendix A. It happens that 6 are in the present (Mat 5.46; 6.1, 2, 5, 16; Jn 4.36), and that 2 have no verbs and are therefore reckoned as present (Mat 5.12, Mk 9.41), and that only three are in the future (Mat 10.41 (bis), Lk 6.32). Here the matter is complicated by the fact that the use of the present in place of the future (especially for things thought absolutely certain and for examples of general laws) is very frequent in koiné, and especially in koiné written under Semitic influence. So it is almost impossible, in such instances as these, to decide which time the writer had in mind.[51] On the other hand, even when the simple future stands in the text, it proves only that the time at which the writer expected the pay to be given was future in relation to the time of writing, or, at least, to the time of the speech which the writing purported to record. Such a future could well refer either to this world or to the world to come. More important are the three passages (Mat 5.11; 6.1; Lk 6.23) which speak of pay in heaven or with God who

is in heaven. It is plausible to suppose that the distance in space carried with it a distance in time, and that 'pay in heaven' here, like 'pay in the world to come' in TL, is pay which the worker will not receive in the immediate future. On the other hand, the passage in Jn, 4.36, discussed above, apparently speaks of pay given already at the time of speaking, but it can be interpreted differently, not only by attaching the word ἤδη to the preceding sentence, but also by understanding λαμβάνει as a present with future significance, like ἔρχεται in the verse preceding. As against these interpretations there is to be said, not only what was said above - that the expectation of pay in this world is found elsewhere both in the Gospels and in TL, but also that if this verse does promise pay at once, then it is a reversal of the famous passage in Peah 1.1: There, he who does good works 'eats their fruits in this world, and the principle is laid up for him in the world to come'; here, he gets paid for them in this world, and eats their fruits in the world to come. So the question as to the meaning of the passage in Jn must remain undecided.

(5) Why is the pay given? I have already discussed the parable in Mat 20, where it appears that the pay is given to all the workers because they went and worked in the vineyard; also Mat 5.12 and Lk 6.23, where it appears that the pay is given the just because, as just, they suffered from slander, and that it was given them to make up for what they had suffered. In Mat 5.46 and Lk 6.43 Jesus counsels his disciples to do extraordinarily good works in order to receive extraordinarily good pay. The question, If they did only moderately good works, would they receive moderately good pay, or no pay at all? cannot be answered with confidence. But anyhow, it is clear from the passage that the pay changes according to the works. The answer to the above discussed question, 'Why are hypocrites paid?' depends on the answer to the question, 'Who gives the pay?' If God, it is not probable that he gives them pay for the works of apparent righteousness, the prayer and fasting, which they do to be seen of men (Mat 6.1); it is more likely that he pays them for other - actually - good deeds which they did without hypocrisy. But if it be other men who give them their pay, then it seems almost certain that the pay is merely the success of their hypocritical practises. Mat 10.41 suggests that there is a particular reward for each particular good deed, or, at least, for each class of good deeds. So each prophet gets a particular kind of reward, and one of the same sort goes to each man who has received a prophet,[52] presumably because he received him. Moreover, I think the purpose of Mat 10.42 and Mk 9.41 is to teach that even the smallest possible good deed has its peculiar pay. Finally in Jn 4.36 the reaper gets paid, presumably because he reaps.

To sum up: Three places speak of pay given hypocrites for obscure reasons; two places, of pay given the disciples of Jesus because of the suffering they underwent qua disciples; all the remaining places, of pay given simply for good deeds. There is no place which justifies Strack-Billerbeck's theory about a Gnadenlohn; on the contrary, it is even said the grace is given as pay. This is the upshot of a review of the Lohnlehre of the Gospels, but it is not possible to base on this a denial that both in the Gospels and, more often, in the letters of the New Testament, there are to be found places in which it is implied that men are saved by grace and not by works for which salvation might be considered payment. For it must be emphasized again that the complex literature which is the Gospels is not to be thought of as expressing individualized and fixed theories between which no contradiction is to be found. On the contrary, the absence of such consistency is characteristic of this literature. Therefore the question arises, How is it that, as to the reason for which the pay was given, all the passages of the Gospels which referred to pay were found to be in almost complete agreement? It may be answered that, as a matter of fact, the teaching about pay is not a peculiar doctrine set off by the natural boundaries of the subject matter, it is merely that part of the teaching of the Gospels which can be distinguished from the rest on the superficial ground that it contains a particular rhetorical figure - the comparison of rewards and punishments to pay. This comparison requires that the author shall speak of giving pay and of receiving pay and of service for which the pay is given. So much fixity and consistency is required by the rhetorical figure, and is therefore to be found, more or less clearly, in all the sources, i.e., in all the various passages of the Gospels where the figure appears. But just because the figure is no more than a rhetorical device, and just because, by its very nature, it requires such little consistency as has been found, we cannot conclude from the places where it occurs that there was a similar consistency in the general theory of rewards and punishments, or of salvation and damnation.

These results must be kept in mind throughout the analysis of the theory of pay to be found in TL. If a similar agreement be found there between passages otherwise different, that will not justify the conclusion that such agreement actually existed in some general Tannaitic theory of salvation. And on the other hand, should no such agreement be found, that would not justify the conclusion that the sources of TL differed one from another more than did the sources of the Gospels, for any such disagreement could be more easily explained by the simple fact that the content of TL, and therefore the likelihood of its expressing disagreement, is far greater than that of the Gospels.

In Appendix B are collected 117 passages in which the word שכר is found in TL. Henceforward these passages will be cited according to their numbers in the appendix. The collection is not intended to illustrate the customary meaning of שכר,[53] and it also neglects the primary extension of that meaning, found most often in the Mishnah,[54] viz: to profit by or derive benefit from. In almost (but not quite) all the passages cited, the pay is given by God, and in almost all, for good or bad deeds; i.e., these passages illustrate the religious, as opposed to the social, meaning of the term. When the same sayings are found in the same places in parallel midrashim, as in Mekilta and Mekilta of Rabbi Simon, I have cited the midrash which exists in MSS as a separate book, and have not referred to the parallel. When the same sayings are found in different places, whether in one or in more midrashim, I have cited one passage, and have added references to the others. Within these limits I think the list very nearly complete for the Mishnah and the midrashim. Some passages in Tosefta may have been missed, but I trust that, at all events, the list as it is will serve for a review of the figurative use of pay in TL.[55] I shall therefore try to sum up the answers to be found in it to the five questions asked above concerning the use of pay in the Gospels, viz: What is it? To whom, by whom, when and why is it given?

1. Just what is the pay? 'Rabbi says,..."Be as careful about an easy commandment as about a difficult one (So Jastrow; but I think the meaning is, "about a (comparatively) unimportant commandment as about an important one") for you do not know how (performance of) a commandment is paid. And reckon the loss (necessary for the performance) of a commandment as against the pay (performance brings), and the pay of a transgression (i.e., the pleasure it makes possible) as against the loss." (107) These words very well express the various theories about pay which are most frequent in TL. On the one hand, pay is given for the performance of commandments - and, in a sense yet more figurative, for their transgression - and there is no doubt that the pay for performance is greater than the loss performance involves, but the matter does not admit of exact calculation; there remains always an element of mystery, a consequence of the arbitrary and unknowable decisions of God, which is not explicable.

Pay for transgressions is found only very rarely, in the passage cited above, for example, and in nos. 113 and 89 (the pay of wicked men), and I think probable that in these places the expression was felt as a deliberate euphemism for 'punishment.' But the opposite opinion could be defended by the fact that the expression 'good pay' (שכר טוב) is very frequent, e.g. 1 (?), 2, 13, 28, 50, 71, 114). However, I do not think that 'good pay' was understood as the opposite of 'bad pay' (שכר רע) which is never found. More than likely, it was a tautology.

Good pay admits of differences of degree or quantity. The Mishnah, especially, speaks of 'much pay' (שכר הרבה) (108, 110, 111, 114), but pay is increased and given in amounts described as 'more' or 'less' in the midrashim also (e.g.: 20, 54, 71, 73). Moreover, the pay and loss involved in performance of a single commandment can be compared as to quantity, e.g.: 107, cited above, also 23, where it is said, 'your pay is consumed by your loss' (יצא שכרך בהפסדך). This

expression and the variant of it found in 117, illustrate a slightly different meaning of 'pay,' which here is not the reward given for a particular action, but the advantage always attendant upon a given temperament or ability. (So, at least, in the first two mishnayot there, in
the third שכר has its customary meaning, and the fact that these
meanings could thus alternate in a list of sayings intended to be thought
parallel, shows how far the concept was from accurate definition.)

Pay is something given to entire generations (v. inf., Why), something given both in this world and in the world to come (v. inf., When).
Here I shall attempt only to list the good (and bad) things which TL
describes as 'pay.'

As for the bad things, the list is very short, for only one is specified, and that only in the saying of Ben Azzai, 'The pay of a transgression is a transgression.' (113, cp. 102).

As for the good things, more details are given:

(A) Physical blessings received in this world: The Old Testament
had long ago promised things of this sort as pay,[56] and in many of the
passages cited below the midrash only says in detail what the Old
Testament had already said in general. The recipient of these promised blessings is often Israel, thus: As pay, Israel was led out of
Egypt (3, 12). As pay, God gave them the manna and provided for them
in the wilderness (15, 22). Their stay at Mt. Sinai was a form of pay
(56). As pay, they subdued the peoples before them (58), and entered
the promised land (24, 63, 74, 91), and subdued it (66), and dwelt in it
(82); and God gives them rains (60) in their season (62?), and doubles
the produce of the land before each seventh year (15), and extends
their borders (64), and cuts off the gentiles from before them (65), and
gives their lands to Israel (15, 61, 68), as it was said, 'Then thou shalt
delight in the Lord, and I shall cause thee to ride upon the high places
of the earth.' (18). Also tribes and families of Israel received pay of
this sort, thus the temple was built in the land of Benjamin and the
kingdom given to Judah as pay (10, 92), the tithe was given to the
Levites as pay (52), the priestly perquisites to the descendants of
Aaron (35), and all the pay of the generation which died in the wilderness went to the daughters of Zelofehad (53), and the family of Jeshbab
received as pay the right to serve in the temple in place of the family
of Bilga (95). Statements of this sort are to be taken as evidences of
the influence of the Old Testament and remnants of the more ancient
conception of the people or the family as suffering or benefitting as a
whole in the sufferings or benefits of each of its parts.

But, of course, the Old Testament contained many places in which
God promised his gifts to individuals, and on these TL built its theories of individual rewards. Particular individuals are specified as
receiving pay: Thus Noah received all the pay of the generation of the
flood, apparently when he escaped from it, and Lot, all the pay of the

generation of Sodom, also, apparently, in his escape (53). Abraham received the pay of ten generations (116), evidently by inheriting this world and the world to come (11), and his pay (like that of Isaac) was extended and given to Israel in Egypt and in the desert: The pay of Isaac in Egypt, when God passed over the houses of the children of Israel, the pay of Abraham in the desert, when God provided for their needs (22). Thus Moses also received, as pay for his service at the altar, a part of the sacrifice (36).

But it is very rarely that such physical blessings are promised as pay to anyone who performs a given commandment, and most often, when they are, the belief that they are is based on the words of the Old Testament. Thus, for example, when long life is promised (19, 61, 73, 86, cp. 103, where the words of the Old Testament are explained as referring to 'the long world'). Similarly childbearing is promised the woman suspected of adultery who emerges successful from her trial, because the Old Testament says, 'She shall be sown seed.' (Num. 5.28), and here too, others interpret otherwise (46). The prayer at circumcision beseeches God to deliver the chosen of the flesh of Israel, as pay for the observance of the commandment (93); and he who studies the Law is protected by it from all evil (106). Also the general rule, 'He who sins is not to be paid.' has a wide range of application in social relationships (104-5), and the expression 'He was alert and was paid.' is used to describe the man who does well in this world because he is alert to use the privileges allowed by the Law. In both these expressions: 'He who sins is not to be paid.' and 'He was alert and was paid.' pay is almost a mistranslation, the correct term would be profit, but their use illustrates one border-land of the concept, and I have therefore cited them, in nos. 106-8, for the sake of completeness as well as for that of the expression 'He was lazy and was paid.' which they define by contrast. Finally, in two instances, 19 and 92, verses of the Old Testament are cited as promising physical pay to all those who perform a given commandment; these two instances, with those listed above, make up all the cases in which physical blessings to be given in this world are promised as pay to every man who performs a given commandment or virtuous action, or who takes advantage of a permission given by the Law.

So far, all these physical blessings have been given to Israel or its native members. But the like are also promised as pay to proselytes. Sifre on Numbers tells a story of a woman proselyte (44) who got a student of the Law as pay in this world, 'And in the world to come I know not how much.' It was Hobab's pay to be called the father-in-law of Moses (48), though this was rather a social than a physical blessing. The families of proselytes also receive blessings of this sort, for the Rechabites were promised that they would always have one member serving in the Temple (41). And not only proselytes, but even gentiles get physical pay. God preserves the gentiles as pay for

His protection of Israel, and looks after their lands as pay for His attention to the land of Israel (59?). The Canaanites were permitted to dwell in their land a year (45) as pay for having honored Abraham (39). Israel was commanded not to abominate an Egyptian, and God gave the Egyptians lost in the Red Sea a place of burial, as pay for their reception of Israel and their recognition that God's judgment on them was just (9, 69). Finally, even the dogs get their pay - טרפה (21).

(B) <u>Spiritual blessings received in this world</u>: Here it is best to begin with blessings given individuals, for the majority of spiritual blessings are promised to each individual who performs a given commandment, or a given good deed, or even to anybody who performs any commandment or good deed whatsoever. So in the well-known saying of Ben Azzai, 'The pay for a commandment is a commandment, and the pay for a transgression is a transgression.' (130) As for particular commandments: Whoever keeps the Sabbath will be kept far from transgression (14). The student of the Law who kept the commandment about fringes on his garments found that his fringes stood between him and sexual impurity (44). Peace is given not only to Abraham and to Pinhas, but also to everyone who obeys the commandment to study the Law and to everyone who practises corporal works of mercy (47). And even when the basis of the promise is found in some story of the Old Testament about all Israel, or in a verse dealing with one of the patriarchs, it is immediately generalized and made an example of the hope of every individual. Thus: 'R. Nehemya said, "Whoever takes one commandment upon himself in faith is worthy that the Holy Spirit should rest upon him, for so we have found in the case of our fathers, for as pay for believing in God our fathers deserved that the Holy Spirit should rest upon them and it did and they uttered the song."' (12, cp. 11)

This is not intended to deny, of course, that spiritual gifts were also given to Israel as a people. God was revealed to them and gave them life (4), Israel is holy to the Lord (6), the Holy Spirit rested on them and caused them to rejoice in song (11-12), and there are verses like 'And the sun of righteousness shall shine on you who fear my name.' such that it cannot be decided whether the Rabbis, reading them, thought of the individual or of the community. Even the gentiles receive, as nations, spiritual pay. That was signified by the statement that there should be an altar to the Lord in the land of Egypt (i.e., that Egypt would be converted? Or were the Rabbis thinking of the altar of Onias?) (9). Nevertheless, there is sufficient evidence to justify the statement that when, in TL, the nature of pay is specified, then, if it be pay given to all Israel as a people, or to one of the great figures of antiquity, it is generally specified as physical, but if it be given to individuals of Israel for their performance of particular commandments, then it is generally specified as spiritual. This conclusion corresponds, first of all, to the needs of religion, for whether or not physical pay is given can be observed, and number 116 shows that efforts were made to answer difficulties raised on the basis of such observation. Second, this conclusion corresponds to the distinction frequently drawn between two different currents in Tannaitic Judaism, on the one hand, the conservative, characterized by the return to the Old Testament, the conception of all Israel as a single individual receiving a single reward or punishment of the sort commonly specified in the Old Testament, i.e., physical; and on the other hand, the liberal, characterized by the conception of Israel as of a collection of individuals of which every one would be paid or punished according to his own actions, and by the conception of pay and punishment as spiritual conditions. But this interpretation of the conclusion depends on the introduction of historical theories. Moreover, as against it, must be emphasized the fact that, if such a difference of tendencies did exist, it was not felt by the sources or editors of TL, in which spiritual and physical pay are often found together, e.g.: 9, 10(?), 11(!), 12, 18, etc.

(C) Blessings to be given in the world to come: TL frequently speaks of pay to be given in the world to come, but only once is the nature of this pay specified, and then the specification comes as an answer to a difficulty, and even in this instance the details are by no means clear, for the passage reads: 'R Akiba says, "You cannot find any commandment in the Law which doesn't have the promise of its pay alongside it and the resurrection of the dead written into it. (Thus for example) it is said (Dt. 22.7), 'Thou shalt certainly let the mother go...that it may be well with thee and that thou mayest prolong thy days.' (A man once obeyed this commandment and shortly afterwards) went up to the top of a tree and fell and died....How was it well with him, and where was his length of days? Hence interpret, 'In order that it may be well with thee' in the good world, 'and that thou mayest prolong thy days' in the long world." ' (103)[57]

(2) To whom is the pay given? This question has already been in large part answered in the section above. There it was seen that pay is given to wicked men (76, 89, 107, 113, cp. 104, 105), and to men possessed of a certain temperament or ability (117), and also to those who take advantage of the privileges given them by the Law (96-8), and to Jeshbab the bad neighbor (95). To this list of those who have received pay for ethical reasons other than their performance of commandments, can be added: Those associated in good actions as unnecessary participants (34, 108); the person upon whom a commandment is performed, i.e., the child circumcized (93); the innocent woman who has undergone the test for adultery (46); one who refrains from committing a transgression (37, 72, 85); one who avoids taking full advantage of the legally permissible, in order to avoid even the

appearance of transgression (97); and those who do good without intending to perform commandments, i.e., the gentiles (40, 59?, 90). These are discussed in detail s.v. Why. The difference between pay given the nation, pay given certain famous individuals, and pay given ordinary individuals, has been discussed above. There were mentioned the peoples to whom pay was promised: Israel (3-6, 11, 12, 15, 17, 22, 24, 25, 56, 63-6, 68, 70, 74, 82), the Egyptians (9, 69) and the Canaanites (39); also the tribes: Judah and Benjamin (10), the Levites (52); also the families: the children of Aaron (35), those of Jonadab ben Rekab (41), the daughters of Zelofehad (53) (though these last might perhaps better be thought of as individuals). Also, most of the individuals specified as recipients of pay have been mentioned above, but the full list is the following: Noah (53), Lot (53), Abraham (11, 20, 22, 47, 53, 116), Isaac (22 - his pay was given to his descendants), Jacob (77), Reuben and Judah (91), Aaron (37), Moses (16, 36, 80, 81, 87, 88), Hobab ben Reuel (48), Pinhas (47), Joshua (45?), Jeshbab (95), one of R. Hiya's pupils and a converted prostitute (44). It is not worth while listing here all the places in which pay is promised to any one who performs some commandment or other, but it is necessary to list the places in which the pay of the otherwise undescribed 'just' (צד״ק׳ם) is mentioned (usually without any indication as to the nature of this pay), viz: 13, 27, 29, 31, 33, 42, 49, 50, 76, 89, 102, 111, 115.

It has also been noted that God gives pay even to dogs (21), and in 48 it is said, 'God gives any instrument which does anything in his service, its pay.' However, here the text is speaking of Hobab ben Reuel, and the notion that pay is given to inanimate objects is contradicted in 55: '(The text) symbolized the wicked by sun and moon and sea, which do not (or: because they do not) receive pay,' and 75 speaks of the earth, the heavens, the sun and the sea and the like as of things 'which were not made for pay (Or: profit? But clearly, profit which they themselves would receive.) and not for loss'; therefore I think that in 48 the word 'instrument' is used figuratively. The same use (i.e., for a proselyte destined to make proselytes of others) is found in Acts 9.15, of Paul: 'This (man) is my chosen instrument to carry my name before nations and kings and the children of Israel.' Note, however, that this conclusion is based only on those passages in which the word שכר appears, but שכר׳, which I have translated pay, is often used as reward, and (in passages which I have not discussed, because they happen not to use the word שכר) the literature does contain the notion that rewards are given to inanimate objects.[58]

(3) By whom is the pay given? Generally by God. (1-4, 6, 13, 15, 18, 20, 22, 26, 28, 38 (!), 40, 41, 47, 48, 50, 51, 59?, 60, 62, 64, etc.) In all these He gives it in person, and 'the Paymaster' (נותן שכר) is one of His most prominent titles, for in 38 the words 'I am the Lord' are explained by the words 'who can be trusted to pay in full.'

(נאמן לשלם שכר). To this general rule, however, there are exceptions. Sometimes God effects payment by means of men, thus in 9 he lays upon Israel commandments from which the Egyptians will benefit, in 21, from which dogs will benefit, in 52, from which the Levites will benefit, and so on. Sometimes the text of the Old Testament (הכתוב) is said to pay (34), or Israel is said to promise the proselyte that there is pay with them (49). I think there is no doubt that these are merely ways of avoiding direct reference to God, and that the pay is here thought of as given by God. Similarly, when it is said, in 11 and 12, that the Holy Spirit rested on Israel, I see no cause to think the Spirit other than a gift of God. (cp. Mekilta 14.13, 'The Shekinah caused the Holy Spirit to rest upon them.') So in 120, where it is said that the Law protects from all evil those who study it, it seems to me certain that God was thought of as doing the protecting. But in other passages matters are otherwise: In 56 it is said that their stay at Sinai was pay for Israel; admittedly, it was God who commanded this stay and made it possible, but it was the Israelites who stayed. In 96-98 the alert man profits by reason of his alertness, and in 117 those easily pacified, hard to make angry, quick to learn and slow to forget are rewarded because of these properties. These changes depend on the changes in the meaning of שכר, alternating between pay and profit, which have already been remarked. But there remain two passages in which are found two theories about pay differing each from the other and both from all the passages above discussed: 88: '(Moses) said before Him, "Master of the world, is it as pay for the trouble which I have taken with Israel that Thou sayest to me, 'You shall not pass over (into the promised land)?' "....The Holy One, blessed be He, said to him, "I have created my world a series of periods ($\alpha\rho\chi\alpha\acute{\iota}$ - in Heb., אורכאות אורכאות בראתי את עולמי). Was it because Abraham sinned that he departed from the world? (No,) but because the period of Isaac came pressing on (דחקה ארכי של יצחק). And now the period of Joshua presses on." ' 113: 'Ben Azzai says, "(The performance of one) commandment brings in its train (the performance of another) commandment, and transgression brings in its train transgression." ' From the use of the word ארכי (= $\alpha\rho\chi\acute{\eta}$) there is no doubt that the administrative theory of 88 comes from the Greek, the source of the psychology of 113 is dubious, it may well have been original observation.

(4) When is the pay given? In most instances pay is given after performance, but a few passages speak of pay, for the performance of commandments, given before the performance. So, explicitly, 15, also 24 and 63, where entrance to the land of Israel is promised as pay for the performance of commandments which can be performed by, or are binding on, only persons already in the land. As for pay given after performance, sometimes it is given in this world,

sometimes in the world to come. When in this world, it is sometimes given almost immediately (4 in the same night, 37 in the same day, 3 after four days), sometimes only to following generations (10, 22, 41). Sometimes, depending on the nature of the pay, the time of its giving is considerably extended, or is not determinable at all. So, for example, in 52 (the payment of the service of the Levites), 9 and 69 (the payment of the Egyptians by the operation of the commandment, 'Thou shalt not abominate an Egyptian.'), and 6 (Israel's holiness to the Lord is a form of pay.) [I think the expression in 117 ('The pay of going is in his hand.') merely a vivid way of saying that he will be paid for going.] As for pay promised in the world to come, details as to the manner and time of its giving are not forthcoming. The expression הֶעָתִיד לָבוֹא ('The destined to come'), refers sometimes to this world, sometimes to the world to come. The clearest example of the former meaning is found in 33: 'If you want to know pay of the just in the destined future, go and learn...(from the case of Adam, whose single transgression was followed by so many deaths. Now God's mercy surpasses his justice, therefore if a man keep one single commandment) a fortiori he obtains merit for himself and for his descendants and for the descendants of his descendants to the end of all the generations.' Even here, the opposite interpretation is possible, but עָתִיד לָבוֹא is often found in the Mishnah meaning simply 'the future'[59] and this meaning seems to me the likeliest in this passage also. The other meaning is exemplified by 50, where the words עָתִיד לָבוֹא are used in contrast to 'this world,' and also in 81 and 87 (for example) it is clear that they mean 'the world to come.' That pay is given in the world to come is said explicitly in 42, 45 and 76. In 103 'the world to come' is signified by 'the good world' and 'the long world.' But a study of eschatological terminology would have to be based on a much larger collection of texts, therefore I shall not attempt to determine the exact meanings of other particular terms, such as לְמָחָר ('tomorrow') in 89. More interesting is the contradiction, as to the time of payment, found between two groups of passages: On the one hand, In 78 and 120 it is said of good actions (particularly of the study of the Law) that those who do them eat their pay in this world, and the principle is laid up for them in the world to come. On the other hand, in 42, 76, 89 and 90 is found the theory that only the wicked get paid in this world, and only the righteous in the world to come. Similarly, only the righteous are punished in this world, and only the wicked in the world to come.

Hitherto the discussion has been limited to the time of payment in its relation to the time at which the commandment was performed. Understandably, those passages which speak of pay without reference to the performance of commandments, require special consideration. In all of them the pay is given in this world; they are 59?, 95 (Jeshbab), 96-98 and 117 (the temperamental differences). 116 is also exceptional, in its suggestion that the pay of 10 wicked generations was given to Abraham (in this world?) because those generations had <u>not</u> done what was good in the eyes of the Lord.

(5) <u>Why is the pay given?</u> The passages which speak of pay given without reference to the performance of commandments or good deeds, have just been cited and, as said above, it is clear that all of them except 97 and 59 are to be explained by the fact that שכר means also <u>profit</u>. 59 is so strange as to defy explanation. 'Lazy and paid' in 97 may be understood in reference to prohibitory commandments (other like examples will appear below). All passages but these speak of pay in reference to some commandment or good deed, but differ widely as to the commandment or good deed for which the pay is promised, and as to the relation between performance and pay.

First of all, there are a great many passages in which pay is promised a man who performs a commandment simply because he performs it, thus 4, 7, 14, 18, 25, 32, 51, 65, 68, 70, 74, 76, 82, 83, 90, 94, 103. Here also belongs the theory, 'The performance of one commandment brings in its train the performance of another.' (117) And apart from these particular examples it is possible to find passages in which this general concept is clearly propounded, e.g., in 26 and 30 it is said the God gives pay according to the Law, and in 44 that every commandment has alongside it the promise to pay, and in 43 that God commanded Israel in order that they might perform and receive pay. (However, even if they don't want the pay, they had better perform in order to avoid punishment.) Similarly it is said, from the other aspect of the theory, that pay is not given for transgression (92), and the general rule that 'The sinner is not to profit.' (104-5) serves as a basis for many halakic details,[60] and in 79 the sages (contradicting R. Hananya ben Gamliel) deny that merit can be used to cancel guilt, or guilt merit, and conclude, 'But pay is given for the performance of the commandments, and punishment for transgressions.' Finally, in 3 it is said explicitly that God was not able to deliver Israel from Egypt because they had not performed any commandments and therefore 'The Holy One, blessed be He, gave them two commandments, (those about) the blood of the Passover and the blood of circumcision, which they could practise so as to be delivered....For pay is not given except on account of practise. (על ידי מעשה)" 'Practise' here clearly means 'the performance of commandments.'

Nevertheless, pay is often given for other reasons than the <u>performance</u> of commandments: (a) As remarked above, in passages like 15, 24 and 63, pay is given for the performance of commandments which are yet to be performed. (b) The innocent woman suspected of adultery, in 46, and the infant who is circumcized, in 93, receive pay for commandments which are performed upon them. (c) In 72 and 85, pay is promised to everyone who refrains from transgression. The

saying about the man who is lazy and gets paid for it supposes the
same theory, except that there the lazy man is paid not because he did
not transgress, but because he avoided even the appearance of transgression. The same theory is found again in 75, according to which
pay is given any man who does not depart from the order of nature
(לא שינה את מידתו - as the sun and moon did not change theirs).
(d) In many passages the pay of one man is given or promised to
another, generally a descendant of the first. Thus in 10, 22, 24, 33,
35, 39, 41, 52, 62, 64, 69 and 77. But other relations are observable.
In 21 the dogs of Israel are rewarded for the behavior of the dogs of
Egypt. In 53 any pure man who arises in a wicked generation receives
the pay of the whole generation, and if there be not even one pure man
in a generation, then its pay is given to (apparently) the first pure man
who comes along. So in 116 Abraham gets the pay of the ten generations of the wicked who preceeded him. In 54 anyone who offers the
sacrifices at the proper times increases the pay due Israel, and in 81
God promises Moses that 'if even one of Israel perform and accomplish
even one of all the commandments which I have given by you, you shall
have a share with him in the future to come.' (e) Sometimes the payment depends not on the physical performance of the commandment,
but on the spiritual condition of the man performing. 37 may, or may
not, be an example of this: 'When Aaron knew that his sons were
known of God he held his tongue and was paid for his silence. Hence
they said, 'If anyone takes his punishment and is silent, it's a good
sign for him.' But certainly 17 belongs here ('If you agree to penalties
gladly you receive pay, and if not, you receive punishment.'), as does
71 (which says that if pay is given for the avoidance of blood which is
naturally loathsome, how much more so for the avoidance of other
sins, which are naturally agreeable), and especially 57: 'The (sacred)
text distinguished between the man who performs from love and the
man who performs from fear; (he who performs) from love - his pay
is doubled and redoubled.' (f) Finally, in many places of TL pay is
given or promised for what I have called 'good deeds,' i.e., actions
for which one receives pay from God, but which are not the performance of commandments. I don't know enough of halakah to distinguish
accurately and always between what is and what is not the performance
of a commandment, so I shall not attempt to cite all the passages of
this sort, but only a few which certainly belong here: 34: (Anyone who
is associated in the performance of a commandment, as a nonessential
figure, is given pay as one who performs a commandment.) 10: (The
Holy Spirit rested on the land of Benjamin because the tribe of Benjamin was the first to go down into the Red Sea, and the tribe of Judah
received the kingdom - i.e., produced the royal house - because at
that time they threw stones at the tribe of Benjamin.) 69: (Pay was
given Egypt because, without intention to perform a meritorious action, they received Israel (into their country).) 9: (The Egyptians

received pay because Pharoah talked of letting Israel go, because they feared the Lord, and because Pharoah admitted the justice of the divine judgment.) 39: (The Canaanites received pay because they honored Abraham.) To these can be added four very important passages. According to Schechter,[61] the Old Testament contains no commandment to believe in God, and even the Tannaïm and Amoraïm, though they postulated that the just man would of necessity believe in God, did not explicitly state such a commandment. Nevertheless the Eighteen Benedictions contain the petition 'Give good pay to all those who truly trust in thy Name.' - apparently because they do trust in it. In 6 Israel is praised because 'they believed and went after Moses.... What pay did they get for that? "Israel is holy to the Lord."' And in 11 it is said, 'As pay for Israel's belief in the Lord, the Holy Spirit rested upon them and they sang the song....And so you find that Abraham our father inherited this world and the world to come only by virtue of faith.' and so on. Almost the same thing is said in 12. So the evidence which Strack-Billerbeck lacked when they tried to prove that according to the Gospels pay was given for faith and not for the performance of commandments, that evidence was in fact to be found in TL.

It seems unnecessary to compare here, point by point, the teachings about pay found in the Gospels and in TL. Anyone who is interested in such a comparison can easily make it by comparing the answers derived from the two literatures to the corresponding questions. In doing so, it will be necessary to keep in mind that the literature of the Gospels is much smaller than that of TL, and therefore cannot be expected to afford the same wealth of detail and the same variety of theory. With allowance made for this fact, I think that no significant differences will be found. That flat contradiction, between one detail in the Gospels and another detail in TL, does exist, has already been pointed out. But similar contradiction is found also between details in the Gospels, and between details in TL, by themselves. For example, in both literatures pay is sometimes given according to the fine points of performance, and at other times not. And when material from other documents of the New Testament is considered along with that of the Gospels, then yet more parallels of detail are found between the New Testament teaching and that of TL. Thus the use of pay to mean pay for transgression, lacking in the Gospels but found in TL, is found also in Acts 1.18: 'He (Judas) bought a field with the pay of his wickedness.' and the belief 'that Abraham our father inherited this world and the world to come only as pay for faith, for it is said, "And he believed in the Lord and it was reckoned to him as righteousness",' lacking in the Gospels but found in TL, is found also, even to the same citation from the Old Testament, in Romans 4.3.

Such are the facts as they appear from an analysis of the documentary evidence which has been preserved. But these facts are not sufficient to justify the historical theory that the similarities and differences between the teachings about pay found in Tannaitic Judaism and those found in early Christianity were identical with those now apparent in the preserved documents. For, on the one hand, these documents represent only a small fragment of the thought of that time, and, on the other hand, the ancient Jewish, or Christian, teaching was known not as a thing discovered by analysis of documents, but as a thing learned by the Jewish, or Christian, child as he grew up at that time. If this Jewish child grew up in one of the little towns[62] of Palestine, and if he were the son of a Pharisee, he probably learned the Law at first, not as law, but as the customary way of life in his father's house. Thus he came to know and love it a long while before he thought much about it as a peculiar law, a system of divine commandments. When, at last, he did come to think of it in this way, he probably thought it altogether fitting and proper that God should have ordained by commandment these familiar and beloved customs. When he went to school, and when he began to move in society he customarily met other young men like himself, the sons of his father's friends. Supposing the fathers to have been farmers or small shop-keepers, and supposing that they brought their sons early to marriage, then the boys were soon occupied with the care of their own families, their own shops, and their own fields. Of course, they gave what spare time they had to the study of the Law, but not as to the study of something new to be learned, for the Law was already known to them, they presupposed it in all their doings, walked in its ways and loved it as a thing known from childhood, the very warp and woof of their daily life. Therefore their study was generally concerned with questions about fine points and minute details, they more often raised these questions for purposes of practise than for determination of theory, and it did not occur to them to talk much about the nature of the Law or its essential and general rules. A fortiori they never thought of, as a single thing, 'das soteriologische System der alten Synagoge';[63] and there is no Aramaic translation of these words which would have made sense to Jacob of the village of Samma[64] or to Jesus of the village of Nazareth.

It seems probable, though, that matters were quite otherwise in the life of a Jewish boy who grew up, at the same period, in one of the smaller Greek cities. Already in childhood - as soon as he left his father's house - he would have begun to be conscious of Jewish customs as of things peculiar, which distinguished him from most people. Almost at once he would have been compelled to explain them, to defend them, to state their purpose and their nature. For such apologetic purposes, especially if he were questioned by philosophers, he would probably have to view all these customs, and all the Law, as a single thing. Such a line of thought would bring him directly and quickly to 'das soteriologische System der alten Synagoge,' and a good

Greek translation of these words would probably have been understandable to Saul of Tarsus.[65]

It may be that such considerations as these will help to solve the
problem, above referred to, which has hitherto been found in Paul's
evidence about Judaism: How was it possible for a Jew, a pupil of
Rabban Gamaliel the Elder, to understand Judaism in a fashion so different from that of the Tannaïm as known to us in TL? Because of
his relations with the gentiles - and philosophers of Tarsus may have
been among these - Paul accustomed himself to sum up the whole Law
in a single system, a very simple one: Commandment, obedience or
transgression, pay or punishment. This system represents very well
the greater part of the thought about the means of salvation to be found
both in TL and in the Gospels. But neither the Jews nor the Christians
of this period lived only according to this system, and both their preserved sayings and the records of their lives contain many details
which cannot be forced into it. When Paul talked about Judaism, however, he talked about the simplified system, made for the purpose of
explaining Judaism to the gentiles. Hence the difference between his
picture of it and that derivable from TL and from the Gospels is the
difference between an account, produced by abstraction, of a philosoph-
ic system, and an account, produced by accumulation of details, of a
complete way of life. This account of the difference, however, is a
historical theory and as such does not admit of proof, nor of disproof.

NOTES

1. The important work in this field is, of course, Strack-Billerbeck.
Strack, in his Einleitung in Talmud u. Midrash (unveränd. Abdr. d. 5....
Aufl. der Einl. i.d. Talmud) pp. 181-3, lists, as the most important
works similar to, but earlier than, Strack-Billberbeck, the collections
made by Lightfoot, Meuschen, Schöttgen, Wettstein, Nork, Delitzsch
and Wünsche, and in the second half of his list cites (inter alia) Dal-
man, Die Worte Jesu. Of the books not mentioned in his list I have
made most use of:
  I. Abrahams, Studies in Pharisaism, Cambridge, 1st Series 1917
                                                       2nd Series 1924
  C. Montefiore, Rabbinic Literature and Gospel Teachings,
       London, 1930
  G. Kittel, Die Problem etc., Stuttgart, 1926.
  P. Fiebig, Jesu Bergpredigt, Göttingen, 1924.
It goes without saying that every book on primitive Christianity and
Tannaïtic Judaism should mention the parallels of meaning which
exist between these two literatures, but in fact one must distinguish
between those which notice the existence of such parallels only in

passing and those which give them special attention. To the latter
class belong the books listed above.

2. v. sup. p. 45.

3. N. Y., 1940.

4. id. p. 11.

5. Thus, for example, I. Lévi, in his article, Le sacrifice d'Isaac
et la mort de Jésus, REJ 64.161 ff. wrote (p. 179) 'Il est superflu de
rappeler la place qu'occupe dans la théologie chrétienne le dogme de
la rédemption. À la verité, les Évangiles n'en font pas mention.' Cp.
Mk 10.45, 'For the Son of Man did not come to be served, but to serve
and to give his life a ransom for many.' Almost the same words are
found in Mat 20.28. Cp. also Mk 14.24 (the words of Jesus to his
disciples at the last supper): 'This is my blood of the covenant, which
is poured out for many.' Almost the same words in Mat 26.28 and in
Lk 22.20. Similar words are preserved as important elements in
every major Christian liturgy.

6. Cambridge, 1917.

7. 23.13.

8. Mat 25.41-42.

9. Mat 8.12; 13.42, 50; 22.13; 24.51; 25.30.

10. 13.28.

11. I think it likely that 'He who despises the set times' (הַמְבַזֶּה
אֶת הַמּוֹעֲדוֹת), here, refers to Paul or to one of his followers. Cp.
Galatians 4.9-10: 'And now, knowing God, or rather, being known by
God, how do you return again to the weak and beggarly elements
(στοιχεῖα), which again, anew, you wish to serve. You observe
days and months and seasons and years.'

12. Zwanzigster Exkurs: Das Gleichnis von den Arbeitern im
Weinberg, Mat 20.1-16 u. die altsynagogale Lohnlehre (Vol. IV, pt. 1,
pp. 484-500).

13. id. p. 485.

14. ib.

15. id. p. 493.

16. s.v. פכה , niphal 3.

17. Prof. Lieberman thinks it clear from the context (in 91.2 and in
ch. 4) that the meaning of the word here agrees with my interpretation.

18. Mat 20.16.

19. id. p. 487.

20. If the contradiction were to that form of the story now known to
us in Sifra, then the story in Mat also would have had to be about a
king. As it is, it argues for the existence of a Jewish story about a
householder. And if it be possible to argue from a comparison of the
parables of the Gospels, of which only a few are about kings, and the
parables of TL, of which only a few are not about kings, it would seem
that the story about a householder was likely to be older than the story
about a king. This fits the theory of Rostovzeff, (The Social and

Economic History of the Roman Empire, Oxford, 1926.), that as the economic structure of the ancient world went from bad to worse, the poorer part of the people learned to turn more and more to the Emperor ($\beta\alpha\sigma\iota\lambda\epsilon\acute{u}s$) as opposed to the rich men of their own cities.

21. Mat 5.21 f., 27 f., 31 f., 33 f., 38 f., 43 f.

22. In Mat 19.30. Note that Mat 20.1 begins: $\acute{o}\mu o\acute{\iota}\alpha\ \gamma\acute{\alpha}\rho\ \acute{\epsilon}\sigma\tau\iota\nu$

23. Mat 19.28-9.

24. Mk 10.29-30, Lk 18.29-30.

25. ib.

26. v. Appendix B, nos. 42, 76, 89, 90.

27. This is the opinion of M. Dibelius, From Tradition to Gospel, (tr. B. Woolf from the rev. 2 ed. of Die Formgeschichte des Evangeliums) London, 1934, p. 3: 'The literary understanding of the synoptics begins with the recognition that they are collections of material. The composers are only to the smallest extent authors. They are principally collectors.'

28. Strack-Billerbeck IV pt. 1, p. 491: 'Diese offizielle Lohnlehre der alten Synagoge lässt natürlich keinen Raum für einen Gnadenlohn.'

29. id. p. 496.

30. For additional examples, see G. Moore, Christian Writers on Judaism, HTR, 14.197 ff.

31. Judaism in the First Christian Centuries, Cambridge, v. II, 1927, p. 95.

32. As against this see the review by K. Lake, Montefiore's 'Judaism and St. Paul,' HTR 9.242 ff. According to Lake the difference between Paul's letters and TL was used by van Maanen to show that the letters were not by Paul, and by Montefiore to show that Paul was not familiar with Judaism. According to Acts 22.3 Paul said that he was in his youth a pupil of Rabban Gamaliel the Elder. This part of Acts was almost certainly written from sources some of which were very close to the events narrated. However, it need not be supposed that Paul's words as reported correspond with stenographic accuracy to what he actually said.

33. According to Moulton and Geden: Mat 5.12, 46; 6.1, 2, 5, 16; 10.41 (bis), 42; 20.8; Mk 9.8; Lk 6.23, 35; 10.7; Jn 4.36.

34. vss. 17, 19, 21.

35. vss. 1, 6-7.

36. According to Huck this text is found in אBDX.

37. P. Fiebig, Altjüdische Gleichnisse u. die Gleichnisse Jesu, Tübingen, 1904, pp. 95-8.

38. e.g.: C. a Lapide, op. cit., in nom. Augustini, Basilii, Gregorii.
    F. Spitta, Das Johannes-Evangelium, Göttingen, 1910.
    J. Belser, Das Evangelium des hl. Johannes, Freiburg i.B. 1905.
    F. Godet, Commentaire sur l'évangile de St. Jean, 4 ed., v. III, Neuchatel, 1905.

Godet thinks that the hired-man represents the priests, but refers to other interpretations, such as, the Pharisees, and also to the opinion that he represents no special group and is introduced only to emphasize by contrast the picture of the good shepherd.

39. μισθόομαι in vss. 1, 6, 7; μισθός in vs. 8.

40. All the instances in the Gospels, except for the story in Mat 20, in which these words are found with meanings other than the customary, are collected in Appendix A, which serves as text for the following annotations in the body of this chapter.

41. The Four Gospels, N.Y., 1933, p. 319; Our Translated Gospels, N.Y., 1936, p. 4.

42. The Four Gospels, p. 319.

43. Mat 9.27-9, Mk 10.29-30, Lk 18.29-30.

44. Abot 5.19.

45. Mat 6.2, 5, 16.

46. v. sup. n. 23 to this chapter.

47. I have already noted, sup. pp. 24-25, the parallel between the Greek here, cp. Mat 5.6, ὅτι Χορτασθήσεσθε, and the Hebrew in Midrash Tannaïm 32.6 (end, cp. Sifre on Deut. ib.), הוא הושיבך על בסיס שלך הלעיטך ביית עמים

48. Distinguish between this notion and the Gnadenlohn of Strack-Billerbeck. Strack-Billerbeck thought of pay given by grace, the Gospels think of grace given as pay.

49. Yet more customary in the epistles is the notion that grace is given in or through (ἐν or διά) Jesus. Two uses, or, perhaps two kinds, of grace must be distinguished, one for salvation and another for particular gifts (prophecy, tongues, etc.).

50. Deut. 24.15 'You shall give his pay in the day he does his work.' (lit. in his - or its - day). See Sifre on Deut. and Midrash Tannaïm ib.

51. See C. Burney, Aramaic Origin, Oxford, 1922, p. 94.

52. δεχόμενος = מקבב see Appendix B, no. 73.

53. See for example Mekilta of R. Simon 22.9-14.

54. See Erubin 4.8, 5.1, Ketubot 10.5, Negaïm 8.10.

55. Of the 134 citations in Appendix B, Strack-Billerbeck, in their article on 'die altsynagogale Lohnlehre' used 15, and added to them 14 citations from TL which they thought relevant to the question because of their content, but which did not contain the word 'pay'; the rest of their material comes from the later literature. In Appendix B I have underlined the references to passages used by Strack-Billerbeck, and have starred the 38 passages cited in J. Bonsirven's Judaisme Palestinien, Paris, 1934-5, in his discussion of pay, i.e., vol. I, pp. 75-80, 107, 199, 204, 505-8, vol. II, pp. 25, 54-74, 251, 256. I have found Bonsirven's work the most satisfactory general treatment of the Judaism of this period.

56. e.g. Num.18.31, and see the comment in Sifre Zutta (in Appendix B, no. 55).

57. Note also no. 50 which speaks of שכר טוב לעולם הבא. It is

interesting to note that it was also when replying to difficulties raised
by the Sadducees that Jesus was most specific about details of life in
the world to come. Cf. Mk 12.18-27 and //s.

58. See V. Aptowitzer, The Rewarding and Punishing of Animals
and Inanimate Objects, HUCA III, 117 ff, esp. pp. 151-2.

59. E.g. Erubin 9.3, Ketubot 9.6, Nedarim 8.1, Shebuot 3.5.

60. On the derivation of halakic details from general rules v. C.
Albeck, Untersuchungen über die Redaktion der Mischna, Berlin, 1923,
pp. 5-8.

61. S. Schechter, Studies in Judaism, N.Y., 1896, pp. 151-2: 'We
are hardly ordered...to believe in the existence of God. I say hardly,
but I do not altogether deny the existence of such a command.' - But
he finds its existence in ancient times implicit rather than explicit.

62. It should go without saying that the large cities and military
posts in Palestine were centers of Greek culture.

63. Strack-Billerbeck IV.1.3.

64. Probably a disciple of Jesus, mentioned in Hullin T 2.22 (503).

65. Acts 9.11.

Chapter 4

PARALLELS OF LITERARY FORM

What are literary forms? For example: Forms of rhetoric which
depend not on a single idiomatic expression nor on the grammatical
peculiarities of the words, but on their meaning; forms of argument,
forms of exegesis - all these are literary forms in the wider sense of
the words; and in their narrower sense they refer to parables, prayers, sayings, sermons, and so on.

This customary use of the word form (as in forms of argument,
figures of speech, Formgeschichte and cognate expressions) is apt to
be misleading, for the essential parallelism of the passages hereinafter to be discussed is one of meaning. For example, between the
story in Mk 3.1-6, which represents Jesus as teaching that it is permissible to heal on the Sabbath, and the words in Shabbat 5.4: 'R.
Elazar ben Azaryah's cow used to go out (of a Sabbath, carrying) the
strap which was between her horns, which (scandalous laxity was) not
according to the wish of the Sages.' there is no important parallelism
in the form of the words, but because of the meaning of the words it is
clear that both passages are stories of particular instances which
serve as evidence for legal theories (and in this instance, for the laws
about the observance of the Sabbath). Similarly, all arguments a fortiori are examples of one literary form, in spite of the fact that some
begin with קל וחומר others conclude with על אחת כמה וכמה others
begin or conclude with מכל שכן and others have none of the customary phrases, e.g., Lk 23.31: 'For if they do these things when the tree
is green, what may happen when it is dry?'

Such being the case, how are these parallels of literary form, which
are actually parallels of meaning, to be distinguished from the parallels of meaning discussed in the chapter above? In its broad outlines,
the answer is simple: Above, the meanings were divided according to
the subjects of knowledge - theology, philosophy, and so on; here they
are divided according to literary classifications - stories, prayers,
arguments, explanations, and so on. As these literary classifications
hereinafter to be discussed have by general convention been called
forms, it must be emphasized at once that literary form, 'the form of
the thought,' has no direct connexion with the forms of the sentences
in which the thought is expressed (for, as has just been pointed out,
there is no peculiar sentence structure common to all stories, nor
even to a single class of argument, but all arguments of a single class
are said to have the same form in spite of the wide formal differences
between the sentences stating them.)

I hope that this statement of the distinction in general terms is clear, for in particular instances it is very difficult to distinguish some parallels of literary form from other parallels of meaning. See, for example, B. Easton's question at the expense of R. Bultmann:[1] 'What form difference is there between the "logion" - "Whosoever exalteth himself shall be humbled." - the "apocalyptic word" - "Whosoever shall be ashamed of me, the Son of man shall be ashamed of him." - and the "church rule" - "Whosoever putteth away his wife and marrieth another, committeth adultery"?' My attention was called to Easton's words by V. Taylor,[2] who quoted them with approval. It cannot be denied that all the sentences given have the same logical form (all x is y) and almost the same grammatical structure. The differences between them lie in their content, but, according to these differences, each one of them belongs to a different class of literary expression - to a different form, as Bultmann said.

In point of fact, two approaches to problems like this are possible. (a) It is possible to set up a class defined by content, and subdivide this class according to external forms. Thus, for example, if the class be 'church rules,' these rules may be subdivided into groups according to the syntactic forms of the sentences in which they are expressed. In this event it would be a mistake to introduce into this class an expression, of whatever syntactic form, which was not a church rule. (b) It is possible to set up a class defined by external forms, and subdivide this class according to the content of its members. Thus, for example, in speaking of the class of 'stories' it is customary to subdivide into stories of miracles, stories of arguments, and so on.

To extend this discussion of the theory of parallelism would be out of place here. I shall therefore go on simply to describe some of the more important parallels of literary form, and to study in detail one group of these, viz. the parallels to be found between the sermons in the Gospels and those in TL.

On the side of rhetoric, parallels of literary form come very close to parallels of idiom, discussed in Ch. 2. Here the theoretical distinction lies in the fact that for parallels of literary form the meaning is the essential, and the words and sentences need not be parallel, whereas in parallels of idiom the parallelism of the words is essential and that of meaning only the conditio sine qua non. It is clear that there are some tricks of verbal arrangement, such as homoioteleuton, which can be discussed without any reference to the meaning of the words concerned, and other conventions of style, such as aporia, of which recognizable examples can be found having no detail of word or word order in common. But, between these extremes, in many cases it is almost impossible to decide just where the examples belong. Thus, for instance, with forms of citation like καθὼς γέγραπται ἐν = ככתוב ב[3] or ἐν τῷ νόμῳ δὲ τῷ ὑμετέρῳ γέγραπται = כתיב בתורתכם.[4]

Here it is almost impossible to decide whether the interest in the verbal parallel derives from the parallel of meaning, or vice versa. I tend to think that in the first the verbal parallel is more important, in the second, the parallel of meaning, but if so, then the two should not be considered examples of the same sort of parallelism - a conclusion which is a reduction to absurdity.

The parallels of rhetorical form which have hitherto received most attention have been 'parallelism' (in its grammatical sense, as a form for poetry) and antithesis. I have listed in the notes[5] the more important of the books known to me which deal at length with these forms. Apart from these a great many parallels in less important forms have been noted in passing by many students, e.g.:[6]

climax: Lk 10.16: ὁ ἀθετῶν ὑμᾶς ἐμὲ ἀθετεῖ ὁ δὲ ἐμὲ ἀθετῶν
         ἀθετεῖ τὸν ἀποστείλαντά με.
         Abot 4:12: יהי.... כבוד חברך כמורך ומורא רבך כמורא שמים

metonomy: Mat 16.17: σὰρξ καὶ αἷμα Mekilta 15.1: בשר ודם [7]

periphrasis: Mat 11.11: οὐκ ἐγήγερται ἐν γεννητοῖς γυναικῶν.
              Sifre on Numbers 9.8: אשרי ילד אשה שכך ה"ה מבטו [8]

pleonasm: Mat 9.16: ἐπιβάλλει ἐπίβλημα
           Kelim 26.2: טלה עליו את המטלת
           28.6: מטלית שטלי"ה.

synecdoche: Jn 4.23: ἔρχεται ὥρα (ὥρα meaning καιρός.)
             Mekilta 15.25: [9] יש שעה לקצר ויש שעה להאריך

                                                    And so on.

It is clear that these are only chance pickings, and that the subject has yet to be studied systematically. I know of no book on the rhetoric (as opposed to the logic and terminology) of TL; a fortiori there is no satisfactory work on its relations to the rhetoric of the Gospels.

One exception to this neglect of the rhetoric of TL has been the considerable discussion of comparisons in the Gospels and in TL, not only of the simple comparisons, but also, and, indeed, rather, the parables and משלים . These are certainly among the best known subjects of the whole field; therefore they need no discussion here, and in order to go on directly to literary forms in the narrower sense of the words I shall also pass over without discussion the parallels to be found in forms of argument and in other, similar, conventional forms of thought, in spite of the fact that here the neglect cannot be justified on the ground that the phenomena are already familiar. On parallels in forms of argument I know of nothing but the note (no. 14) by Fiebig in his Pirqe 'aboth,[10] p. 2, to the effect that arguments a fortiori are frequent both in the Gospels and TL, the few passages cited by Strack-Billerbeck as parallels to some of the arguments in the Gospels, and their note on the argument a fortiori and its like in their commentary on Romans 5.9. The basic book on the subject has still to be written, but here more of the preparatory work has been done on the Jewish side, and there is considerable material on the forms of argument in TL.

The study of literary forms, in the narrower sense of the words, has also been very spotty. Some, like prayers and sayings, have already been discussed at length. Others, like introductions to stories and forms of transition have had only such one-sided consideration as these got from K. Schmidt in Der Rahmen der Geschichte Jesu.[11] Of others nothing at all has been written, and of yet others, too much.

Prominent in the last group are the miracle stories, to which Fiebig devoted an entire book (Jüdische Wundergeschichten des neutestamentlichen Zeitalters[12]) of which the essential conclusions are completely false. Fiebig writes (p. 72): '1. dies Material zeigt, dass auch in Palästina...in der Zeit Jesu...Wundergeschichten etwas Geläufiges waren, dass die Juden jener Gegenden und jener Zeit Wunder von ihren Lehrern erzählten...dass also das Milieu, in dem Jesus lebte, derartig war....2. dass es falsch ist, die Wunder Jesu allein, oder vorzugsweise aus seiner Messianität abzuleiten. Gewiss erwarteten die Juden der Zeit Jesu vom Messias Wunder, aber sie sagten sie doch auch von ihren Rabbinen aus, ohne dabei an Messianisches zu denken.' The words I have underlined are basic to Fiebig's thought and are quite unjustifiable. For as a matter of fact TL contains almost no stories of miracles performed by Tannaïm, and this not because the authorities behind the literature did not believe in miracles, nor yet because they did not like to talk of them, for when they commented on the stories of the Old Testament - which already contain enough miracles for the average man - they added to their accounts many more miracles of the most miraculous sort, but when they came to tell of the doings of the Tannaïm they ceased almost altogether to tell miracle stories, and this fact is strikingly obvious from the collection of stories made by Fiebig in his book. There he discusses 13 passages from TL, as follows:

Mekilta 23.7[13]: Judah ben Tabbai 'went into a cave and found there a murdered man (still) wriggling and the sword dripping blood from the hand of the murderer. He said to him...."May (evil) come upon me if neither I nor you killed him. (Ergo, since I didn't, you must have.) But what shall I do, for behold, the Law said, 'Let (every)thing be established by two witnesses.' But He who knows and (who is) Lord of thoughts, will take vengeance upon that man." Before he had finished leaving the place a snake bit him (the murderer) and he died.'

Now (1) Judah ben Tabbai belongs to the borderland between the Tannaïm and the legendary. (2) He did not perform the 'miracle.' (3) The miracle was not miraculous in respect of what happened, but only in respect to the time and appropriateness of a quite natural event.

Sanhedrin T 6.6 (424): This contains nothing in any way miraculous.

Taanit 3.8: The story of Honi 'the circle-drawer,' who got his prayers for rain answered by drawing a circle, standing in it, and threatening God that he would not move till they were. (1) Honi also belongs to the period of Judah ben Tabbai. (2) Again, this is not a story of the performance of a miracle. That God sends rain, and that he sends it in answer to prayer, is nothing special. Such miraculous element as the story contains is derived, again, from the appropriate time and manner in which the desired takes place.

Berakot T. 3.20 (8): A story about R. Hanina ben Dosa - a snake bit him when he was praying and the snake died. (Fiebig cites it from the Babylonian Talmud.)

Sotah T 13.8 (319): 'Once upon a time there was a man from Sepphoris who took his share and his companion's share and nevertheless got only double, and people called him 'the grabber' down to this day.' (The Vienna MS and the printed eds: 'Down to the year in which Simon the Just died.' Simon the Just considerably antedates ben Tabbai, and the following story almost certainly concerns him.) 'He said to them, "I am going to die in the course of this year." They said, "Whence do you know?" He said to them, "Each Day of Atonement an old man dressed in white and covering his head with white used to meet me. He went in with me (to the Holy of Holies) and came out with me. This year he went in with me and did not come out with me." After the feast he was sick a week and died.' (1) Again from the legendary period. (2) There is a wide difference between seeing spirits and doing miracles.

Hullin T 2.22 (503): 'Once upon a time a snake bit R. Elazar ben Damah, and Jacob, a man of the village of Samma, came to cure him in the name of Jeshua ben Pantera, and R. Ishmael did not permit him. They said to him, "You are not permitted, ben Dama." He said to him, "I shall prove to you that he may cure me." And before he finished the proof, he died.' (1) The miracle was not performed, (2) The man who wanted to perform it was not one of the Tannaïm, but was - presumably - a follower of Jesus;[14] therefore the story cannot be used to prove that miracles were attributed to the Tannaïm as well as to Jesus and his followers. (The attribution of miracles to his followers is well known from Acts.)

Mekilta 17.9: A story about Gehazi, the servant of Elisha - hardly evidence for belief about the Tannaïm.

Sifre on Deut. 32.4 (end): The story of R. Hananyah ben Teradyon, remarkable for the fact that it contains no miraculous element, whereas Christian accounts of martyrdom abound in them.

Mekilta 23.8: 'Anyone who takes money and perverts justice will
not leave the world till he lack the light of his eyes (i.e., have gone
blind.) R. Nathan says, "Until he experience one of these three things:
Either his knowledge of the Law will be confused...or he will be supported by public charity, or he will go blind." ' What is the miracle
here? And which of the Tannaïm performed it?

Yoma 4.1: No miracle.

Yoma 6.8: 'And whence did they know that the goat (of the Day of
Atonement) had reached the desert?...R. Judah says, "And had they
not another sign? A strip of red cloth was tied to the gate of the temple and when the goat reached the desert the strip turned white, for it
was said, 'Though your sins be as scarlet, they shall be white as
snow.' This miracle, also, was neither done by nor attributed to any
of the Tannaïm.

Eduyot 7.7: No miracle.

Kelim 5.10: No miracle.

Thus of these thirteen passages there are only 6 containing accounts of what can possibly be called 'miracles,' and of these 6 one
concerns a figure from the Old Testament, while another is not related to any of the Tannaïm. That leaves four. Of these four, one is
from the time of Simon the Just, and two are from the time of Judah
ben Tabbai, and none - except perhaps the story about Honi - represents the Rabbi as performing the miracle. On the contrary, as the
customary terminology has it, the miracle is performed for him
(נעשה לו!). To sum up: Simon the Just saw a spirit, Judah ben
Tabbai saw a murderer killed by snake-bite, Honi prayed for rain and
it came, a snake bit Hanina ben Dosa and the snake died, and Fiebig
represented these facts as proof that the Jews of the Tannaïtic period
were accustomed to tell, about the Tannaïm, such miracle stories as
Jesus' followers told about him.[15]

I do not deny that TL contains other stories, not cited by Fiebig,
which tell of miracles performed by, or for, one or another of the
Tannaïm. For example, there is Pesahim T 1.27 (157): 'Once upon a
time Rabban Gamliel and R. Ilai were walking from Akko to Kazib and
(Rabban Gamliel) saw a loaf of fine bread. He said to Tabi his servant, "Take this bread." He saw a gentile and said to him, "Mabgai,
take this bread." R. Ilai ran after him; he said to him...."What is
your name?" He said to him, "My name is Mabgai." He said to him,
"Did Rabban Gamliel ever know you?" He said to him, "No." Hence
we learned that Rabban Gamliel directed (his actions) with (the in-
spiration of) the Holy Spirit.' And stories like this were told not only
about the Tannaïm of those days, but also about other men of the same
period, for example the story about the gates of Nikanor, of which one
was thrown into the sea and cast up in the harbor of Jaffa (Yom

Hakkippurim T 2.4 (183) - though Nikanor is, in fact, a little early and
didn't perform the miracle.) And beside these there are other stories
which, although they do not tell of the strictly miraculous, yet show how
God brings on the wicked the doom they deserve. To this class belonged, as I said, the story cited by Fiebig from Mekilta 23.7. Another
example of the class is found in Sifre on Num. 28.26: 'R. Tarefon says,
"Since the (offering of the) omer (of barley - v. Lev. 23.10 ff.) makes
it permissible (to use the new crop for ordinary food) and (the offering of) the two loaves of bread (Lev. 23.15 ff.) makes it permissible
(to use the new crop for sacrifices), if I have learned, as to vegetable
offerings (from the new crop) coming prior to (the offering of) the
omer, that they are unfit, (then) also vegetable offerings coming prior
to (the offering of) the two loaves of bread will be unfit (פסולות)."
R. Judah b. Nahman said to him, 'No, if you stated (a conclusion holding) in (the case of) vegetable offerings coming prior to the omer,
which are not fit to be used either for the Temple or for a private individual, shall you state (the same conclusion as holding) in (the case
of) vegetable offerings coming prior to the two loaves of bread, which,
although they were not fitted to be used for the Temple, were fitted
for use by private individuals?" R. Akiba looked at him and (saw that)
his face shone; he said to him, "Judah ben Nahman, your face shone
because you refuted the old man; I wonder if your days will be long in
the world. (or, I shall wonder at you if you prolong your days in the
world.)" R. Judah the son of R. Ilai said, "This happened at Passover
and when I came for Pentecost I said, 'Where is Judah ben Nahman?'
They told me, 'He is gone.'"' But even stories of this sort are very
few in number, and as for stories of real miracles done by one or
another of the Tannaim, I remember none, unless there be one among
those already cited. And even should there be one or two I have
missed, their existence would not alter the general conclusion,[16] viz.:
That as for stories of miracles done by men of that period (as opposed
to the figures of the Old Testament), the parallels between the Gospels
and TL are not so important as the difference between them, and that
difference is, that stories like these are very frequent in the Gospels
and almost totally lacking in TL.

However, as opposed to this difference, there are also important
parallels of literary forms to be found between the Gospels and TL.
As an illustration of these parallels I have chosen the sermons to be
found in the two literatures.

The sermons in the Gospels have not hitherto been much discussed
qua sermons - on their content, of course, and especially on the content of the sermon on the mount, whole libraries have been written;
on their literary form, something has been said by some commentators,[17] but almost always with the purpose of demonstrating the sequence of thought in the particular sermon under discussion, and not
of showing how its form was like the form of the other sermons in the

Gospels, or how it differed from them. Even the representatives of
Formgeschichte were more interested in Geschichte than in Form,[18]
and attempted less to describe the forms now found in the Gospels
than to go back through history, by means of a comparison of the parts
composing these forms, to the 'original' forms which are knowable
only as inferences. So even Dibelius, according to whose opinion sermons were[19] 'the original seat of all tradition about Jesus,' wrote
nothing about the structure of the sermons now found in the Gospels,
but devoted all his discussion to those which he found in Acts.

Similarly E. Norden, in Agnostos Theos,[20] although he called the
book 'Untersuchungen zur Formengeschichte religiöser Rede,' wrote
nothing about the sermons in the Gospels and does not seem to have
considered them, for his analysis of the sermon in Acts 17. 22-31
contains an important error which would have been almost impossible
to anyone who, while reading the sermon attributed to Paul, kept in
mind the sermons attributed to Jesus. According to Norden's analysis[21] the sermon in Acts 17 consists of four parts: (1) 17.23: 'What,
then, you worship without knowing it, this I proclaim to you.'
(2) 17.24 ff.: God is to be revered, not as an image, but as a spirit.
(3) 17.30: 'So God, overlooking the times of ignorance, now warns all
men everywhere to repent.' (4) 17.31: 'The resurrection of Christ
from the dead.' Here there is no visible relationship between the
resurrection of Jesus from the dead and the philosophical preach-
ment preceding it. And when Norden seeks in Poimandres[22] for a
parallel to the resurrection of Jesus, he finds only the promise of
eternal life to those who succeed in knowing the divine. There is a
clear difference between the past resurrection of a single individual
from actual death, and the present promise to all men that they can
escape from ignorance of things divine. And in the particular parallel
found by Norden this difference is more striking than the similarity.
Of course, the promise of eternal life is found often in the New Testament, and although it is not explicit in the sermon in Acts which Norden was discussing, it is doubtless there presupposed. But just because it is presupposed there, it is itself the parallel to the promise
in Poimandres, and the resurrection of Jesus remains unparalleled,
and the question arises, Why was Jesus mentioned in the sermon in
Acts? The answer is clear from the real structure of the sermon,
which is clear from the text, vss. 30-31: 'So God, overlooking the
times of ignorance, now warns all men everywhere to repent, inasmuch as he has set a day in which he is about to judge the world by a
man whom he has determined, providing evidence (of this determination) to all (by) raising him from the dead.' The underlined words,
which are not mentioned in Norden's analysis, constitute an essential
part of the sermon, and contain the theme most emphasized in the
sermons in the Gospels. In a word, Norden overlooked one of the
most typically Jewish elements in primitive Christianity, for the

sermons in <u>Acts</u> taught, not only salvation by means of a new knowledge of the divine – something taught also by gentile philosophy – but also salvation <u>by means of the Messiah</u> from the dangers <u>of the day of judgment</u>.[23] And in the sermons of the Gospels this theme, the day of judgment, is more emphasized than any other.

The question, What are the sermons in the Gospels? may be given several answers, depending on the several different definitions of 'sermon.' For the purposes of this thesis a sermon in the Gospels shall be an element (1) of greater length than the 'logion' or the 'parable,' (2) introduced by an editorial statement that a certain man said these words (as it happens, this man is always Jesus, but the Gospels narrowly missed having a sermon by John the Baptist) and (3) composed of several parts so connected by the structure of the thought as to constitute beginning, middle and end; therefore a parable, being all of one piece, will not count as a sermon, in spite of being long (as is the parable about the prodigal son, in Lk 15.11 ff), nor will an abbreviation of a bona-fide sermon, now reduced to three or four verses (and therefore I have not considered the summary in Mk 6.8-11, of the sermon to the Twelve, nor the summary of the sermon in Lk 9.3-5), nor will strings of parables nor strings of sayings, which do not show at once unity, structure and development of thought (such as the collection of parables in Mk 4, Mat 13, Lk 8, and the collections of sayings about John the Baptist in Mat 11, Lk 7, about spirits in Mat 12, Lk 11, about pay in Mk 9, Mat 18, and the like – although I think it probable that much of the material contained in them came originally from sermons).

The concern of this chapter, in a word, is to discuss, not the material from sermons contained in the Gospels, nor the original sermons of Jesus, nor the sermons from which the authors of the sources of the Gospels obtained their material, but the sermons <u>now found</u> in the Gospels. These constitute the answer to the question, When the final editors of the Gospels wished to represent Jesus as preaching a sermon, and to outline his sermon in full, what did they make him say?

Here, of course, it can be objected that my procedure is an example of <u>hysteron-proteron,</u> for, wishing to determine the form of the sermons in the Gospels, I have decided to take account only of that material which shows a certain form. This objection is correct, but can be brought against all studies of literary forms, for it is impossible to study, say, stories, without knowing what 'stories' are. And how is the story known except from its literary form? (See the distinction between literary and syntactic form, made at the beginning of this chapter.) Every student of literary forms brings to the material before him his own concepts of the forms he wishes to find in it, and distinguishes the forms of one book from those of another only according to the differences between those parts which he thinks important as examples corresponding to his concepts. This system leaves ample opportunity for differences of opinion, as can be seen from a comparison of the opinions of three scholars about one or more of the sermons to be discussed.

R. Bultmann denies that the Gospels contain any passages of unified structure. He says,[24] "auch in den schriftlichen Sammlungen sind die Prinzipien der Bildung grösserer Einheiten zunächst keine andern, als sie es schon in der mündlichen Tradition waren, d. h. es kommt nur zu einer recht primitiven Aneinanderreihung einzelner kleinen Einheiten, wobei stoffliche Verwandtschaft oder äussere Ähnlichkeit (Stichwortdisposition) leitend ist und mitunter auch nur der Zufall waltet. Auf diese Weise...kann auch wohl ein gewisser Gedankengang leitend sein. Aber es konnte nicht zu organischen Kompositionen, zu einheitlichen Reden, kommen."

As against this, A. Schweitzer[25] thinks the sermon to the Twelve (Mat 10) a summary of the words of Jesus himself, arranged in the order in which he spoke them in the original sermon. After his exposition of the sequence of thought in this sermon, he writes,[26] 'Hiernach beurteile man, mit welchem Recht die moderne Theologie die grossen matthäischen Reden kurzerhand als "Redenkompositionen" hinstellt. Man beweise doch einmal, wie der Evangelist, der sich abmühte, eine Aussendungsrede aus überlieferten Sprüchen u. aus der 'Gemeindetheologie' halb zusammenzustellen, halb zu erfinden, auf den seltsamen Gedanken kommen konnte, den Herrn von lauter unzeitgemässen und unsachlichen Dingen reden zu lassen, und nachher selber zu konstatieren, dass sie nicht in Erfüllung gingen.'

Between these opinions stands that of T. Soiron, who wrote, as the conclusion of his study, 'Somit stellt sich die Bergpredigt bei Matthäus als ein Ganzes dar, das durch zwei mnemotechnische Mittel zusammengehalten ist. Zum Teil sind es gleichartige, systematische Gedanken, welche die Sprüche wie an einen Faden aufreihen. Und wo die Gleichartigkeit der Gedanken fehlt, um die Sprüche zusammenzuhalten, da bilden Stichworte die Klammern, die die Teile der Spruchgruppe kunstvoll verbinden.'[27] Soiron examined also the remaining sermons in the synoptics, and found in them all the same two sorts of structural connection, which he found also in rabbinical literature, and which he thought evidence of verbal tradition; but his purpose was not to examine the structure of the sermons, but to demonstrate the ways in which the sayings that compose them are held together. He also was more concerned with Geschichte than with Form, and was especially concerned with the history of the sources.

As against this, I shall not here compare the individual sayings in the sermons with their synoptic parallels, nor attempt by such comparison to determine their original forms or the sources from which they were taken, nor shall I discuss the connection of the individual sayings except when it happens to be important for an understanding of the structure of the sermon as a whole, for I wish to examine the sermons as they are now, to see if there be a form common to all of them, or several different forms, each found in one or more, and thereafter to see if such form or forms be found also in TL.

Here I have limited the study to the sermons in the synoptics. According to the criteria stated above, these sermons are nine: The sermon on the mount (Mat 5-7) and two parallels in Lk (6.20-49; 12.22-40), the sermon to the Twelve (Mat 10) and its parallel to the Seventy (Lk 10), the attack on the scribes and Pharisees (Mat 23), and the three prophecies of the last things (Mk 13, Mat 24-5, Lk 21). The parallels of content, mentioned here, will henceforward be important only insofar as they help to indicate parallelism in structure of thought. I shall first give outlines of the sermons, with a few annotations, and then point out the similarities of their structures. As to all the sermons in the synoptics, and also as to the passages of TL which I think sermons, it is good to keep in mind what Dibelius said of the sermons in <u>Acts</u>:[28] 'What Acts offers as the content of a speech which was really delivered, is proved by its brevity to be rather the skeleton than the substance.' Therefore it is presumable that if there ever were sermons corresponding to those now found in the Gospels, the short generalities[29] these now contain stand for considerable sections of the originals, for they admit of expansion more easily than do the parables and rhetorical ornament.

But even if the present sermons be not abbreviations of longer originals, it is yet possible to suppose that the editors of the Gospels, when writing the outline of an imaginary sermon, wrote it according to the customary form of the sermons known in their days. But even this supposition is here unnecessary, for it is a historical theory, and here I shall be content to show that collections of sayings, of similar form, appear several times in the Gospels and in TL. Whether these collections should be called 'sermons' or 'outlines of sermons' is itself a historical question, if understood to imply a theory as to their origin or purpose. Not wishing to become involved in the discussion of such a question, I have nevertheless used the term 'sermon' for the sake of convenience.

Outlines:

A. <u>The sermon on the mount, Mat 5.3-7.27</u>.   <u>A.</u>

(I. Introduction to the sermon:
Mat 5.1-2 <u>'Seeing the crowds...he taught them, saying:'</u>)

II. The introduction of the sermon, viz. a challenge to the listeners.
Mat 5.3-10 <u>'The...are fortunate, for'</u>...
.11 <u>'You are fortunate, when men revile you...for my sake.'</u>
.12 <u>'Be glad and rejoice, for your pay is great.'</u>
.13 <u>'You are the salt of the earth.'</u>
.14 <u>'You are the light of the world.'</u>
(The last verse of the section, 16, serves as a transition to the subject of the body of the sermon: <u>'Let your light so shine</u>

before men that they may see your good works and glorify your
Father who is in Heaven.'

III. The body of the sermon: Concerning the Law.
  (a) The Law is important.
      Mat 5.17 'I have not come to destroy (the Law or the proph-
      ets) but to fulfill.'
           .18 'For...not the smallest letter or sign shall pass
      from the Law till all be fulfilled.'
           .19 'Whoever, then, abolish one of the least of these
      commandments...shall be called least in the kingdom of
      Heaven...and whoever shall do and teach, he shall be
      called great in the kingdom.'
           .20 'For I tell you that unless your righteousness sur-
      pass that of the scribes and Pharisees, you shall not en-
      ter the kingdom' (Here again the last vs. serves as a
      transition to the next section.)
  (b) Principles of the Law, taught, as usual in TL, by reference
      to particular commandments.
      1. The purpose, rather than the letter, of the Law is to be
         obeyed. (No doubt any distinction between purpose and
         letter would have been denied, but the modern concept
         states conveniently the upshot of the ancient teaching.)
         Mat 5.21-47 'You have heard that it was said....But I tell
         you.' (The prohibitions of murder, adultery and perjury
         are to be understood as prohibiting anger, lust and swear-
         ing; the permissions of divorce, revenge and hatred are
         either drastically limited (divorce) or abolished (revenge
         and hatred).)
              5.48 (Summary) 'Be therefore perfect as your heaven-
         ly Father is perfect.'
      2. Obedience must be motivated by proper intention.
         Mat 6.1 (Rule) 'Beware of practicing your piety before men
         in order to be seen by them; if you do not (beware of this)
         you have no pay from the Father.'
              6.2-18 (3 examples: almsgiving, prayer, fasting.)
      3. Intention must be based on trust.
         Mat 6.19-24a (Three comparisons) Lay not up treasures on
         earth but in heaven, for where your treasure is, there will
         your heart be. The light of the body is the eye, if that be
         evil the body is dark. None can serve two masters.
              6.24b (General rule, derived from the last of the com-
         parisons) 'You cannot serve God and mammon.'
              6.25-34 (Consequences following from the rule):
                   6.25 (A second rule) 'Because of this I say to you,
                   take no thought for your life...nor for your
                   body'...

6.26-30 (Arguments to support the rule) 'Consider the birds...the lilies'...

6.31 (The rule repeated) 'Therefore, take no thought'...

6.32 (More arguments for it) The gentiles take thought for physical needs, but your Father will take care of yours.

6.33 (The rule restated) 'Seek first his kingdom and his righteousness.'

[4. Against fault-finding (and thence, on humility)

Mat 7.1 (Rule) 'Judge not, that you be not judged.'

7.3-5 (Comparison) How can you see the mote in your neighbor's eye till you have removed the beam from your own?

5. Against those who profane holy things

Mat 7.6 'Give not that which is holy to the dogs'...] [30]

6. Trust implies prayer[31]

Mat 7.7 (Rule) 'Ask and it shall be given you.' (Restated in .8)

.9 (Argument to support the rule) If you, being men, give your children what they ask for, a fortiori God....

7. Summary: Definition of the Law of which the principles have thus been outlined.

Mat 7.12 'Therefore do for men such things as you wish men should do for you, for this is the Law and the prophets.' (Here also the last verse of the section, by its emphasis on do, serves as a transition to the following. section.)

IV. The conclusion of the sermon: Salvation is given, not for the acceptance of the Law, but for its practice.

Mat 7.13-14 (Comparison) Enter through the narrow gate, for narrow is the gate which leads to life. The two roads.

[.15 (Warning) Beware of false prophets[32]]

.16 (Second comparison) 'From their fruits you shall know them.'

.21 (The rule stated directly) 'Not everyone who says to me, Lord, Lord, shall enter the kingdom...but he who does the will of my Father.'

.22-3 (Warning) 'On that day, many will say to me, Lord, Lord,....And then I shall say to them, I never knew you, depart from me, you workers of iniquity.'

.24-27 (Comparison) He who hears my words and does them is like a wise man who built his house on a rock, and he who hears but does not do, like a fool who built on the sand.

V. Conclusion after the sermon:
Mat 7.28-9 'And it came to pass, when Jesus finished these
    words, the crowds were astonished at his teaching, for he
    taught them as one having authority, and not as their scribes.'

B. <u>Lk 6.20-49</u>   **B.**

(I. Introduction to the sermon:
Lk 6.20a 'And he, looking at his disciples, said:')

II. The introduction of the sermon: How pay and punishment are
awarded. (The first part of this material corresponds roughly
to some of that used in Mat for the address to the listeners.
But here the application to the listeners is overshadowed by the
general implications of vss. 24 ff.)
(a) Pay: Lk 6.20b - 21: 'The...are fortunate, for'
              .22 'You are fortunate when...and when'...
              .23 'Be glad, then, and rejoice, for, behold, your
                    pay.'
(b) Punishment: 6.24-5 'But woe to you, the...for'...
              .26 'Woe, when'...

III. The body of the sermon:
(a) An address to the listeners
Lk 6.27a 'But I say to you who hear'...
(b) Obedience to the purpose, as well as to the letter, of the
Law is required of those who would receive pay.
Lk 6.27b-31 (A list of commandments) 'Love your enemies'
              etc.
      .32 ff. (Supporting argument) 'And if you love your
                friends, what grace have you, for ever sinners
                love their friends?'
      .35 'But love your enemies...and your pay will be great.'
(c) Pay is given according to practise.
Lk 6.36 ff. (A list of commandments) 'Be merciful' etc.
      .38b 'For the measure you give will be the measure you
                get.'
(Here the sequence of thought is completely broken, and Lk 6.39
contains a new introduction. However, such introductions in the
middle of a subject, or even in the middle of a speech, are found
elsewhere in Lk, v. Lk 18.6,[33] for example. Thus, though it is
possible to argue that the sermon in Lk 6 was intended to conclude with vs. 38, and that the remainder of the chapter contains
a separate collection of sayings, yet, because a conclusion <u>after</u>
a sermon is found in 7.1, and because 6.39-49 can be understood as the conclusion of the preceding sermon (and certain
parts of the material unquestionably serve this purpose in Mat)

I think the text is better interpreted by regarding the whole section from 20-49 as the outline of a single speech.)

IV. The conclusion of the sermon:
(Lk 6.39a (Editorial transition) 'And he also told them a parable')
.39b (Comparison) 'Can the blind lead the blind?'
[.40 (Corruption?) 'A disciple is not above his teacher.'[34]]
.41 ff. (Further comparisons, all illustrating the necessity of personal practise) The mote and the beam, the tree and the fruit, the houses on the rock and on the sand. The point is made directly in .46 'Why do you call me, Lord, Lord, and not do what I say?'

V. Conclusion after the sermon:
Lk 7.1 'And when he finished all these words...he entered Capernaum.'

C. Lk 12.15-40   C.

(The greater part of the material in Lk 11 and 12 is arranged not in sermons, but in collections of sayings introduced by short stories. I suppose this may reflect the form of teaching common in the Christian circles known to the author, and the author may have supposed it the form of teaching used by Jesus. At any event, there is no doubt that Lk has here in short sections much of the material which appears in Mat in longer sermons. Only one of these sections of Lk's seems to me sufficiently large and developed to satisfy the requirements above laid down for a 'sermon.' It follows:)

(I. Introduction to the sermon:
Lk 12.15a 'And he said to them:')

(The sermon itself has no introduction.)

II. The body of the sermon:
(a) Antithesis: Do not seek the good things of this world.
Lk 12.15b (General rule) 'Look out and guard yourselves from all covetousness.'
.16 ff. (Illustrative parable - the rich fool)
.22 f. (Consequences drawn from the parable, the detailed application of the rule) 'And he said to his disciples, Therefore I tell you, take no thought for your life...nor for your body'...
.24-28 (Arguments confirming the rule) Consider the ravens and the lilies.
.29 (The rule repeated) 'And as for you, do not seek what you shall eat and what you shall drink' etc.
.30 (A final pair of arguments) 'For the gentiles of the

world seek all these things, but your Father
knows that you need them.'

(b) Thesis: But seek the kingdom and be ready for its coming.
Lk 12.31 (General rule) 'But seek His kingdom and these
   things will be added to you.'
.32 (Encouragement) 'Do not fear, little flock, for it is
   your Father's good pleasure to give you the kingdom.'
.33 ff. (The rule translated, first into practical terms,
   then into comparisons) Sell what you have and
   give to the poor, make yourselves purses that do
   not grow old, an unfailing treasure in the heavens,
   let your loins be girded and be like men awaiting
   their master's return, or like a householder
   awake to prevent a thief.
.40 (The rule restated) 'And, you also, be ready, for
   the Son of Man is coming in that hour in which
   you do not expect (him).'
(The sermon has no conclusion.)

D. Mat 10.5-42   D.

(I. Introduction to the sermon:
Mat 10.5a 'These twelve Jesus sent out and charged them, saying:')

(The sermon has no introduction.)

II. The body of the sermon:
(a) To whom they are sent.
Mat 10.5b (Antithesis) 'Do not go into a road of the gentiles,
   and do not enter a city of the Samaritans'
.6 (Thesis) 'But rather go to the lost sheep of the
   house of Israel.'
(b) What they are to do.
Mat 10.7-8a Proclaim that the kingdom of God is near, heal
   the sick, raise the dead, cleanse lepers, cast out
   demons.
(c) How they are to behave.
Mat 10.8b-15 Give freely, get no money, carry no provisions;
   stay where you are received; where you are not,
   shake the dust from your feet.
(d) What will happen to them. (This is intimately connected with
the preceding section, for their behaviour must, of course,
be determined by what does happen to them. Therefore this
section also contains rules for behaviour, especially vs. 16
which serves as a transition between the two sections, containing, as it does, both the prophecy of persecution and the
instruction how it is to be met.)

Mat 10.16 (General) 'Behold, I send you forth as sheep
among wolves, be therefore wise as serpents and
innocent as doves.'

10.17-34 (Special)

   (1) .17-.23 You will be persecuted, but he who endures to the end will be saved, and the end is
near.

   (2) .24-.27 You will be slandered, but the truth
will be known in the end.

   (3) .28-.32 You will be killed, but even this will
not happen without your Father's knowledge
(the comparison of the sparrows) and everyone who acknowledges or denies the Son of
Man will receive due reward or punishment in
the future.

10.34-39 (General) The first coming of the Messiah is
only to precipitate the pains of the Messianic
era, and there is no way of salvation but
through suffering.

III. The conclusion of the sermon: The promise of pay.

Mat 10.40 'He who receives you, receives me'...

.41 'He who receives a prophet in the name of a prophet
shall get the pay of a prophet' etc.

.42 ...'I tell you truly, he shall not lose his pay.'

(IV. Conclusion after the sermon:

Mat 11.1 'And when Jesus finished giving directions to his 12
disciples, he went thence to teach and preach in their cities.'

E. Lk 10.2-16   E.

(I. Introduction to the sermon:

Lk 10.1-2a 'After these things the Lord appointed 70 others and
sent them ahead of him...and said to them:')

II. The introduction of the sermon: The general conditions of the
mission.

Lk 10.2b-3 The harvest is large, the laborers few, pray God
send more. I send you out as sheep among wolves.

III. The body of the sermon:

(a) How they are to behave.

Lk 10.4-12: What to take with them (nothing), how to behave
on the road, how to behave where they are received, and how where they are not ('I tell you,
it will be more tolerable for Sodom in that day
than for that city (which does not receive you).')

(b) A digression, occasioned by the preceding verse, on the cities which had not received Him.
Lk 10.13-15 Woe to you, Chorazin, woe to you, Bethsaida, Capernaum.

IV. The conclusion of the sermon: The importance of the apostles.
Lk 10.16 'He who hears you, hears me, and he who rejects you, rejects me, and he who rejects me, rejects him who sent me.'

F. Mat 23.2-39   F.

(I. Introduction to the sermon:
Mat 23.1-2a 'Then Jesus spoke to the crowds and to his disciples, saying: ')

II. The introduction of the sermon: (Antithesis) The words of the sages are as the words of Moses.
Mat 23.2-3a 'The scribes and the Pharisees sit on Moses' seat, whatever, then, they say to you, that do and obey.'

III. The body of the sermon: (Thesis) The sages themselves are hypocrites.
Mat 23.3b (General rule) 'But do not do as they do.'
  .3c (Reason justifying the rule) 'For they say and do not.'
  .4 (Illustration of the reason) 'They bind heavy burdens... (on others) but themselves will not move them'...
  .5a (A second reason) 'And all they do, they do to be seen by men.'
  .5b-7 (Illustrations) They make broad their phylacteries, and love the best seats, and love to be called 'Rabbi.'
  .8-11 (Digression) 'But you, be not called "Rabbi,"...nor "Father" '...and let the greatest among you be your servant.
  .13-33 (Additional reasons and illustrations, repeating the pattern made by these first.)

IV. The conclusion of the sermon:
(a) Consequences of the thesis:
Mat 23.34 'Therefore, behold, I send you prophets and sages and scribes; some of them you shall kill' etc.
  .35 In order that you may be punished for all the murders of just men ('that all just blood may come upon you') from...to...
(b) Address to Jerusalem (Consequences of the consequences).
Mat 23.37-9 'Jerusalem, Jerusalem, who killeth the prophets...behold, your house is left...desolate...you shall see me no more, till you say, "Blessed be he that cometh..." '

G. Mat 24.4-25.46   G.

(I. Introduction to the sermon:

Mat 24.3-4a 'And as he was sitting on the Mt. of Olives, his disciples came to him, saying, "Tell us when these things shall be, and what is the sign?"...And Jesus, answering, said to them:')

II. The introduction of the sermon: (Antithesis) What are not the signs.

Mat 24.4b (Warning) 'Beware lest any lead you astray.'

.5-12 (Reason for the warning, the false signs) 'For many shall come in my name...and you shall hear wars, and rumors of wars...but the end is not yet... then...and then'...

[.13 (Digression, or corruption?) 'And he who endures till the end shall be saved.'[35]]

.14 'And...then shall come the end.'

III. The body of the sermon:

(a) (Thesis) The signs of the coming, and the coming.

Mat 24.15-30 (The signs) 'When, therefore, you see the abomination...then...for then...then...and immediately after'...

.30-31 'And then shall be seen the sign of the Son of Man in heaven, and then...and he shall send out his angels...and they shall gather together his elect'...

(b) The time of this coming is near, but unknown.

1. Near: Mat 24.32-3 (Comparison): 'Learn from the fig tree'...

.34-5 'This generation shall not pass till all...be fulfilled.

2. Unknown: Mat 24.36 'But of that day and hour, no one knows'...

.37-9 (Comparison) 'As the day of Noah, so'...

.40-41 (Illustrations) 'Then there shall be two'...

(c) Therefore beware, that you be found in good works.

Mat 24.42 (Rule) 'Beware, then, because you do not know the day'

[.43 f. (Comparison)[36] 'But you know...that if the householder knew when the thief were coming'...]

.45 ff. (Comparison) 'Who, then, is the faithful servant?'

25.1 ff. (Comparison) 'Then the kingdom of Heaven shall be likened to ten virgins'...

.13 (The rule repeated) 'Beware, then, for you know neither the day nor the hour.'
(d) For when he comes, the Messiah will reward men according to their works.
    Mat 25.14 ff. (The parable of the talents)
    .31 ff.(The last judgment compared to the separation of sheep from goats.)

(IV. Conclusion after the sermon:
    Mat 26.1 'And...when Jesus spoke all these words, he said to his disciples'...)

H. <u>Mk 13.5-37</u>   H.

(I. Introduction to the sermon:
    Mk 13.3-5a 'And while he was sitting on the Mt. of Olives... Peter and James and John and Andrew asked him privately, "Tell us when these things will be and what is the sign?"... And Jesus began to say to them'...)

II. The introduction of the sermon: Warning.
    (a) Lest they be led astray:
        Mk 13.5b (General) 'Beware lest any lead you astray'
        .6 (Particular- by false prophets)
        .7-8 (Particular- by false signs)
    (b) Lest they be discouraged by persecution:
        Mk 13.9a (General) 'Beware also for yourselves'
        .9b-11 (Particulars) For they shall hand you over to sanhedrins and you shall be beaten in synagogues etc.
        .13 'But he who endure till the end, he shall be saved.'

III. The body of the sermon: The signs of the coming and the coming.
    (a) The signs: Mk 13.14-25 'And when you see the abomination ...then...for in those days there shall be...And then...But in those days, after'...
    (b) The coming: Mk 13.26-7 'And then they shall see the Son of Man coming...and then he shall send out the angels.'

IV. The conclusion of the sermon: The time is near, therefore beware!
    Mk 13.28 f. (Comparison) 'From the fig-tree learn the parable'
    .30 'For this generation shall not pass away till all these things occur.'
    .32 (Warning) 'Beware, be watchful, for you know not the time'

97

.34 (Comparison) 'As a man, going away,...commanded his porter to watch'

.35 ff. (The warning repeated) 'Watch, therefore'...

I. Lk 21.8-36   I.

(I. Introduction to the sermon:

Lk 21.7-8a 'They asked him, saying, "Teacher, when, therefore, shall these things be, and what is the sign?"...And he said':)

II. The introduction of the sermon: (Antithesis) What are not the signs.

Lk 21.8b (Warning) 'Beware lest ye be led astray.'

.8c-9 (Details, false prophets and false signs)

III. The body of the sermon: (Thesis) The signs of the coming and the coming.

(Lk 21.10a Editorial transition: 'Then he said to them')

(a) The signs: Lk 21.10b-26: Disturbances in the world, persecutions of the disciples, destruction of Jerusalem, signs in the sky.

(b) The coming: Lk 21.27-8 'And then you shall see the Son... coming...When these things begin to happen,...lift up your heads'...

IV. The conclusion of the sermon: The time is near, therefore beware and pray that you may be saved.

(Lk 21.29a Editorial transition: 'And he told them a parable')

Lk 21.29b-31 (Comparison) 'You see the fig tree' etc.

.32 'I tell you truly that this generation shall not pass away until all take place.'

.34 ff. (Warnings) 'Beware...lest the day come upon you suddenly...be always watchful, praying that you may escape all these things which are about to happen, and may stand before the Son of Man.'

When these sermons are compared, the following facts appear:

1. Introductions: A has for its introduction an address to the listeners. In B a part of the same material is changed by the addition of other material to make an introduction of general reference, stating vividly the great principle which underlies the award of pay and punishment: that a man's condition in this world is reversed in the world to come. But the body of B has a small introduction which is also a direct address to the listeners. (Such address is found elsewhere in the bodies and conclusions of these sermons, cf. E ('Woe to you, Chorazin'), and F ('Jerusalem, Jerusalem').) C and D begin without special

introductions, but E has a little introduction stating the general conditions of the ministry - the need for apostles, and their condition in the
world. In G, F and I the introduction is the antithesis of what is to be
said in the body of the sermon, and also in H this is true for the first
part of the introduction, but there the second part intervenes between
it and the thesis stated in the body and thus the antithetical force is
not so clear. There is no doubt that antithesis is one of the basic
elements of the rhetoric of the Gospels, and, in particular, it is found
everywhere throughout the sermons. Thus in the introduction of A
the sentences are mostly antithetical, contrasting the present condition of the disciples with their destined future. In the body of A the
first sentence is antithetical: 'Think not that I came to destroy...I
came not to destroy, but to fulfill.' After this comes the list: 'You
have heard that it was said...but I tell you.' After that, a series of
of descriptions in which the behaviour of the wicked, in almsgiving,
fasting and prayer, is antithetically opposed to that of the good (Mat
6.1-18). And so on throughout the sermon, which concludes with the
parable in which the house built on the sand is presented as antithesis
to that built on the rock. On the same principle the whole of C is divided into two parts: Antithesis - do not seek the goods of this world;
and thesis - seek those of the world to come. But to return to the introductions: In sum there are nine sermons, of these three have antithetical introductions, two are introduced by statements of general
principles, and one by direct address to the listeners, one begins with
a warning as introduction, and two have no introduction whatsoever.

2. Bodies: The structure of C - antithesis and thesis - has already
been noted. Yet simpler is that of E, a mere list of commandments
with a saying which serves for transition to the digression with which
it concludes, and that of B, two lists of commandments connected by
their subject matter. In F also the body of the sermon is merely a
list of proofs for one rule; the consequences of the rule appear only
as a part of the conclusion of the sermon. In G, H, and I, the eschatological sermons, the body of the sermon is always a prophecy, i.e., a
story of the future, and as in every story the subject develops. In H
the development is only in time, first things come first and latter
later; but I shows a transition, in vs. 28, from the mere description
of what is destined to happen, to the hope which will be justified only
by the happening; and in G the body of the sermon is much developed
by the addition of material, suggesting the consequences of the events
prophesied, which in turn introduces a new prophecy, Mat 25.31-46.
In H and I only the first of these consequences appeared, and there
only in the conclusions of the sermons. D and A also show development of the subject-matter in the body of the sermon, but this in different ways. In D the development begins with the arrangement of the
commands given the apostles according to their subjects. As a

consequence of this, the question, What should the apostles do in certain instances? leads to the second question, What will happen to them? and the answer to this second question is developed by related ideas on divine providence, the coming of the Messiah and the connection between suffering and salvation. In A, on the other hand, the development begins in the realm of concepts and only ultimately reaches the details of practical life, the beginning being the general concept of the importance of the law, and the description of the law in terms of practise appearing only as a consequence of its importance.

3. Conclusions: It has already been remarked that in H and I the conclusions are composed of consequences which follow from the stories given in the bodies. More accurately: in both these sermons the beginning of the conclusion consists of the declaration that the events prophesied above will soon take place, and from this declaration arises the true conclusion, Therefore beware! In G all this material is included in the body of the sermon, and were there a formal conclusion - I think there is none - it would consist of the second prophecy. This second prophecy describes the last judgment and, by means of this description, inculcates caution. In F, as in H and I, the conclusion of the sermon is a consequence following from what is stated in the body, but here is added an address to Jerusalem, i.e., to the listeners, for, by Mat, the sermon is laid in Jerusalem. E closes with the general rule that the apostles are to be respected as Jesus, and Jesus as God (according to the well-known principle of Jewish law that a man's agent is legally equivalent to the man himself). In D, to this thought is added the promise of pay. In both, the conclusion of the sermon follows a digression or near-digression, and has no close connection with the ideas expressed in the body. This is also the state of affairs in B, but there the text is probably corrupt, and as in A, so also in B, the essential element of the conclusion is an exhortation to obey the law described in the body of the sermon. C has been reckoned as without conclusion, but there also that side of the subject which is best adapted to exhortation is the side most emphasized at the end. This fact is typical of the sermons in the synoptics. Of nine, seven close with references to the day of judgment, of the two others, D closes with the promise of pay and E with a reference to final punishment which, though not specific, is sufficiently clear ('He who rejects you rejects me, and he who rejects me rejects Him who sent me.') and which immediately follows the prophecy warning the cities of Galilee as to the fate in store for them, should they not repent, at the last judgment. Moreover, not only do these sermons close with reference to the last judgment, but most of them close with what in the outline I have called 'comparisons,' arbitrarily extending the term to include also metaphors. It is interesting to note that D and E, which were the exceptions to the first rule, are also the exceptions to this

second. The metaphor at the end of F does not appear in the outline, it is 'How often have I wished to gather your children together, as a hen gathers her chickens under her wings.' Here, as in G, the comparison at the end of the sermon is neither extended nor important, but it is there.

These being the facts, it can be said in summary that the structure of the sermons in the synoptics is generally simple. Most often (but not always - C, D -) there is a short introduction (extended to two sections only in B and H) which generally contains either the antithesis or the underlying principles of what is to be said in the body. The body itself is generally composed of a list or a story; only in exceptional cases does it contain any important development of the thought, but the completely simple form may be varied in any of several ways - for example, made a double list, of which one part is the antithesis of the other (C), or extended by digression (E) - and may be elaborated, of course, by such customary forms of rhetoric as antithesis, comparison, metaphor, and direct address to the listeners. Of these the most frequent is antithesis, but comparisons and metaphors are also very common, especially towards the conclusions of the sermons. These conclusions sometimes state the consequences of what was said in the body, sometimes are exhortations to the listeners to act according to the rules laid down in the body, but almost always contain warnings, and especially warnings about the punishment in store for the wicked, or promises, of the pay destined for the saints, on the day of judgment.

If, now, forms like these be sought in TL, the criteria set up for them must be slightly changed, for TL does not generally contain such introductions before its elements, and conclusions after them, as are found in the Gospels. Sometimes, it is true, such introductions are found in TL, for example in <u>Yoma</u> 8.9 (the passage has been cited by Zunz[37]), but they generally introduce, as does that in <u>Yoma</u>, summaries so very summary that nothing can be known from them as to the structure of the one-time sermon. Only in three passages does TL introduce as sermons somewhat fuller outlines. These passages are:

<u>Taanit 2.1</u>:

(I. <u>Introduction to the sermon</u>: 'The eldest among them admonishes them to repent:'

II. <u>The body of the sermon</u>: 'Our brethren, it was not said of the men of Nineveh, "And God saw their sackcloth and their fast," but, "And God saw their works, that they turned from their evil way." And in the post-Mosaic books He says, "Rend your heart and not your garments." '

The address, 'Our brethren' is interesting. Little can be decided as to the structure of the sermon, what there is of it looks like the beginning of a list of proof-texts from the Old Testament.

Sotah 8.1:

(I. <u>Introduction to the sermon</u>: (Dt. 20.2 ff.) ' "And when you come
near to the battle the priest shall approach," this is the priest
(specially) anointed (for the) war. "And he shall speak to the people," in Hebrew (<u>lit.</u> in the holy language). "And shall say to
them":'

II. <u>The body of the sermon</u>: ' "Hear, O Israel, you to-day draw near
to battle against your enemies." Against your enemies, and not
against your brethren, not Judah against Simeon and not Simeon
against Benjamin, (your brethren) who, if you fell into their power,
would have mercy on you, as it was said, "And the named men
arose" etc. (the men of Samaria who - according to II Chron. 28.15
- fed, clothed and sent home the prisoners from Judah). You are
going against your enemies who, if you fall into their hands, will
not have mercy on you. "Let not your hearts faint, fear not and do
not tremble" etc. Let not your hearts faint because of the neighing
of horses and the glitter of swords, fear not because of the noise
made by fastening cuirasses and the tramp of the military boots,
tremble not because of the noise of the trumpets and be not terri-
fied because of the noise of the shouts. "For it is the Lord your
God who goes with you." They come (trusting) in the victory of
flesh and blood, and you come (trusting) in the victory of God. The
Philistines came (trusting) in the victory of Goliath. What was his
end? In the end, he fell by the sword and they fell with him. The
children of Ammon came trusting in the victory of Shobak. What
was his end? In the end, he fell by the sword and they fell with
him. And you, you are not like them, for "It is the Lord your God
who goes with you to fight for you." etc. This is the camp of the
Ark.'

Here the matter is complicated, because the essentials of the sermon
are taken from the Old Testament. Therefore in spite of the fact that
the address 'Hear, O Israel' - for example - is here found in TL, it
is not possible to take this occurrence as a certain example of Tannaïtic usage. So also the larger structure, by which the sermon is
divided into three parts (You are going against your enemies....Do not
fear....For the Lord your God goes with you.) is also determined by
the division of the phrases in Deut. 20.3-4. But the exegesis is unquestionably Tannaïtic, and it contains some things found also in the
sermons in the Gospels, for example, the way in which the phrase,
'You are going against your enemies.' is made to recur at the end of
the comment upon it, compare the recurrence of 'Take no thought' in
Mat 6.25, 31, 34, and of 'Watch, therefore' in Mat 24.42; 25.13.
Another similarity is the antithetical structure of the first and last
sections: 'Against your enemies, and not against your brethren';
'They came...but you, you are not like them.'

102

Taanit T. 1.8 (215)[38]

(I. <u>Introduction to the sermon:</u> 'The eldest among them admonishes them to repent:')

II. <u>The introduction of the sermon:</u> 'My sons, let not a man be ashamed of his companion, and let not a man be ashamed of what he has done.'

III. <u>The body of the sermon:</u> '(Yet) it is better that a man should be ashamed of his companion and of what he has done, than that he and his sons should be distressed by famine, as it is said "Why have we fasted and Thou hast not seen?" etc. "Is it a fast of this sort that I shall chose?" etc. But of what sort is the fast which I find acceptable? "To loose the bands of wickedness, to undo the heavy burdens." etc. If a man hold a reptile in his hand, even though he immerse himself in the waters of Siloam (שׁילוֹחַ) and in all the waters of creation he is never clean (so long as he continue to hold the reptile); if he cast away the reptile, immersion in forty seah suffices him. For it is said, "And he who confesses and abandons (his evil ways) will find mercy," and it says, "To lift up our hearts upon our hands." '

Here the most interesting thing in the structure of the sermon is the antithetical introduction, cp. F and also D, G, and I of the synoptic sermons. In this instance antithesis is also found in the body of the sermon ('But of what sort is the fast which I find acceptable?' - inspired, of course, by <u>Isaiah</u> 58.3 ff. - and the - original - structure of the comparison to immersion). Notice also the use of comparison at the end of the sermon, and the address, 'My sons.'

From these three passages of TL, which are marked out as sermons by their introductions, it is clear that the sermons in TL show some of the characteristics of the sermons found in the synoptics. Hereinafter are cited from the midrashim five passages which lack special introductions but which show, more or less, the characteristics of the synoptic sermons.

<u>Mekilta 14.10.</u>

I. <u>The introduction of the sermon: Prayer was the craft of the patriarchs:</u> ' "(And the children of Israel lifted up their eyes and, behold, Egypt came after them), and they feared greatly, and the children of Israel cried unto the Lord." They at once took to the craft of their ancestors, the craft of Abraham, Isaac and Jacob. Of Abraham it says....Of Isaac it says....Of Jacob, what does it say?...

II. <u>The body of the sermon: Prayer is the single and sufficient trust of Israel:</u>
(a) <u>Single:</u> 'And so it says, "Fear not, thou worm Jacob, men of

103

Israel." As the worm smites the cedar only with its mouth, so Israel has nothing else but prayer. And it says, "And I have given you Shechem...which I took...with my sword and with my bow." And did he in fact take it with his sword and with his bow? (No,) but (these words were used) to tell you (that) "my sword," this is prayer, "my bow," this is petition.'

(b) <u>Sufficient:</u> 'And so Jeremiah said, "Blessed is the man who trusteth in the Lord."....And so David said....And so, of Asa, it says, "And Asa called upon the name of the Lord." '

III. <u>The conclusion of the sermon: So it was in the past, so it will be in the future:</u>
'What does it say of Moses, "And Moses sent messengers from Kadesh to the King of Edom"[39]....He said to them, "You are proud because of what your father Isaac left you as inheritance, for it is written....'And you shall live by your sword.' " This (is the meaning of) that which is written, "And Edom said to him, you shall not pass over through my land lest I come out with the sword to meet you.", that they trust only in the sword. And here also you (interpret correctly in) saying...."And the children of Israel cried unto the Lord"....They took to the craft of their ancestors, the craft of Abraham, Isaac and Jacob.' (Note: Where I have written 'took (themselves) to' the Hebrew has 'took to themselves.' Both idioms indicate resort for need.)

Here must be noted (apart from the progress of thought, adapted to the needs of a sermon) the general structure, which is typical of forms like this in TL, viz: a general rule followed by a list of proof passages from the Old Testament. This way of using the Old Testament is not found in the Gospels, but the use of a list as basis of the structure of a sermon is frequent there, see especially B, E and F. The use of recurrent expressions has already been noted. Here the verse with which the sermon began is recalled at the end, a custom dear to preachers down to this day. The appearance of Edom (i.e., Rome) at the end was, in the early centuries, a clear reference to the eschatological future, and the regular appearance of that theme at the end of sermons has already been remarked in the synoptics.

Mekilta 22.20[40]

I. <u>The introduction of the sermon: An exposition of the legal meaning of the commandment, 'And you shall not vex a proselyte.'</u>
(גר in TL regularly means 'proselyte,' not 'stranger.'): ' "And you shall not vex a proselyte and you shall not oppress him, for you were proselytes in the land of Egypt." You shalt not vex him, with words, and you shalt not oppress him, in financial transactions. (This commandment implies) that you shalt not say to him, "Last night you were a servant of Baal Kores Nebo." etc. And

whence (do we learn) that if you vex him he is able to vex you? The text says, "For you were proselytes." On (the basis of) this (text) R. Nathan used to say, "Do not reproach your neighbor with a fault which is also your own." '

II. The body of the sermon: Proselytes are dear to God:
   'Proselytes are dear (to God).'
   (a) 'Because (the text) everywhere comes back (to speak) of them: "And you shall not oppress a proselyte." "And you shall love the proselyte." etc.....R. Eliezer says, "Because the original nature of the proselyte is bad, therefore (the text) always comes back to him"...
   (b) R. Simon ben Yohai says, "Behold, it says, 'And those who love Him (shall shine) as the coming forth of the sun in its strength.' But who is greater, he who loves the king, or he whom the king loves?" ' etc.
   'Proselytes are dear (to God).'
   (c) Because they were called by the names used for Israel.
   (d) 'Abraham called himself a proselyte, for it is said....David called himself a proselyte, for it is said'...
   'Proselytes are dear (to God).'
   (e) 'Because Abraham our father was circumcised only at ninety-nine, for had he been circumcised at twenty or at thirty no one could have become a proselyte unless under thirty, therefore God staved off the day in his case until he reached ninety-nine years, in order not to lock the door in the face of the future proselytes, and to give pay for days and years, and to increase the pay of those who do His will, for it is said'....

III. The conclusion of the sermon: The proselytes shall also be paid:
   'And so you find (proselytes) among the four groups which answer and say before Him-who-spoke-and-the-world-was, "I am the Lord's," for it is said, "This one will say, 'I am the Lord's,' and the next will call on the name of Jacob, and the next will devote his hand to the Lord's (service) and will be called by the name of Israel." "I am the Lord's," and sin shall not be mixed with me. "And the next will call on the name of Jacob," these are the righteous proselytes. "And the next will devote his hand to the Lord," these are the penitent. "And will be called by the name of Israel," these are those who fear Heaven.' (Cp. the terminology in Acts 13.)

Here also the structure contains a list, a key phrase repeated, and a conclusion concerned with the promise of pay (cp. D) - matters already discussed. It is interesting that here the last sentence of the body of the sermon serves as a transition to the content of the section following; similar transitions are found several times in Mat, e.g. A, 5.14, 20; 7.12.

Sifre on Numbers 6.26

I. The introduction of the sermon: (Antithesis) Grace is given only
in the return for works:
' "The Lord lift up his countenance upon thee." One text says,
"The Lord will lift up his countenance upon thee," and another text
says, "Who will not lift up countenance" (i.e., who will not play
favorites - ישא פנים). How (can both) these two texts prove
true? When Israel do the will of God, "the Lord will lift up his
countenance upon you," and when Israel do not do the will of God,
(God becomes one) "who will not lift up countenance." '

II. The body of the sermon: (Thesis) On the contrary, grace is given
those who repent in time, (therefore repent now):
'Another explanation: So long as the decree of judgment has not
been sealed, He will...after the decree of judgment has been sealed,
He will not'...

(a) 'One text says, "Who hearest prayer," and another text says,
"Thou hast covered Thyself with cloud, that prayer should not
pass through." How can both these two texts prove true? So
long as the decree of judgment has not been sealed, He "hears
prayer," after the decree of judgment has been sealed, "Thou
hast covered Thyself with a cloud."

(b) 'One text says, "The Lord is near,"...and one text says, "Why
wilt Thou stand afar off?" How can both these two texts prove
true? So long as the decree of judgment has not been sealed,
"the Lord is near," after the decree of judgment has been
sealed, "Why wilt Thou stand afar off?"

(c) 'One text says, "Evil shall not go forth from before the Highest"...and one text says, "The Lord has watched over the evil
(and brought it upon us)", one text says, "Wash your heart from
evil, O Jerusalem, that thou mayest be saved" and one text
says, "For shouldst thou wash with nitre...thine iniquity is as
a blotch before me"; one text says, "Repent, backsliding children"...and one text says, "He will repent and he will not repent." How can both these two texts prove true? So long as
the decree of judgment has not been sealed, "repent, backsliding children," after the decree of judgment has been sealed, he
"he will repent and he will not repent." '

(d) 'One text says, "Seek the Lord while He may be found" and one
text says, "As I live, I shall not be sought of you" (i.e., I shall
not let you find Me. אם אדרש לכם) How can both these two
texts prove true? So long as the decree of judgment has not
been sealed, "seek ye the Lord while He may be found"; after
the decree of judgment has been sealed, "As I live, I shall not
let you find Me."

III. The conclusion of the sermon: (Warning) There will be no opportunity for repentance in the world to come. (Therefore, repent
now.):
'One text says, "For I shall not desire the death of him who dies."
and one text says, "For the Lord desired to kill them." One text
says, "The Lord will lift up his countenance upon you." and one
text says, "Who will not lift up countenance." How can both these
two texts prove true? "The Lord will lift up his countenance upon
you" in this world, (He becomes one) "who will not lift up countenance" in the world to come." '

Here the striking element is the antithetical introduction similar to
the introductions of F, G, I etc.. The structure of the body (a list of
proof texts following a general rule) has been noticed above. Every
section of the list shows the same form - a phenomenon found already
in A ('You have heard that it was said') and in F ('Woe to you, Scribes
and Pharisees'). The proof text used first returns at the end of the
sermon, and the conclusion is a warning of the danger of the day of
judgment - these points also require no further comment.

Sifre on Deut. 3.23

I. The body of the sermon: Let no man, however righteous, rely on
his righteousness; rather let him beseech mercy:
' "And I (Moses) besought mercy of the Lord at that time, saying."
This illustrates the meaning of the text: "The poor man will utter
entreaties and the rich will reply with hard words." Two excellent
guardians arose for Israel, Moses and David the King of Israel.
Moses said before the Holy One, blessed be He, "Master of the
world, let the transgression which I have committed be written
down (for the time) after me, that men may not be saying, 'Moses
probably counterfeited the Law.' or, 'He said something which was
not commanded.' " A comparison....The Holy One, blessed be He,
said to him, "Behold, I shall write it down, that it was only about
the water." for it is said....(R. Simon said, "A comparison"...[41])
David said before God, "Let not the transgression which I have
committed be written down after me." God said to him, "It is not
worthy of you that men should be saying, 'Because he loved him he
forgave him.' " A comparison....(So) also all the punishments
which came upon David were doubled, for it is said, "And he shall
pay the (value of the) lamb fourfold." '....

II. The conclusion of the sermon: A. Summary of the body. B. Consequences:
A. 'Two excellent guardians arose for Israel, Moses and David the
King of Israel and they could have suspended the world by their
good works (i.e., their good works outweighed - lifted up - cancelled, or could have cancelled - all the transgressions of the

world? Very dubious.), and (yet) they did not beseech God that
He should give them (aught), save gratuitously.'

B. '(Hence) is there not an argument a fortiori? If these, who were
able to suspend the world by their good works, did not beseech
God that He should give them aught, save gratuitously, (then as
for) one who is only one of a thousand thousands of thousands
and myriads of myriads of the disciples of their disciples, a
fortiori he should not beseech the Holy One, blessed be He, to
give him aught, save gratuitously.'[42]

The structure of the body of the sermon (a rule, two examples, one
comparison to each example) is much like the structure of the conclusion of the sermon on the mount (A 7.21 ff.). The habit of repeating
at the end of a sermon the words used at its beginning, has been noted
above.[43] The use of consequences, derived from the body, for the
conclusion of a sermon is found in H and I.

Sifre on Deut. 11.13

I. The introduction of the sermon: The study of the Law is required
at times when practise is not required:
' "And if ye surely hearken to my commandments." Why was this
said? Inasmuch as it was said, "And you shall learn them and you
shall take care to do them," I should infer ((Antithesis)) that they
were not obligated to study until they were obligated to practise.
The text says ((Thesis)), "And if you shall surely hearken"...it declares that they were obligated to study immediately....And (from
this) I cannot (conclude about any) commandments but those (which
were capable of practice) while Israel had not yet entered the
(promised) land, such as....Whence (can I conclude about) commandments (which were capable of practice only) after they entered...such as...? The text says, "And if you shall surely hearken
to my commandments." (mentioning commandments unnecessarily)
in order to indicate the inclusion of the rest of the commandments
(in the obligation of study). (And from this) I cannot (conclude
about any commandments) but (those which admitted of practise)
while Israel had not yet subdued and settled (the land); whence (can
I conclude about those which admitted of practise only) after they
had subdued and settled, such as....The text says, "And if" etc., to
add to those (already mentioned) yet other commandments.

II. The body of the sermon: Practise depends on study and study does
not depend on practise:
' "And you shall learn them and you shall take care to do them,"
(this) teaches that practise depends on study and study does not depend on practise.'
(Proof a) 'And in accordance with this we have found that He punished for the (neglect of) study more than for the (neglect of)

practise, for it is said, "Hear the word of the Lord, O house of Israel, for the Lord has a quarrel with the inhabitants of the land, for there is no truth and there is no mercy and there is no knowledge of God in the land." "There is no truth," (i.e.) the words of truth are not spoken, for it is said'....('Mercy' and 'knowledge of God' are similarly explained as referring to the study of the Law.) 'And it says, "Therefore as eating straw a tongue of fire" etc. (so shall Israel be consumed, "because they have despised the Law of the Lord of Hosts.") And can you find straw which consumes fire?[44] But this 'straw' is evil-doing which rules over Israel whenever they neglect the study of the commandments (lit. 'slacken their hands from the commandments,' but this regularly refers to the neglect of study). And it says....And it says....[45] And once R. Tarpon and R. Akiba and R. Jose the Galilean were reclining in a summer-house made of a grape-arbour in Lydda. This question was asked before them, 'Which is greater, study or practise?'....They all answered and said, 'Study is greater.' (Their reasons follow.) (Proof b) 'And just as He punished for the neglect of study more than for the neglect of practise, so He gave more pay for study than for practise, for it is said, "And you shall teach them to your sons that they may talk of them." And what does it say? (i.e., How does the text continue?) "In order that your days and the days of your sons may be multiplied." And it says, "And he will give them the lands of gentiles, and they shall inherit the toil of nations." etc.'

The antithetical structure of the introduction recalls the introduction of B. The interesting relation of the introduction to the body (such that the introduction constitutes one detail of the consequences of the rule stated in the body) is not found in the synoptic sermons. The structure of the body (rule and proofs) is also found in F. The last section of the body serves as a conclusion for the whole sermon, as in C and G; its content is the award of pay, with special reference to eschatology, as in D and in G. Note that the tenses of the verbs 'He punished,' 'He gave more pay,' refer to the time at which the punishment and the pay were promised, at the giving of the Law or the utterance of the prophecy, not to the time at which they will be effected. This sort of reference to the Old Testament (or its Author) as having already done what it (or He) threatens or promises, is frequent in TL.

I think it clear from the above passages that TL contains forms parallel to the forms introduced in the synoptics as sermons. It is therefore plausible to suppose that such forms of TL were also derived from the sermons customary in those days. But it cannot be concluded that any one of these 'sermons' is in fact an outline of something once actually preached, for an editor might easily compose a sermon (most probably, according to the rules of sermon composition known to him, but perhaps otherwise) merely for the benefit of his book. Therefore it is impossible to conclude that the sources of the Gospels or of TL contained such forms as are now found in the edited works. This is especially true as regards the synoptic sermons, which are among the forms of the Gospels most suspect of ad hoc composition by the editors, and which may show either the rules for the composition of a single form, or the rules which governed generally the grouping of all synoptic material. In the latter case, their similarity to the forms found in TL would have to be explained by the fact that the general rules of association, by which both literatures were built up, were similar. Again we come back to the question of cause, the historical question which admits of no certain answer.

NOTES

1. The Gospel before the Gospels, New York, 1928, p. 74.

2. The Formation of the Gospel Tradition, London, 1933, p. 31.

3. Mk 1.2, Yoma 6.2, cited in Strack-Billerbeck.

4. Jn 8.17, Mekilta 20.5, cited in Fiebig, Altjüdische Gleichnisse, Tübingen, 1904, p. 15, n. 4.

5. The older books are listed by L. Newman, Parallelism in Amos, (Part I of Studies in Biblical Parallelism, Univ. of Cal. Pubs. in Sem. Philol., vol. I, nos. 2-3) pp. 121-2. The most important of them are Jebb, Sacred Literature and Forbes, Symmetrical Structure of Scripture. Of more recent books the most important are C. Burney, The Poetry of Our Lord, (Oxford, 1925) and P. Fiebig, Der Erzahlungs-stil der Evangelien, (Leipzig, 1925).

6. The names of the groups here are taken from a list of 'figures' in H. Smythe's Greek Grammar for Colleges (N. Y., n. d.) pp. 671-83, and the examples here given for each group correspond to the examples given by Smythe for the same group. The first and fourth examples are noted by Strack-Billerbeck on the verses cited.

7. The passage in Mat is referred to by Fiebig (A. G. p. 17, n. 4) as a parallel to Mekilta 20.5, but there 'flesh and blood' is used adjectivally. Schlatter, S. u. H., pp. 21-22, cites the passage I have cited from Mekilta, together with a passage from Sifre on Deut. (19.17) as parallels to Jn 1.13, where only σάρξ is found. The "Jewish" phrase is also cited as a parallel to the usage of the Gospels by W. C. Allen in his article, The Book of Sayings, which was printed in Studies in the Synoptic Problem, ed. W. Sanday, Oxford, 1911, pp. 234 ff., cit. on p. 286. Allen gives no particular examples.

8. P. Levertoff, Midrash Sifre on Numbers, London, N.D. (1926), p. 45, n. 2. Another example, p. 69, n. 1.

9. Schlatter, Sprache u. Heimat, p. 59; other examples p. 33, but not such good ones. The same expression, with yet other examples,

is noted by P. Fiebig in Altjüdische Gleichnisse, p. 31, n. 8, and in Pirque 'aboth, p. 6, n. 8, to Abot 2.3.

10. Tübingen, 1906.

11. Berlin, 1919.

12. Tübingen, 1911.

13. The same story is found again in Sanhedrin T 8.3 (427), though Fiebig does not cite the passage in his list of parallels.

14. Or a man who, without being of his disciples, yet used his name for healing. See Mk 9.38: 'John said to him, "Teacher, we saw someone, who does not go about with us (or: who does not follow our practices) casting out demons in your name, and we forbade him"....Jesus said, "Do not forbid him."' See also Acts 19.13.

15. M. Dibelius, in his book From Tradition to Gospel (tr. B. Woolf, London, 1934) followed Fiebig in this error and devoted almost half of his section on rabbinic analogies (pp. 133-151) to parallels of miracle-stories. In eight pages he cites one example from TL: Taanit 3.8.

16. It must always be remembered that TL is ten or twenty times larger than the Gospels (about 300 pages of Greek as against about 3000 of Hebrew, but one page of Hebrew - especially Tannaïtic Hebrew - contains about twice as much material as one page of Greek).

17. The works of the more important exegetes who have done so have been cited above.

18. So, for example, V. Taylor, The Formation of the Gospel Tradition, London, 1933, pp. 22-37: 'The first task of form criticism is to classify the Synoptic material according to its form....The next step is to try to recover the original form....The third task...is to seek for the Sitz im Leben...out of which the material springs.' i.e., two parts of history to one part of fact.

19. M. Dibelius, op. cit., p. 14.

20. Berlin, 1913.

21. idem. p. 6.

22. ib.

23. In Acts see also 2.40; 3.20; 10.42

24. Die Geschichte der synoptischen Tradition, Göttingen, 1921, pp. 194-5.

25. Geschichte der Leben-Jesu-Forschung, 4 ed. Tübingen, 1926, pp. 408-410.

26. idem. p. 410.

27. T. Soiron, Die Logia Jesu, Münster i.W. 1916 Neutestamentliche Abhandlungen, VI, 4 Heft.), p. 60. Father Benoit brought this book to my attention.

28. From Tradition to Gospel, London, 1934, p. 25.

29. Generally, but not always, these rules are commandments.

30. I fail to see the place of these verses in the sequence of the thought, and think likely that they were added after the 'sermon,' as such, was complete.

31. The parallel in Lk 11.9-13 closes thus (vs. 13): 'How much more will the Father from heaven give the Holy Spirit to those who ask Him.'; and I think that the 'good things' of Mat had some hidden significance, as understatement, corresponding to the apparent meaning of Lk. Specifically, I think that Mat wished, not the gift of the Holy Spirit, but the second coming of the Messiah, and that for this reason he placed the commandment, to pray for good things, at the end of his outline of the Law. But in the present state of the text the truth or falsity of this theory is not demonstrable.

32. Of this verse also I do not see the place in the sequence of thought and must again suppose it a later addition. It is clear that αὐτῶν of vs. 16 could refer, if vs. 15 were deleted, to the 'many' and the 'few' of vss. 13-14.

33. A similar use of introductions in the middle of a speech dealing with a single subject is found twice in the sermon in Lk 12 (16 and 22), but there also it is possible to question whether or not the passage should be taken as a single speech. Therefore I have cited the passage in 18, as clearer. In Lk 21, vss. 10 and 29 introductions certainly do come in the midst of speeches, but as introductions to the body and the conclusion. Here also, therefore, I take, 'And he told them a parable' as constituting an introduction to the conclusion of the sermon.

34. I do not see the relation of this verse to the vss. before and after it, and therefore, and also because of the break between vss. 38 and 39 it seems to me likely that there was some corruption in the text used by the editor of Lk.

35. I think these words were inserted here from the parallel in Mk 13.13, after the sermon was complete, for they interrupt a list of signs and cannot be understood save as a digression, and as a digression they spoil the climactic effect of the list.

36. This parable interrupts between 42 and 45, the lord and the servant.

37. Die gottesdienstlichen Vorträge der Juden, 2 ed., ed. N. Brüll, Frankfurt a.M., 1892, p. 354, note. The whole of Zunz' chapter on the 'Vortragswesen des Altertums' (ch. 20, pp. 342 ff.) is the locus classicus on the sermon as the background of the haggadah, and I need not review here the proofs given there of the widespread use of the sermon in the society reflected in TL. Here I wish only to add something to Zunz' discussion by investigating the forms of the largest of those sections which are presented as sermons in TL and to discover, among the passages not so presented, some which have forms similar to those of the sermons in the synoptics.

38. A most interesting problem is posed by the relation of this passage to that from Taanit cited above, for the passages are parallel, the introductions are identical, but the sermons are completely different. How can it be explained that the editors of the later document took over the introduction, but changed the sermon introduced? I think,

by the fact that here the introduction is the essential, and the sermon incidental. Cp. - for similar change of content following parallel introductions - Mat 26.13 // Mk 14.3-7 // Lk 7.36-38 // Jn 12.1-8.

39. Edom, of course, is Rome.

40. This passage is mentioned by I. Lévi in the second part of his article, Le prosélytisme juif, REJ, 51.1 ff. On p. 21 he says, 'Nous (le) tenons pour un fragment de discours des missionnaires juifs.' and bases his judgment on a consideration of the content, not on the form of the passage. As a gentile, I doubt that the introduction of the sermon is well calculated to convert the hearers. Therefore I think more probable that it was intended for a Jewish audience. And if one can trust to the indications of the form, it is not a fragment of a sermon, but the summary of a complete sermon.

Apart from this article by Lévi, and Zunz' chapter mentioned above, I know of no work which attempts to pick out as sermons or parts of sermons particular passages of TL, let alone of any in which such an attempt is based on a consideration of the form of the passages. The general notion, that the 'Sitz im Leben' of the haggadah was the sermon, has been widespread since the time of Zunz, but it does not justify the conclusion that all haggadic passages are outlines of sermons, for in spite of the fact that the material which they contain is (or may be) suitable for homiletic use, the present form in which it is found is not at all that of a sermon, see for example the chapter on peace (Sifre on Numbers 6.26 end) or that on punishment (Sifre on Deut. 6.5). And it is just this fact which makes the passages I have picked out most interesting. For when other passages, of which the content is strikingly homiletic, fail to show the form which these show, the question arises why these particular passages, of which the content happens to be suitable for preaching, happen to show this form, which happens to be just the form of the passages represented as sermons by the synoptics.

41. I follow the opinion of Finklestein that the structure of the passage is clear and shows that the words of R. Simon are a later addition, therefore I have added the parentheses.

42. By the way, I think it very likely that the beginning of this sermon - the Lord published the sin of Moses in order that men might not say he had falsified the Law - is directed against some opponents of the Law who said just that, and who may well have been Christians. From this it might be argued that the conclusion of the sermon is also directed against Christians, particularly against Paulinism.

43. I think this fact a sufficient refutation of the theory of Finklestein (that the introduction and body of this sermon are later additions to the text of Sifre on Deut.), especially since the theory is founded only on the fact that in four MSS the words 'and they could have suspended the world by their good deeds' appear also at the beginning of the sermon, after the words 'Moses and David the King of Israel.'

Finklestein also thinks that there is no relation between the parts which I have called the introduction and the body of the sermon, on the one hand, and that, on the other, which I have called the conclusion. The relation seems to me obvious.

44. Of course the meaning of the text in Isaiah 5.24 is that the fire eats the straw, but the order of words there is inverted - as in the translation just given - and the commentary takes advantage of this inversion to suggest that Israel should normally overcome sin.

45. I think that proof b originally followed closer on proof a, and that the words from here to proof b are a later interpolation.

Chapter 5

PARALLELS IN TYPES OF ASSOCIATION

It must be admitted, to begin with, that the question, How is the material in a given book (or part of a book) associated; what principle of association can be seen in its selection and arrangement? is a question which can be given several different answers according to the several opinions of different scholars. It would take a small book even to list the various theories hitherto propounded as to the composition of the Gospels, and Schweitzer, in his large book,[1] was able to describe only briefly the greater number of the more recent examples. Similarly, on the structure of the Mishnah, there is a literature rich not only in content but also in conflicts of opinion.[2] But it happens that little hitherto has been written about the parallels to be found in these matters between the Gospels and TL. Of the books which do discuss them the most important known to me is that of T. Soiron, Die Logia Jesu.[3] Soiron finds the essentials of the types of association apparent in the synoptics to be 'systematische Gesichtspunkte' and 'Stichwortdisposition'; and in the second part of his book[4] he attempts to demonstrate that these are also the principles underlying the composition of the Mishnah.[5] The demonstration depends on an analysis of Yoma and this analysis suffices at least to show that it is possible to understand many of the connections in this tractate as consequences of these two types of association. I therefore take Soiron's work as the basis of what is to be said in this chapter.

As against Soiron's theory, which is on the whole correct, must be mentioned that of G. Klein in his article, Zur Erläuterung der Evangelien aus Talmud u. Midrasch,[6] of which the essential is the statement, 'Sicher (!) hat Jesus seine Lehren, den jüdischen Schriftgelehrten gleich, an Schriftworte angelehnt. Leider sind uns diese "Deraschot" weder in seiner Muttersprache, noch in einer Übersetzung so überliefert, wie Jesus sie in Wirklichkeit gesprochen hat....Die Evangelien, die wir besitzen, sind in griechischer Sprache bearbeitete Midraschim.'[7] This hardly requires refutation. In the previous chapter were discussed the sermons now actually found in the synoptics, and their parallels in TL. The most important and striking difference between these two groups of sermons was precisely the difference of the ways in which they used the Old Testament.

Apart from this theory about the midrashic source of the Gospels, Klein remarks in the beginning of his article two particular parallels from TL to types of association found in the Gospels:[8] 'Man hat weiter eine Sammlung der Meschalim, der Gleichnisse und Parabeln, die

Jesus...gesprochen, angelegt. Ein Analogon dafür besitzen wir (sic) in der Meschalimsammlung des R. Meir aus der hadrianischen Zeit.' (This collection is unknown to me.) 'Nach Papias hat man zuerst "Worte Jesu" gesammelt. Was darunter zu verstehen ist, könnte man ...aus Pirke Aboth schliessen.' This is, in fact, possible, but caution is necessary, for we cannot be sure that the term used by Papias described accurately all the material which, according to Eusebius, he said that Matthew συνετάξατο.[9] The term 'sayings' may have been correct only as a description a potiori, and it is known that Papias was given to using words in this way, for (still according to Eusebius) he spoke of the material which he himself had collected as 'commandments' (ἐντολαί),[10] but Eusebius cites from it[11] a story of a fine miracle done by Justus bar Sabba, and says,[12] 'And the same (author) (i.e., Papias) has put down besides, as (derived) from unwritten tradition which reached him, other things: some outlandish parables of the Saviour, and teachings of His, and some other rather legendary things.' Therefore it cannot certainly be concluded from the words of Papias that Matthew's collection contained only 'sayings' (λόγια), just as it cannot certainly be concluded from his words that his own collection contained only 'commandments.' Many scholars have been accustomed to call the material lacking in Mk but found in Mat and Lk by the name 'Q' and to suppose it related to the Matthaean collection of sayings mentioned by Papias. The greater part of this material is, in fact, sayings, but it also contains some stories of miracles, and therefore other scholars have denied that all of it could have been derived from a single source, and have wished to divide it so as to get one source, all sayings, and another source, or several other sources, all stories.[13] Clearly, these are historical theories; I shall therefore not discuss them further.

In spite of these efforts to find parallels between the types of association found in the Gospels and those found in TL, the most striking fact remains not the parallelism of the two literatures in this respect, but their difference. This difference was well remarked by Marmorstein in his article Les Rabbins et les Évangiles:[14] 'Tandis que dans les Évangiles ne figure qu' une personne...les textes parallèles du Talmud et du Midrasch sont attribués à divers auteurs et maîtres.' In other words, the material in the Gospels is connected by reason of its association with a single man, whereas the material in TL is connected generally by associations of form or associations of content, and only very rarely, among these associations of content, are found a few in which the common element of content happens to be relation to a single man. However, even in TL a few such passages are to be found, and both Marmorstein[15] and Dibelius[16] thought of the possibility that at one time there were collections of stories or sayings which were connected by reason of the association with a single rabbi of all the material they contained. But neither of these scholars supported

his supposition by means of proofs from TL. Therefore I think it
worth while to cite here what have seemed to me the most important
passages of TL in which this type of association appears. It should
go without saying that I am not concerned with the question, Were
there, at one time, complete books of which the material was thus associated? That is a historical question dependent for its answer not
only on facts, but on theories more or less imaginative. I wish only
to list and to describe certain passages from TL which show a type of
association parallel to that most common in the Gospels. Therefore I
shall not attempt to list all the facts which could be used in the support of the theories, for - e.g. - the expressions 'the house of Shammai' and 'the house of Hillel' give occasion to think that at one time
the Law was divided into two Laws and that in each the material was
associated primarily by the fact that so it had been taught in the
school of the great master, i.e., by its relation to a certain man (either
directly or through his pupils). And the traditions preserved in the
Talmuds provide yet other bases for such theories: such statements
as, 'Sifra, when it does not specify the speaker, reports the opinions
of R. Judah (ben Ilai).'[17] - statements which are quite specific about
the unknown.[18] Moreover, both specific statements[19] and the tradition
which has recorded the names of the Tanna'im along with their sayings,
make it possible to associate certain sayings and certain ways of exposition with the schools of R. Akiba and of R. Ishmael, to divide the
midrashim according to these criteria, and to discover that entire
sections or books originated in one or the other school, i.e., that their
content is associated as the teaching of one man and of his pupils.[20]

Even from this summary it is clear that the historical question:
How far did the relation to particular teachers influence the connection of material in TL? is very different from the philological question: What passages now found in TL show clearly the connection of
the material by virtue of its relation to a single man? It is this second question which must now be answered.

These passages are of two sorts: On the one hand there are complete sections of books in which references of the material to the
same man (or the same men) appear so often that it seems almost
certain that one of the sources of the book was a collection of that
man's (or those men's) sayings. The best known example of this sort
is the use of sayings by R. Elazar of Modiim and R. Joshua (ben
Hananiah) in Mekilta and especially in Mekilta of R. Simon, in the section common to it and to Mekilta. There the frequency of recurrence
of these two names, which are hardly found at all in other parts of the
book, is most striking. This can be seen from the index of names in
Hoffmann's edition of Mekilta of R. Simon,[21] in which the numbers of
pages containing the names twice or more times are starred. The
lists for the two names are as follows:[22]

R. Joshua: 1*, 4, 28, 38, 40, 47, 71, 72*, 73*, 74*, 75*, 76*, 77*, 78*,
R. Elazar: .... 48, ... 72*, 73*, 74*, 75*, 76*, 77*, 78*

R. J.:   79*, 80*, 81*, 82*, 83*, 84*, 85*, 86*, 87*, 88, 89*, 90*, 91*..
R. E.:   79*, 80*, 81*, 82*, 83*, 84*, 85*, 86*, 87*, ... 89*, 90*, 91*..

R. J.: ....
R. E.: ... 170.

Mekilta of R. Simon contains (with the appendix) 173 pages of text.

But, even in examples striking as these, the connection of the material is not primarily dependent on the association with the men. For even should we suppose (as Hoffmann supposed[23]) that in this section the editor of Mekilta of R. Simon used a written source(s), and should we also suppose (as Hoffmann did not suppose) that this (these) source(s) contained a (several) midrash(im) from these rabbis on the chapters in question - yet it would have to be admitted that in this (these) source(s) the essential connection of the material was effected, not by its relation to the man expounding, but by its relation to the text expounded. The comments of R. Elazar of Modiim on Exodus, if they ever constituted, by themselves, a separate book, were connected primarily by reason of their relationship to Exodus, and the fact that they were all written by one man had no influence whatsoever on their arrangement. And such, certainly, is the state of affairs in Mekilta of R. Simon as we have it now. For in spite of the fact that these two names there appear almost exclusively in one section, yet the comments in this section are arranged altogether according to the text of the Old Testament, and had the names been lost and the tradition relating the comments to these particular Tannaïm disappeared, the order of the comments would have been no less and no more understandable than it is now; whereas on the contrary, had the names been lost from the material in several chapters of the Gospels, there would have been no apparent relationship between the various sections they contain. Consequently, in passages like these in Mekilta of R. Simon the relation to the man is not the essential of the connection of the material, but is merely an accident of that connection, and in order to find true parallels to the type of association found generally in the Gospels we must pass on to the second group of passages from TL, which show a different sort of 'association by man.'

The smallest passages of this second group are those in which several sayings (or explanations or parables or the like) attributed to one man appear in sequence, with little or no interruption by any material attributed to another man. But in selecting passages like these it is necessary to beware of textual corruptions. For example, in Sifre on Deut. 11.22 the text of Friedmann reads: 'R. Simon (ben Yohai) used to say....R. Simon ben Yohai says...R. Simon ben Yohai says....Another explanation....R. Judah says....R. Simon ben Yohai says'... This looks, at first blush, like a section of the traditional teaching of R. Simon, of which the various elements would be connected by the fact that he taught them. But Friedmann himself remarks in the notes that in the Yalkut the third of these elements is cited as from R. Simon ben Menasya, and Hoffmann cites it so in Midrash Tannaïm, and in Midrash Tannaïm on the same passage the first section appears as a saying of R. Ishmael's, and so in Sifre on Deut. in Finklestein's edition. Friedmann's text of Sifre on Deut. is therefore not, in this instance, reliable, and what appeared at first to be a collection of material from the tradition of R. Simon is now seen to be a piece of evidence for the fact that these elements were at first related by their content (they all deal with the study of the Law), were drawn by virtue of this relationship from the traditions of several Tannaïm, and were afterwards related by textual corruption to R. Simon, whose name replaced in one instance that of R. Ishmael, in another that of R. Simon ben Menasya.

But even after the elimination of passages suspect by reason of textual variations, there remain very many passages of this class, though they constitute only a small part of TL. They can be divided into several types. Of these types the commonest is that in which are found several sayings (or the like) from the same man on the same subject. Understandably, this is also the type least helpful for the purpose of the present investigation, for there is no telling whether the similarity of the content or the common relation to the teacher determined the association in the text. An example more interesting than usual is afforded by the passage in Erubin 2.6: 'R. Ilai said, "I heard from R. Eliezer....And I also heard from him....And I also heard from him....And I went around to all his pupils and sought a companion for myself (i.e., one who had heard the same) and found none." ' (What he heard was two laws concerning erubin and one concerning the bitter herbs of Passover.) I think this passage more interesting than most because it shows that R. Ilai kept together in his memory these three laws as a part of the teaching of R. Eliezer, and not simply as Law. For completely simple examples see the 16 passages in which the expression אמר ועוד ('And he also said') is found in the Mishnah.[24]

A slight variant from this type is found in those passages composed of several elements having a common subject and cited, not as the teachings of one man, but as the teachings of two or more men personally related, e.g., Sifra 7.33: 'And R. Simon said....R. Simon said....and so R. Simon used to say....R. Elazar the son of R. Simon says'....(All the elements are concerned with the Levitical privileges and can be understood as examples of polemic against the priests.) Another example from Moed Katan T 2.15 ff. (231): 'A story about Rabban Gamliel.....A story about Judah and Hillel the sons of Rabban Gamliel.....Another story about Judah and Hillel the sons of Rabban Gamliel'....(All these stories show that Rabban Gamliel and his sons followed the customs of

the cities in which they found themselves, even when these customs denied them privileges which the Law, as they interpreted it, permitted.)
Hitherto I have spoken of the tradition of a given man - the material
which he handed down or introduced in his own teaching. Clearly, this
can be distinguished from the tradition about a man - the stories in which
he figures as a character. Clearly, too, this distinction is only superficial, for many stories, especially in the midrashim and in the Gospels, serve merely as introductions to sayings, and even in the cases
of stories which do not introduce sayings, and of sayings preserved
without any reference to place or occasion, it is impossible to draw a
fundamental distinction between teaching effected by words and teaching effected by actions. Moreover, as far as the subject of this chapter is concerned, the presence of either sort of tradition may be sufficient to show that the sections of text in which it occurs may have been
connected by virtue of their relation to the man it concerns, therefore
I shall pay no more attention to this difference between the sorts of
tradition and shall return to the subject of the chapter.

The examples cited above show that stories about several different
men may be connected by virtue of their relation to a single man.
However, in all the examples cited above, all the stories (or sayings
or whatever) had also a common subject. But both in the Gospels and
in TL are found passages in which, although the basis of the connection is the relationship to a single man, the stories not only concern
several different men, but also have several different subjects. The
examples best known in the Gospels are the stories about John the
Baptist, which appear only by reason of his historical connection with
Jesus. In TL there are a considerable number of small passages, of
which one example will suffice: Mekilta of R. Simon 20.8: 'Shammai
the Elder said....And they said about him (about Shammai the Elder)....
And they said about Shammai the Elder....But (as for) Hillel the Elder,
he had a different characteristic, for all his deeds were done for the
service of God.' All three of the stories about Shammai are concerned
with reverence for the Sabbath, and it is clear that Hillel is mentioned
here only because his name is generally associated with that of Shammai.

The passage just cited will serve as a transition to another class
of passages more important for the subject of this chapter: Those
containing elements which differ in content, but which are connected
in the text by reason of their direct relation to a single man. Sometimes these passages are very simple, like the stories about Rabban
Gamliel in Berakot 2.5-7 ('He read the Shema on the first night of his
marriage....He washed the first night after his wife's death....And
when Tabi his servant died, he received formal visits of consolation')
or the charming stories about R. Ishmael in Nedarim 9.10, end, ('And
there is a story about a man who swore that he would not receive
benefit from the daughter of his sister. So they took her into the house

of R. Ishmael and made her beautiful. R. Ishmael said to him, "My son, was it from <u>this</u> that you swore to receive no benefit?" He said to him, "No." And R. Ishmael declared him free (to marry her). At that time R. Ishmael wept and said, "The daughters of Israel are lovely, but poverty disfigures them." And when R. Ishmael died the daughters of Israel sang songs of mourning and said, "Daughters of Israel weep for (reading עַל for אֶל) R. Ishmael." And so the Scripture says of Saul"...). It is clear that passages like this give no occasion to think that there may have existed a collection of stories about the same man. The first story here got into the text because of its relation to the subject, the others were added to it as showing the same side of the same man's personality. At the very most, such passages as these can show that the personalities of the Tannaïm were distinguished and that some stories were remembered not only as legal precedents but also as typical of the teacher who figured in them. This can also be learned from the material connected by reason of its association with other men. For example, the sayings added to the words of Hillel in <u>Abot</u> 1.13-14 ('He used to say....He used to say'....) and in 2.5-7 ('He used to say....He also saw....He said....He used to say'...). Here there is no need to suppose a prior collection of the sayings of Hillel. It is sufficient, to explain the passage, that the sayings cited were known as his and were thought so typical of his teaching that, when a summary representation of his teaching was desired, they were added to the first saying.

But there are passages in which this is not so, passages in which the material is connected by reason of its relation to a man, in spite of the fact that the context gave no sufficient reason to describe this man's teaching or personality. An example is Sifre on Deut. 32.2 (end): 'R. Simai used to say, "Whence (do we know) that as Moses called heaven and earth to witness against Israel, so he called the four winds to witness against them?....For it is said, 'My doctrine will drop as the rain, (my speech will distil as the dew, as the small rain upon the tender herb, and as the showers upon the grass.' " ' Evidently R. Simai supposed a different wind for each different kind of rain?) 'Another explanation, "My doctrine will drop as the rain": And R. Simai used to say thus, "These four winds were mentioned only as against the four winds of heaven."....And R. Simai used to say thus, "The souls and bodies of all creatures created from the heavens are from the heavens, and the souls and bodies of all creatures created from the earth are from the earth, except for this (creature) man, whose soul is from the heavens and his body from the earth. Accordingly if a man performs the Law and does the will of his Father who is in the heavens, behold, he is like the creatures of the upper regions, for it is said, 'I have said, "You are gods." ';...if he does not perform the Law and does not do the will of his Father who is in the heavens, behold, he is like the creatures of the lower regions, for it is said,

121

'None the less you shall die like men.'" And R. Simai used to say
thus, "You cannot find any section (of the Old Testament) which does
not imply the resurrection of the dead...for it is said...'Come, wind,
from the four winds.'"' Here the latter sayings appear only because
of their relation to R. Simai who was the source of the former ones.
But the passage gave no occasion for a further description of R. Simai
or of his teaching. Why, then, were the latter sayings inserted? One
possible answer is, because R. Simai's teachings were known in a giv-
en sequence - even if not in a given text - and when the editor of Sifre
on Deut. took the first sections he took along with them the two sections following, connected with them not only by subject but also by
reason of their place in the order of the teaching. Of course, such a
hypothesis as this about the reasons for the connections already
verges on the history of the material. Within the limitations of the
subject of this thesis, it can only be said that in Sifre on Deut. 32.2
the material is connected by its relation to a single man, and this in a
fashion quite singular in that text, and one which adds little to our
knowledge of the man.

Other passages like this are found both in Eduyot and in Eduyot T.
The key to the type of association found in these two tractates is given
by the words in the Mishnah: 'Why do they record the words of a single man who differs from the majority?'[25] The answers given there
and in the parallel passage in Eduyot T[26] are in brief: (A) To dis-
credit them, (B) To enable some future court to cite them as prece-
dent. Thus the whole tractate is essentially a collection of opinions
held by isolated men as against the opinions of the majority. Thus
also it is understandably divided into two large sections: (A) Individual or minority opinions overruled by the decisions of the majority
(and the opinions of the school of Shammai contradicted by those of the
school of Hillel form a special subject within this section); (B)[27] 'Testimonies' a class of individual opinions possessed of a special authority, such that occasionally[28] they overrule the opinions of the majority.
This is the underlying structure of the tractate, both in the Mishnah
and in Tosefta, but both in the Mishnah and in Tosefta there are in the
middle[29] of the first section a number of details concerning the sayings of R. Ishmael and of R. Akiba, which are not introduced as individual opinions overruled by those of the majority, and in connection
with which the opinion of the majority either is not cited at all, or at
least is no essential element of the tradition.[30] Concerning some it
is even reported that the Sages admitted them to be true.[31] At all
events, it is clear that it was not their legal nature which led to
their connection as a group. From the text of the Mishnah it appears that the essential connection between them was that of relationship to particular men: As a transition from the opinions of R.
Ishmael to those of R. Akiba appear three 'things which R. Ishmael
said and R. Akiba did not admit their truth.' (Incidentally, the Law in

these three matters is 'according to R. Ishmael'). Along with the relationship to particular individuals, the number 3 appears as an important connective element. The introductions are as follows: 'R.
Ishmael said three things before the Sages in the vineyard in Jabneh....
Three things were said before R. Ishmael and he neither permitted
nor forbade them....R. Ishmael said three things and R. Akiba did not
admit their truth....Three things were said before R. Akiba....R.
Akiba said three things....He used to say....He also used to say five
things'... In Eduyot T the connection is based only on the relations to
R. Ishmael and R. Akiba, the use of the number is not perceptibly important. The introductions are as follows: 'Three things were said
before R. Ishmael....R. Ishmael says....And R. Akiba says (the contrary)....Three things were said before R. Akiba....(An opinion known
from the Mishnah to be R. Akiba's but here cited without his name)....
R. Akiba used to give a haggadic exposition of five things'....However,
it seems to me that the relation of this digression to the tractate in
which it is found can be explained only from the text of Tosefta, where,
immediately before it, is written:[32] 'There are six things which R.
Akiba declares unclean and which the Sages declare clean....There are
six cases of doubt in which R. Akiba declares that the object is to be
considered unclean and the Sages, clean'....Here the opinions of R.
Akiba appear - in groups of fixed number - as individual opinions
overruled by those of the majority - and it has already been remarked
that such opinions are the subject of this first section of the tractate.
Thus it is possible to understand that, if there were once a collection
of the sayings of R. Ishmael and R. Akiba, the editor who took from it
the passage recording the two differences of opinion between R. Akiba
and the Sages, took from it also the following passage in spite of the
fact that the differences of opinion which it contained were not of the
same sort.

Here another detail of the text of Tosefta proves interesting - the
introduction to Eduyot T 1.14 (456): 'R. Akiba used to give a haggadic
exposition of five things.' For this is one of the passages in which the
material is connected not only by association with a particular man,
but also by reason of the literary form which this man gave it. If the
'testimony' be thought a literary form - or a legal one - then the
tractate Eduyot (Testimonies) shows several examples of this sort of
association. Yet another example is, e.g., Gittin 5.5: 'R. Johanan
ben Gudgada testified concerning...and concerning...and concerning'....
Other examples of the same sort of association are found in the four
passages about the three things which R. Ishmael expounded as parables,[33] and the largest example of all is the collection of Jesus' parables in Mk 4 and parallels. But yet more important for the subject of
this chapter are the passages of TL in which are collected a number
of expositions (of Old Testament verses) by a single man. As was
seen in the preceding chapter, those sections of TL which look most

like sermons are largely composed of Biblical exegesis, and the exegesis found in many other sections has a strongly homiletic character. The relation between expounding and preaching is further emphasized by the fact that the word which meant, in TL, 'expound' (דרש) means, in modern Hebrew, 'preach,' and the two meanings are not to be very sharply distinguished, for in such passages as Mekilta 14.29, where the words, 'Papus expounded (or preached)....R. Akiba said to him, "That's enough, Papus,"' appear as introduction and transition in four expositions, it cannot be decided whether the verb means 'preach' or 'expound' or both together.

Of all the passages of TL in which expositions of this sort are connected by virtue of their association with a single expositor, there is one in which the relation between the collection and the surrounding text is most peculiar. This is the passage in Sotah T 5.13-6.11 (302-6). A large part of the material found here is found also in Sifre on Deut. 6.4,[34] and a part of this in Sifre on Numbers 11.22 and in Sifre Zutta ib. These passages were already referred to as containing parallels to the expression, 'But I say,' for in them R. Simon ben Yohai rates his own opinions above those of R. Akiba. In Sifre on Numbers and Sifre Zutta he speaks only of his exposition on Numbers 11.22 as compared to that of R. Akiba, but in Sifre on Deut. he begins, 'R. Akiba used to expound four things, and I expound them, and I prefer my words to his.' The things expounded are: Why Sarah wished to drive away Ishmael, the text 'Shall sheep and cattle be slaughtered for them and will it suffice them?', the saying, 'Abraham was one man and he inherited the land, and we are many, to us the land is given for inheritance,' and what is 'the tenth fast.' From this list it is clear that these expositions are connected only by the fact that in each of them R. Simon corrected R. Akiba. Moreover, in Sifre on Deut. the whole passage appears as a digression and interrupts the progress of the thought, only the first of R. Simon's expositions has some slight relation to the subject there under discussion (viz. Jacob's fear lest some of his offspring should prove unworthy), and when the group of expositions is completed the text returns to its original subject without any sign of a transition, as though, indeed, the original subject had never been abandoned. In Sotah T 5.13-6.11 R. Simon's saying about R. Akiba's expositions appears in a form expanded by added opinions of other teachers, but even so it constitutes only the second part of the passage (pp. 304 ff.); before it appear four other expositions by R. Akiba, two of them with the simple introduction 'R. Akiba expounded' (5.13; 6.2) and two as handed down by R. Judah ben Paturi and R. Joshua. In this part of the passage, also, the basic material has been expanded by the addition of many opinions of other teachers, but it is indubitable that the essential connection running through it is the association of the expositions with R. Akiba, and this association also accounts for the fact that three of them are found connected in the

Mishnah (Sotah 5.2-4) where appears an additional connective element, the phrase 'On that same day' which will be discussed hereinafter. This element is lacking in Tosefta, but otherwise the text of Tosefta is much fuller than that of the Mishnah - so much fuller that it is impossible to think the two different forms of a single text. Another interesting point is the fact that in Tosefta this passage interrupts the course of the thought by which Sotah T 5.12 (302) is connected with the first of R. Simon's expositions in Sotah T 6.6 (304).

Thus it is possible to sum up the evidence and conclude that there were in the days of the Tannaim two collections of the expositions of R. Akiba, each of which is now known to us in two versions - and versions so different that they cannot be explained as different forms of a single text. One collection is now found in Sotah 5.2-4 and in Sotah T 5.13-6.5, the other collection is now found in Sifre on Deut. 6.4 and in Sotah T 6.6-11. In Tosefta the first collection interrupts the course of the thought which passes directly from 5.12 to 6.6. If it be asked why the material in Tosefta is arranged as it is, the answer would seem to be, either that the first collection was there added to the second because of the common relation to R. Akiba, and was placed before the second carelessly, without notice of the fact that it there came between the text expounded and the exposition, or that the two collections were found already connected (apparently in some larger collection of R. Akiba's expositions) and that the editor of the Tosefta in taking the second of them took the first also as context. (The like was done often in the composition of the Mishnah.[35]) The second of these possibilities seems to me the more plausible and therefore I think this passage in Sotah T almost a proof that among the sources from which the tractate was composed was a fairly extensive collection of R. Akiba's expositions, connected by reason of their relationship to the single expositor, R. Akiba, just as among the sources of Mk was a considerable collection of parables connected by reason of their association with the single preacher, Jesus. However, discussion of the causes of the connection already verges on the historical, i.e., the imaginative. The textual basis of all this construction is merely the passage in Sotah T and its parallels, in which the material is connected in a fashion other than usual.

If TL show no very important instance of that type of association general in the Gospels - i.e., by relation to a single man - it nevertheless shows very frequent parallels to those types of association which appear in the Gospels as of minor importance. The course of the chapter has already led to the notice of parallels between lists of sayings (e.g., Abot 1.12-14: 'Hillel says....He used to say....He used to say'....parallel Mk 4.21-30: 'And he said to them....And he said to them....And he said....And he said'...), lists of parables (Mk ib. parallel the three parables of R. Ishmael in Mekilta 21.19 and its parallels.), etc. Here, to round off this chapter, I shall discuss one other of these types of association which are found only in certain sections of the Gospels:[36] Association by relation to a single day. In this discussion it is necessary to distinguish between those instances in which the doings of a single day are related as a group for some other reason, and those in which they are kept together only because they all happened on one day. For example, all the long sermons in the Gospels, which were discussed in the preceding chapter, appear there as having been, each one, preached in a single day, but it is clear that the essential connection of the material they contain is not its relation to that day, rather it is the structure of the sermon. Another example - this time a dubious one: The story of the last supper and the passion covers, in all, one day, from evening to evening (Mk 14.12-15.47), but here the material is connected by the course of events represented as historical and not by the relation to that particular day. (Thus, had Jesus been left in prison for a week, the story would have included the doings of a week.) However, there are some signs that this story served as devotional reading (haggadah) for Passover in the earliest church,[37] and therefore it is natural to think of the question, 'How does this day differ from all the (other) days?' Nevertheless, I do not think the story of Jesus' last day an example of material connected by reason of its relation to a particular day, and a fortiori I do not think the story of the entrance of Jerusalem (Mk 11.1-11 and parallels) such an example.

These passages being put out of account, there remain in Mk the following, in which, without any excuse being provided by the content, the happenings are grouped according to the days on which they occurred:

A. Mk 1.21-39:
.21 'And they enter Capernaum and at once, on the Sabbath, entering the synagogue, he taught...
.23 And thereupon there was in their synagogue a man in an unclean spirit. (And Jesus healed him.)
.29 And at once, going out of the synagogue, they came into Simon's house. (And Jesus healed Simon's mother-in-law.)
.32 And when it was late...they brought to him all the sick. (And he healed them.)
.35 And very early in the morning, while it was yet dark, he got up and went out...and...and...and'...

B. Mk 3.20-35:
.20 'And he comes into the house and the crowd again gathers....
.21 And his family, hearing of it, went out to seize him, for they said, "He is out of his head."...
.22 And the scribes...said, "He has Beelzebub."....
.23 And, calling them, he spoke to them in parables...

.31 And his mother and his brothers come and, standing outside, they sent to him, calling him.

.32 And a crowd was sitting around him, and they say to him, "Behold, your mother and your brothers...are outside looking for you." '

C. Mk 4.1-10, 4.33-5.20:

.1 'And again he started to teach by the sea. And a very great crowd is gathered to him so that, going into a boat, he sat (in it) on the sea...

.2 And he taught them many things in parables....(Here much teaching material has been added.)

.35 And he says to them, on that day, when it is late, "Let's go over to the other side."

.36 And, leaving the crowd, they take him with them, as he was, in the boat....

.37 And a storm arises (And he stills it.)...

5.1 And they came to the other side of the sea, to the land of the Gerasenes.' (And Jesus healed a man in an unclean spirit.)

D. Mk 5.21-43:

.21 'And when Jesus again went across in the boat to the other side....And there comes one of the rulers of the Synagogue, by name Jaïrus.' (And Jesus went with him to heal his daughter, and while he was going a woman touched him and was healed of her issue of blood. He dismissed her and thereafter healed the girl.)

E. Mk 6.31-56:

.31 'And he (Jesus) says to them (his disciples), "Come by yourselves into a desert spot and rest."....

.32 And they went away in the boat....

.33 And many saw them going and followed them, and on foot from all the cities they ran together there....

.34 And he started to teach them....

.35 And when it was already late his disciples, coming to him, said, "The spot is desert and it is already late. (.36) Let them go, in order that, going away,...they may buy themselves something to eat. (But Jesus fed them from the five loaves and two fishes.)

.45 And he at once compelled his disciples to enter the boat and proceed to the other side....

.47 And when it was late the boat was in the middle of the sea. (And he came to them, walking on the sea.)

.53 And when they had crossed over they came to land at Gennesaret and anchored.' (And crowds came to them and Jesus healed their sick.)

F. Mk 9.2-29:

.2 'And after six days Jesus takes Peter and James and
John, and brings them up into a high mountain by themselves
alone.

.3 And he was transfigured before them....

.9 And when they were coming down...he ordered them that
they should recount to no one what they had seen....

.14 And coming to the disciples they saw a great crowd
around them and scribes (etc. And Jesus healed a demoniac
boy.)

.28 And when he went inside his disciples asked him pri-
vately, "Why could not we cast it out?"

.29 And he said to them, "This sort can be cast out by
nothing but prayer." '

Clearly, in all these cases there is reason to doubt how far the one
day served as an essential element of association and how far its appearance is merely accidental. The representatives of 'form-criticism' - especially Bultmann and K. Schmidt - thought the connection
of events to a single day a thing wholly unimportant, added in the last
stage of the development of the Gospels. On the contrary, V. Taylor,
in his book on the tradition of the Gospels[38] emphasized the actual
connection of the stories in the sections I have lettered A, C, D, and
E. However, he took C and D together as the events of a single day -
a supposition not necessitated by the text as it stands - and added
several stories to E, since he wished only to find sections based on a
chronological order, and did not demand that the events they recounted
should all transpire in one day. Here, of course, it is unnecessary to
inquire as to the historical basis of these passages, and also as to the
period in which the material of the Gospels was so arranged as to
constitute them, for it is never necessary to ask unanswerable questions. It is enough that the material of the Gospels is now so arranged that in some passages the events are connected, apparently,
by their association with a single day, and that this same method of
connection is fairly frequent in TL. Of these two points the first requires no further proof than the above analysis of Markan passages,
the second remains to be demonstrated.

When TL records the day on which a particular event took place or
on which a particular teaching was laid down, it most often happens
that the event was determined by the necessary course of events or
that the statement of such a law at such a time was determined by its
content; and that, consequently, the mention of the day is superfluous
or, at most, serves merely to date the material. For example (a
date): Pesahim T 4.2 (162-3): 'Hillel says, "It is said, in the case of
the Passover, 'in its season,' and it is said, in the case of the daily
offering, 'in its season,' (therefore, as the duty of offering the daily

offering takes precedence of the duty of observing the Sabbath, so will
that of offering the Passover.)...And further, a fortiori....And further,
I have received from my teachers"... They said to him, "If so, what
shall be done about the people, for they did not bring their knives and
their animals for the Passover sacrifice to the Temple (during the
week, and if the Passover is to be sacrificed to-morrow, which is a
Sabbath, they will not be permitted to carry them)?" He said to them,
"Let them alone. The Holy Spirit is upon them. If they are not prophets they are the sons of the prophets." Next day what did they do?
He whose Passover sacrifice was a lamb stuck (the knife) in its wool,
and (he whose Passover sacrifice was a) kid fixed it in its horns (and
the animals came under their own power. Thus) they brought knives
and animals for Passover sacrifices to the Temple and made their
Passover sacrifices. On that same day they appointed Hillel Patriarch
and he was teaching them the laws of the Passover.'

Such is the general rule, but sometimes there are found diverse
laws - or expositions or the like - connected by reason of their association with the day on which they were taught. Most often they are
also connected by reason of their association with the man who taught
them. In such instances the structure of the passage is exactly that of
passages in the Gospels where the material is connected not only by
reason of its association with Jesus, but also by reason of its association with a particular day. Of the many such passages to be found in
TL I cite only a few examples:

Berakot T 4.16-18 (10-11) (Another form of the same material in
Mekilta of R. Simon 14.22 end.): 'Once upon a time R. Tarefon was
sitting in the shadow of a dove-cote, on a Sabbath, at the time of the
afternoon prayer. They brought before him a bucket of cold water.
R. Tarefon said to them - to his disciples - "He who drinks water to
(satisfy) his thirst, what form of blessing does he say?" they said to
him, "Our Master, teach us." He said to them, "(Blessed be Thou....)
Who createst living things and their need." He said to them, "I shall
ask a question." They said to him, "Teach us." He said to them,
"Behold it says, 'And they sat down to eat and they lifted up their eyes
and saw and behold a company of Ishmaelites' etc. And isn't it the
fact that it is not the custom of Arabs to be carrying anything but foul-
smelling skins and resin? (Whereas these, to whom Joseph was sold,
are said to have been carrying "spicery and balm and myrrh.") But
(this shows) that they put that just man among precious things. And
see, it is possible to argue a fortiori: If, when fortune frowns upon
the just, they yet are treated mercifully, how much more so will they
be when mercy prevail? Similarly....Similarly"... He said to them,
"I shall ask a question." They said to him, "Our Master, teach us."
He said to them, "Why did Judah deserve the kingdom" (i.e., deserve
to produce the royal family)? They said to him, "Because he admitted
the truth about Tamar."....He said to them, "Is pay given for

transgression? But why did Judah deserve the kingdom?....Because
(the tribe of Judah) hallowed the Name of God (i.e., were zealous to
obey Him) at the (Red) Sea." '

Pesahim T 1.27-28 (157): 'If one find leavened substance in the
road, if the greater part of it be leavened it is permitted, and if not,
it is prohibited. Once upon a time Rabban Gamliel and R. Ilai were
walking from Akko to Kazib and (Rabban Gamliel) saw a loaf of fine
bread. He said to Tabi his servant, "Take this bread." He saw a
gentile and said to him, "Mabgai, take this bread." R. Ilai ran after
him (and) said to him, "What sort of man are you?" (and found out
that his name actually was Mabgai and that he was unknown to Rabban
Gamliel)....Hence we learned that Rabban Gamliel was guided by the
Holy Spirit, and from his words we learned three things: That the
leaven of a gentile may be used immediately after the Passover-sea-
son, and (that) one should not pass by food (but should take it along),
and (that, in judging the legal status of things found by the way-side,)
one goes by the majority of the travellers. He reached Kazib and a
man came and asked him (to determine whether or not) his vow (were
binding). He said to one of those who were with him, "Didn't we drink
a fourth (of a log) of Italian wine?" He said to him, "Yes." He said
to him, "If so, let (the petitioner) walk after us until (the effect of) our
wine pass away." He walked with him until they came to the Ladder
of Tyre. He got down from the donkey and wrapped himself (in his
judge's cloak) and sat down and loosed him of his vow. And we
learned many things in that day: We learned that a quarter (of a log)
of wine intoxicates, and (that) travelling drives away (the effects of)
the wine, and (that) one should not teach after drinking wine, and (that)
one should not loose (men of their) vows while walking nor while riding nor while standing, but while wearing (a judge's cloak) and seated.'

Sifra 4.2, middle. (Ch. 1, from middle to end): 'R. Akiba said, "I
asked Rabban Gamliel and R. Joshua at the fair of Emmaus, where
they went to get an animal for his son's (wedding) feast....R. Akiba
asked them (Reading שאלין for שאלו and so hereafter.)....And again
R. Akiba asked them....R. Joshua said, "I have heard"....R. Simon
said, "And what is the proof?"....R. Joshua said, "I have heard"....
R. Akiba said, "If this be legal tradition we will accept it, or is (it
permitted to) answer the argument?" He said to him, "Answer." He
said to him....R. Akiba said, "I asked R. Elazar....He said to me....I
said to him, 'No.' " ' etc. All of these questions deal with actions performed in ignorance of important relevant facts, they are therefore
connected by subject as well as by relationship to a single man.
Nevertheless, the relationship to a particular day appears in the first
three as an additional bond of association.

But sometimes in TL the relationship to a particular day appears
(when the elements are not connected by relationship to a single man,
nor by a common subject) as the essential connective element of a

relatively large chapter. Assuredly, there are few such chapters, but those few are among the most important. In particular must be mentioned the following: (1) Shabbat 1.4,5 = Shabbat T 1.16 ff. (111): The eighteen things they said in the upper room of Hananyah ben Hezkiyah ben Garon on the day when they were numbered and the House of Shammai outnumbered the House of Hillel. (2) Sotah 5.2-5: Three things expounded by R. Akiba and one expounded by R. Judah ben Hyrcanus (The parallel in Sotah T has already been discussed. It lacks the expression 'In that same day.') (3) Yadayim 4.1-4 = Yadayim T 16-18 (683): Things done 'in that same day' in which they installed R. Elazar ben Azaryah in the assembly. (These are again explicitly mentioned in Zebahim 1.3, and Bartinurah thinks that the matters mentioned in Sotah 5 were also expounded on that same day.)[39] These passages suffice at least to show that it was customary to remember as a group the teachings learned from a given Rabbi on a given day. Evidently, this custom was shared by the sources of TL and the sources of the Gospels, for in both literatures are found collections, sometimes fairly large, of quite diverse elements associated chiefly by their relationship to a single day. In discussion of the Gospels, I passed over those stories of which the elements were associated by the necessary sequence of events, and in discussion of TL, I have not mentioned those tractates of which all the material is connected as dealing with a single day (or several days) of festival, nor those passages of the midrashim (such as Sifre on Numbers 7.1) in which the commentator explains that large number of events, related in different parts of the Old Testament, took place all on the same day. I did not wish to make the demonstration depend on such dubious material. But I think that, given the demonstration, such material may be used to strengthen it, for in spite of the fact that, in these instances, causes other than literary served to associate the material with the day, yet the final association remains undeniable, and it seems to me probable that both in the Gospels and in TL this form of association, so prominent in such important sections of the literature, influenced the structure of the other sections also.

NOTES

1. A. Schweitzer, Geschichte der Leben-Jesu-Forschung, 4 ed., Tübingen, 1926, 642 pp.
2. e.g., articles in MGWJ 1934, pp. 119 ff, 438 ff; 1932, pp. 241 ff; 1931, pp. 401 ff; 1926, pp. 376 ff; 1925, pp. 171 ff, 311 ff, 401 ff., etc. Of the more important books, I have read:
   D. Hoffmann, Die erste Mischna, Berlin, 1881.
   C. Albeck, Untersuchungen über die Redaktion der Mischna,

Berlin, 1923 (<u>Veröffentl. d. Ak. f.d. Wissen. d. Jtms., Talm. Sektion</u>, Bd. 2).

3. Münster i.W. 1916.

4. pp. 145 ff.

5. p. 157: 'Diese Methode (der mündl. Überlieferung ausfindig zu machen)....bestand darin, dass man Halachoth, die sich auf das gleiche Gebot oder Verbot bezogen, zusammenfasste, dass man ungleichartige Halachoth unter Stichworten einer Gruppe einordnete, oder Halachoth mit gleichem Anfang zusammenstellte oder nach bestimmten Zahlen-verhältnissen gruppierte.' It must be added that this is said, not of the structure of the Mishnah itself, but of the structure of the sources from which it is said that the sections of the Mishnah were taken without any considerable change of the sequence of the individual laws.

6. ZNW 5.144 ff. (The same opinion has appeared recently in the article of S. Feigin, <u>The Oriental Language of the Gospels</u>, in 'Journal of Near Eastern Studies,' II. 188a).

7. <u>idem</u> p. 145.

8. <u>ib.</u> I have inverted the order of Klein's sentences because the remark about <u>Abot</u> required discussion, while that about R. Meir did not.

9. Eusebius, <u>Kirchengeschichte</u>, 3.39.16 (ed. Schwartz, Leipzig, 1903).

10. <u>id.</u> 3.39.3.

11. <u>id.</u> 3.39.9.

12. <u>id.</u> 3.39.11.

13. See, for example, the article by V. Bartlett, <u>The Sources of St. Luke's Gospel</u>, in 'Studies in the Synoptic Problem,' ed. W. Sanday, Oxford, 1911, pp. 315 ff.

14. REJ 92.31 ff. (The citation is from p. 33.)

15. <u>ib.</u> p. 34: 'Qui sait si ces restes (les fragments biographiques sur les rabbins) ne proviennent pas effectivement de biographies de ce genre qu'on appelle, dans l'Église, des Évangiles?' (A very dubious use of the word 'biographies.')

16. <u>From Tradition to Gospel</u>, London, 1934, p. 136: 'We catch sight of pre-canonical connections amongst the Rabbinic stories. It is really self-apparent that not only material, but often also personal, connections existed which were preserved together in the <u>stories about a Rabbi</u>.' (Underlining by Dibelius.)

17. (<u>Babli</u>) Erubin 96b. I cite from C. Albeck, <u>Untersuchungen über die hal. Midraschim</u>, Berlin, 1927 (<u>Veröffentl. der. Ak. f.d. Wiss. d. Judtms., Talm. Sektion</u>, Bd. III.) p. 88.

18. According to Albeck, <u>idem</u>, p. 89: 'Auch in den Stellen, wo der ספרא סתם des Babli in unser Sifra vorkommt, dem Talmud <u>nicht</u> unser Sifrabuch vorgelegen haben musste.' (Underlining by Albeck.) E. Melamed, in his book, <u>Halachic Midrashim of the Tannaïm in the Talmud Babli</u>, (Jerusalem, 1943, pp. 31-2) emphasizes the fact that

the talmudic tradition must be tested tractate by tractate, and excuses himself from the attempt because of its difficulty.

19. Numerous examples in D. Hoffmann, Zur Einleitung in die hal. Midraschim, Berlin, 1887, pp. 6-12.

20. Hoffmann, ib., relied on such signs as these. In this he was followed by H. Horowitz in his introduction to Sifre on Numbers (Corpus Tannaiticum, sectio tertia, pars tertia, fasc. I, pp. V-X, Lipsiae, 1917). On the contrary, Albeck (Midraschim, p. 86) has maintained, 'dass in den Tannaitenschulen keine feststehende Terminologie geherrscht hat, dass sie vielmehr erst allmählich in den Quellen sich entwickelt und in unseren Midraschim fest Gestalt angenommen hat, da die Redaktoren die Terminologie der Baraitot...in die ihnen geläufige Terminologie umgeändert haben.' Melamed, (op. cit., pp. 33-6) takes the signs singled out by Hoffmann, Albeck and others as signs peculiar to different schools, but raises so many difficulties as to make it practically impossible to rely on them.

21. Mekilta of R. Simon pp. 174-5.

22. The pages on which the names are frequent contain the commentary on Ex. 15.20-18.27.

23. Mekilta of R. Simon, Introduction, p. XI, end. 'And when the Amoraïm came to put in order the Tannaïtic exegesis they found the haggadot already written and added them, in a uniform style, to their collection. But the legal traditions differed each in its own way.' It is clear that Hoffmann thought of a written source, not in order to explain the appearance of the names in one section only, but in order to explain the fact that Mekilta parallels Mekilta of R. Simon (and Sifre on Numbers parallels Sifre Zutta) far more closely in haggadic than in halakic sections.

24. According to KM s.v. ו_עוד

25. Eduyot 1.5.

26. 1.4 (455).

27. The second section begins with the testimony of Akabya ben Mehallelel, Eduyot 5.6, Eduyot T 2.9, middle (458).

28. The Law agrees with the testimony: Eduyot 1.3; 2.3; 7.3, 4, 6, 7 (!), 8 (!), Eduyot T 1.3 (455); 3.1 (459) bis (!). The exclamation marks indicate the passages in which it is said that the testimony there recorded contradicted the majority opinion. The Law differs from the testimony: Eduyot 2.2; 5.6; 7.1; 8.2, 3, 4(?).

29. Eduyot T 1.8 (455) - 15 (456), Eduyot 2.4-10. Apart from these two sections almost all the material of the two tractates belongs to one or the other of the two parts I have described. Other than these there is only the introduction to Eduyot T and the conclusions to both the tractates, which are composed of haggadic material, the two passages, already mentioned, on the use of the tractates, and a very few isolated sentences. The details of the order of the material would, of course, admit of much further discussion which would be out of place here.

30. Apart from the last two traditions concerning the words of R. Akiba which appear in Eduyot T 1.12-15 along with the disagreement of the majority.

31. Eduyot 2.8 ('R. Akiba said three things; they admitted to the truth of two and denied the truth of one.' According to Eduyot T 1.13 (456) they admitted to the truth of one and did not admit to the truth of another.)

32. Eduyot T 1.7 (455).

33. Mekilta 21.19; 22.2. Sifre on Deut. 22.17. Midrash Tannaïm ib.

34. See Finkelstein's note ib.

35. See Albeck, Untersuchungen uber die Redaktion der Mischna, Berlin, 1923, Einleitung, pp. 3-13, esp. p. 13.

36. As opposed to association by relationship to a single man, which is the essential connection of all the sections of the Gospels.

37. See esp. I Cor. 5.7-8.

38. V. Taylor, The Formation of the Gospel Tradition, London, 1933, pp. 39 f.

39. However, S. Zeitlin thinks to find a common subject in the eighteen things. See his article, Les 'dix-huit mesures,' REJ 68.22 ff. (And note that there are practically two volumes 68 of REJ. The numeration begins anew in the July-Sept. issue, where Zeitlin's article is found.) Even should Zeitlin be correct it would remain to show why these laws were kept separate in the tradition from the other laws dealing with the same subjects (or, as he thinks, subject). Probably, I suppose, because they were laid down together, on one memorable day.

Chapter 6

COMPLETE PARALLELS

Last in the list of simple parallels are those which I have called 'complete' - passages which are parallel at once in words and in structure, in content and in literary form. The best known and also the most striking example of this class to be found between the Gospels and TL is the parallel between Mk 4.24 (= Mat 7.2 = Lk 6.38): 'In the measure in which you mete it shall be measured to you.' and the rabbinical saying, 'In the measure in which a man metes it is measured[1] to him.' which is found in Mekilta 13.19 ff., Sotah 1.7, Sotah T 3.1 (295), Sifre on Numbers 12.15 ff., in forms little different one from another. Clearly, even here there is a slight difference: In the Gospels the saying is said of a particular group, the hearers; in TL, of everyone. So it would be possible to conceive of a yet more complete parallel, and since, logically, completeness does not admit of degrees, this chapter might more accurately have been called 'Parallels showing many types of parallelism' - or something else equally cumbersome.

Actually, one passage may be parallel to another in one or more ways, and more or less closely in each way. For example, in ch. III, above, was discussed the parallelism between the story of the king and his servants, in Sifra 26.9, and that in Mat 20.1-15 of the householder and his servants. Clearly these two passages display verbal parallelism (e.g., both contain words meaning 'workers'), parallelism of literary form (both are 'parables'), and parallelism of content (both are concerned with the question of pay; both use pay, given for work done to suit a man, as a symbol for the reward given for work done according to the will of God). Therefore these two passages show what might be called, in all, a very high degree of parallelism. Nevertheless there are between them very striking and important differences: Striking - one speaks of a king and one of a householder. Important - the theory of pay found in the one flatly contradicts that found in the other. Another example is afforded by Mk 4.25 (= Mat 13.12; 25.29, Lk 8.18; 19.26): 'For he who has, to him shall be given, and who has not, from him shall be taken even what he has.' which parallels Mekilta 15.26 (and very many other passages, see Horovitz' commentary in loc.) 'If a man hear (i.e., obey) one commandment he is made to hear many commandments, for it is said, "If hearing you will hear," if a man forget one commandment he is made to forget many commandments, for it is said..."If forgetting you will forget." ' Here there is parallelism in form - saying - and in structure - antithesis - and in

content - the good come first and the evil second in both, moreover
they both express the rather interesting theory, not found in all sys-
tems of moral theology, that God helps the good to become better and
the bad worse. The latter element of this theory is expressed in the
Gospels also by - for example - Mk 4.11-12 and its parallels: 'To
those who are outside all things are in parables, in order that they
may surely look and not see,[2] and may surely hear and not understand,
lest they should turn back and be forgiven.' and in TL - for example -
by the rule 'That the virtuous are caused to perform acts of virtue,
and sinners acts of sin.' (Sifre on Numbers 9.8; 15.36; 27.5; ff.), but
it is not, at very least, the commonest notion in the later literature
either of Judaism or of Christianity.[3] Therefore it is interesting that
the formal parallelism of the first mentioned passages should be so
close, in spite of the fact that there is no verbal parallelism between
them.

From the above discussion it should be clear that it would be possible, theoretically, to classify parallel passages according to the
number of types of parallelism they manifest: Parallels of one type
(e.g., all parables, being all of them parallel in form), of two types
(all parables dealing with the same subject), of three types (all parables dealing with the same subject and using stories about the same
objects) etc.

Perhaps, were there a sufficient number of such parallels, such a
classification as the above would be worth-while, for all theories of
direct literary relationship between two literatures depend on passages
manifesting simultaneously several types of parallelism. But as things
are, such parallels between the Gospels and TL are so infrequent that
I have thought it best to collect all the most important in a single list
of 'complete parallels,' which list follows. It contains no passages,
however close in other respects, which do not display some verbal
parallelism, and no passages of which the parallelism consists only
in the use of some familiar literary ornament, such as the passages
on the 'two ways' (mentioned in ch. III), and those on 'treasures in
heaven' (Mat 6.19, 21. Lk 12.33-4. Peah T 4.18 ff. (24)). When such
passages are excluded, very few are left. They are:[4]

Mat 5.34: 'Swear not at all.'
Sifre on Deut. 23.23 (and Midrash Tannaïm ib. and Hullin T 2.17) 'It
        were good...that you vow not at all.' (Admittedly 'swear,'
        השבע, is not 'vow', נדר - but the two Hebrew verbs are some-
        what confused in TL,[5] and I therefore thought best to list the
        pair of passages as a dubious case.)

Mat 6.9 (Lk 11.2): 'Hallowed be Thy Name.'
The Kaddish: 'Let the Great Name be magnified and hallowed.'

Mat 6.10: 'Thy will be done, as in heaven, also on earth.'
Berakot T 3.7 (6): 'Do Thy will in the heavens above and give tran-
    quility of spirit to those who fear Thee on earth.'

Mat 6.13 (Lacking in the oldest MSS.): 'For Thine is the kingdom.'
Alenu: 'For Thine is the kingdom.'

Mat 6.14 (cf. Mk 11.25): 'For if you pardon men their transgressions,
    your heavenly Father will pardon you also.'
Sifre on Deut. 13.18 (Midrash Tannaïm ib.): 'Whenever you have
    mercy on other creatures, they from heaven (i.e., God) have
    mercy on you.'

*Mat 6.15: 'But if you do not forgive men, neither will your father
    forgive your trespasses.'
Midrash Tannaïm 15.11: 'As you withhold mercy, so they (i.e., God)
    withhold mercy from you.'

Mat 6.26 (Lk 12.24): 'Look at the birds of heaven, they do now sow,
    neither do they reap...and your heavenly Father feeds them.
    Do you not much surpass them?'
Kiddushin 4.14 (Kiddushin T 5.15 (343)): 'Did you ever in your life see
    an animal or a bird which had a trade? And they support them-
    selves without trouble. And were they not created only to serve
    me? And I was created to serve my maker. Does it not follow
    that I shall be supported without trouble?' (The verbal parallel
    is not particularly close.)

Mat 6.30-4 (the beginning in Lk 12.28-9): 'Ye of little faith, do not,
    then, take thought, saying, "What shall we eat?"....Take,
    therefore, no thought for the morrow. For the morrow will
    take thought for itself. Sufficient to the day is the evil thereof.'
Mekilta 16.4 (Mekilta of R. Simon ib.): 'He who has what he will eat
    to-day and says "What shall I eat to-morrow,?" behold, this
    man lacks faith, (for it is said, "The day's lot in its day." ')
    (The citation is only in Mekilta of R. Simon, in Mekilta a differ-
    ent text is cited. To bring together the two elements of the
    Matthaean parallel, two verses have been omitted.)

Mat 7.2 (Mk 4.24, Lk 6.38): 'In the measure in which you mete it shall
    be measured to you.'
Mekilta 13.19 (ff., Sotah 1.7, Sotah T 3.1 (295), Sifre on Numbers 12.15
    ff.): 'In the measure in which a man metes it is measured to
    him.'

*Mat 7.7 (Lk 11.9): 'Seek and ye shall find.'
Sifre on Deut. 12.5: 'Seek and find.' (The immediate reference of
    these words is to 'the place which the Lord your God will
    choose,' but they are not closely connected with the context

and appear rather as a popular saying there given particular
application. So also they appear in Mat and in Lk, therefore I
have listed these passages as a dubious instance, cp. Ben Sira
(Heb.) 6.27)

*Mat 7.11 (Lk 11.13): 'If, then, you, being evil, know how to give good
gifts to your children, how much more will your Father in the
heavens give good things to those who ask Him?'
Sifre on Numbers 10.29: 'If a member of the household of a man is
well treated, a fortiori a member of the household of Him-
Who-spoke-and-the-world-was.' (Again, the verbal parallel is
not particularly close, and it is further disguised by translation. The Hebrew reads: אם לבן ביתו של בשר ודם מטיבין
לו קל וחומר לבן ביתו של מי שאמר והיה העולם.

((Mat 22.38: 'This is the great and first commandment.'
Sifra 19.18: 'This is the great rule in the Law.' (Sifra speaks of Lev.
19.18, Mat of Deut. 6.5; 'rule' is not 'commandment'; 'great'
in Sifra means 'logically prior' - that rule which includes by
implication all the rest, 'great' in Mat means 'morally pre-
eminent' - the most important. In short, the two sentences
have nothing in common but their structure and the word
'great,' and I have cited the pair of them only to exclude them
specifically from this list - an exclusion made necessary by
the custom of supposing them equivalent.)))

Mk 2.27: 'The Sabbath came into being for man, and not man for the
Sabbath.'
Mekilta 31.13, 14 (Mekilta of R. Simon ib.): 'The Sabbath is com-
mitted to you, and you are not committed to the Sabbath.'
(Little verbal parallelism.)

*Lk 23.35: 'And the rulers, too, mocked (Jesus as he hung on the
cross), saying, "He saved others, let him save himself." '
Midrash Tannaim 3.23: 'Before a man put his trust on flesh and blood
and ask him to save him, let him save himself from death
first.'

Jn 7.23: 'If a man receive circumcision on the Sabbath in order that
the Law of Moses be not broken, are you angry at me because
I made a whole man sound on the Sabbath?'
Shabbat T 15.16 (134): 'Circumcision takes precedence of the Sabbath.
Why? Because the neglect of it makes a man liable to be cut
off in time to come. And cannot one argue a fortiori? One
member of him takes precedence of the Sabbath, shall not all
of him take precedence of the Sabbath?' (An argument proving
that the duty of saving life - as, of digging a man out of a col-
lapsed building - takes precedence of the Sabbath.)

*Jn 11.50 (cf. 18.14): 'It is to your advantage that one man die for the people and that the whole nation be not destroyed.'
Midrash Tannaîm 21.21: 'The Law said it is better that one life should be lost and that many lives should not be lost.'

Of course, in drawing up such lists as this, there are always border-line cases which must be included or excluded, and it is impossible that the judgment of the editor should always be consistent. It may have happened, therefore, that I have excluded in one place what I have included in another. In particular, there were three sorts of parallels which I decided only after much hesitation to exclude, viz:

(1) Important parallels which, however, lacked completely one sort of parallelism, generally verbal, e.g.:

*Lk 6.38: 'Give and it shall be given to you.'
Midrash Tannaîm 15.8: 'As you open (your hand to the poor), so (others shall) open to you.' (Reading לך for לו)

but sometimes of another sort, e.g.:

Mat 13.44: 'The kingdom of Heaven is like a treasure hid in a field, which a man who found it hid, and from his joy he goes away and sells all he has and buys that field.'
Mekilta 14.5 (Mekilta of R. Simon ib.): '(It is like) one to whom there fell in inheritance a residence in a sea-port city and he sold it for a small sum and the purchaser went and dug through it and found in it treasures of silver and treasures of gold and precious stones and pearls. The seller almost strangled (of rage and grief). So did Egypt because they sent away (Israel) and did not know what they sent away.'

Here should also be mentioned the most interesting of the parallels of idiom, such as 'And I say,' which have not sufficient content to be considered complete parallels.

(2) Parallels in which it seemed to me that a passage of one literature deliberately reversed the words of a well-known passage of the other, and this for the sake of parody. The famous parody of Alenu found in the Pharisee's prayer in Lk 18.10 is not here in question, for the verbal parallelism between Lk and the present text of Alenu is not sufficiently close to make the parallelism 'complete' and, in any case, the parody there is effected not by reversal of the words, but by external additions, especially a different conclusion. But other passages certainly lead one to suspect parody by reversal. One such, the story in Mat 20.1-16, has already been discussed. Another is found in Lk 16.12, 'If you were not trustworthy in others' (affairs), who will give you your* own?' The opposite is found in Demai 2.2: 'R. Judah

---

*So א, D, Θ, latin, syriac. Nestle reads our, with B.

says, "He who stays as guest in the house of a man who neglects the Law (an am-haarez) is (also) trustworthy."[6] They said to him, "He is not trustworthy about himself, how will he be trustworthy about others' (belongings)?" ' Lk 16.1-13 is one of the most difficult passages of the Gospels. I think to make sense of it thus: The rich man is Satan, the lord of this world; the steward is everyman. If the steward use the master's goods for the master's benefit, he will in the end be driven out anyhow, and none will receive him; but if he squander them on the poor he will in the end be driven out of this world, but they will receive him in the world to come. Therefore one must deal deceitfully with the mammon of unrighteousness in order to receive the true treasure. Verses 10 and 11 reverse ironically the rules of every-day ethics; vs. 12 similarly reverses this rule of rabbinical law. The irony is emphasized by a rule from the ethics of Jesus, which appears in vs. 13: 'No servant can serve two masters...you cannot serve God and mammon.'[7] That ethical rules are used ironically in the Gospels is known from the use of 'Repay if you owe anything.' in Mat 18.28, and that Lk 16.12 is also ironical is made more probable by the fact that the words it reverses appear in Demai as if they were a well-known rule.[8]

(3) Parallels of the class which I have called 'parallels with a fixed difference.' This whole class will be discussed in the final chapter and there will be cited a number of examples of passages almost completely parallel, but referring, in TL to God and His Law, in the Gospels to Jesus and his teaching. But there are other differences seen in other examples, of which one may be cited here:

*Lk 17.34: 'In that night there will be two men in one bed, the one will be taken and the other will be left.' (Referring to the day of judgment.)

Mekilta of R. Simon 12.27: 'If an Egyptian and an Israelite were lying in bed, only the Israelite was passed over.' (Referring to the last plague on Egypt.)

But even were all the closest parallels of these three sorts to be collected and added to the list of those which I have called 'complete' the total would yet remain very small, especially in consideration of the fact that these parallels are collected from more than three hundred pages of Greek and from almost three thousand pages of Hebrew. If it be recalled again that these 'complete' parallels would have to be the most important element in the proof of any theory hypothecating a direct literary relationship between the Gospels and TL, then it will be seen that the most important fact demonstrated by the study of these parallels is their absence.

NOTES

1. Literally, 'They measure' - the regular Hebrew impersonal of which the subject, like the unmentioned agent of the Greek impersonal passive, may be God, or other men, or both.

2. Or, literally, 'that, seeing, they may not see, and, hearing, they may not hear.' Since the literal translation fits the context better, it may be that the Old Testament idiom has been misunderstood - or deliberately 'interpreted' - by the New Testament authors.

3. Prof. Lieberman tells me that the same thought is found in the Yerushalmi, Sanhedrin 9.27 and in Babli Shabbat 104.1 and their parallels.

4. From here on to the end of the chapter I have marked with an asterisk the parallels which I have not found mentioned in scholarly works.

5. Such is the opinion of Prof. Lieberman, Greek in Jewish Palestine, N.Y., 1942, p. 117 (and notes 14-17).

6. Especially, in the matter of tithing.

7. Of course, I am describing only what I think the meaning of Lk. As to the historical question, whether or not Lk 16.13 came from the mouth of Jesus, I am not concerned to answer it. But it is interesting to note that this verse is the only one in the whole story which is found almost word for word in another Gospel (in Mat 6.24). This would make it seem probable that Lk here used one of the sayings then known as 'sayings of Jesus,' in order to emphasize the irony of the preceding vss.

8. Which is not the case with their inverted form found in Bekorot 5.4, which seems to me mere accident.

Chapter 7

PARALLELS OF PARALLELISM

In the parallels hitherto discussed one passage in one literature
has been parallel to one passage in the other literature, more specifically, one passage in the Gospels to one in TL. Sometimes there has
been occasion to mention other passages in the Gospels parallel to the
one under discussion, sometimes other passages in TL parallel to the
one being discussed, but such occasion has produced at best incidental
remarks which could have been deleted without any loss to the essential content of the work. But every literature consisting of several
books - such as the Gospels or TL - makes possible the discussion of
the relationship which exists between the books, and in the comparison of literatures it is possible to compare the relationship which
exists between the books of one literature with the relationship which
exists between the books of a second literature. Now both in the Gospels and in TL the most striking characteristic of this relationship is
the fact of parallelism, and especially the large number of 'complete'
parallels found between the different books.

Of course all the Gospels are parallel one to another in all the
various manners of parallelism which have hitherto been discussed.
Between Mat and Mk, for instance, there are to be found parallels of
words, of idiom, of content, of literary forms, and of types of association. But scholars frequently neglect these partial parallels, depending on only one or two aspects of the material, because there are, between the two books, so many complete parallels, and these so noticeable and so important. And such is the relation of each of the synoptic
Gospels to the other; and such, also, is the relationship of each one of
them to Jn, for only because the synoptics are so close one to another
does Jn seem far from them. As a matter of fact all of the four are
very close to each other, and the more they are studied the more superficial their differences and the more important their similarities
are seen to be. Such also is the state of affairs in TL: The striking
fact is the large numbers of complete parallels to be found between
its various books, especially between the Mishnah and Tosefta, Mekilta
of R. Simon and Sifre on Deut, Sifre Zutta and Sifra, Mekilta and Sifre
on Numbers.[1] But, apart from these pairs, there are to be found many
passages common to all the midrashim.[2]

It is obvious on reflection that most European literatures do not,
for the most part, consist of books thus related. In classical Greek
literature, for instance, there are not many complete parallels to be
found between one book and another, neither are there in classical

142

Latin literature, nor in the better known parts of French, German or
English literature. And when such relationship is found, it is found
usually in works outside the normal canon of literature, such as magi-
cal texts or folk tales. Yet, in spite of these facts, scholars have paid
little attention to this parallel which exists between the Gospels on the
one hand and that of the books of TL on the other, viz: that in both
literatures the books are related to one another chiefly by 'complete'
parallelism.

On the Christian side, P. Fiebig wrote in his Jüdische Wundergeschichten:[3] 'Die meisten Überlieferungen liegen uns in Paralleltexten
vor, die die grösste Ähnlichkeit mit den in unseren neutestamentlichen
Evangelien vorhandenen Paralleltexten haben.' and when he printed the
Hebrew texts which he had discussed in this book he added,[4] 'Das
Studium solcher Paralleltexte ist sehr lehrreich zur Beurteilung der
synoptischen Parallelen.' but gave no details whatsoever. G. Kittel,
in his book, Die Probleme des palästinischen Spätjudentums und das
Urchristentum,[5] wrote,[6] 'Das synoptische Problem, ja das ganze Tra-
ditionsproblem der Evangelien, ist nicht ein singuläres....Dieselbe
Art der Traditionsvarianten die wir aus den Paralleltexten der Evangelien kennen, ist für die rabbinische Tradition charakteristisch....So
muss man, wenn man die Überlieferung irgendeines der Rabbinen
sichten will, in jedem Fall eine Synopse der Paralleltraditionen her-
stellen. Man erkennt dann, wie Traditionen über weite Zeitspannen
hin in parallelen Kanälen laufen.' u.s.w. And he cited several examples of complete parallels found in rabbinical literature, but compared
with them none of the parallels found in the Gospels.

Moreover, as against his remarks, it must be noted that the problem of parallelism is not simplified by confusion with the problem of
tradition. The question, 'What are the parallels?' is a philological
question which can be answered exactly by analysis and comparison
of the preserved documents. The question, 'Which theory about the
nature of the tradition can best be supported by such parallels as have
been preserved?' is a historical question which admits of various
answers according to the various abilities and inclinations of the persons answering.

But if the Christians have done little to describe this important
parallel between the Gospels and TL, the Jews have done nothing. I
cannot recall even a word by any Jewish scholar remarking - for example - that the problem of the relationship between Tosefta and the
Mishnah is similar to the synoptic problem, and this in spite of the
fact that they are so similar as to be practically inseparable, and that
any theory begun from a study of the one literature should have immediate application in the study of the other.

But if neither Jews nor Christians have written much on this parallel of parallelism which exists between the two literatures, at least
both groups have written at great length on the complete parallels

which exist between the books of either literature, considered singly. In particular, numberless books have been written by Christians on the synoptic problem, and the literature has been reviewed by A. Schweitzer[7] and P. Wernle[8]; it need not, therefore, be discussed here. Schweitzer reviews also the war waged throughout the nineteenth century over the question of the relationship of Jn to the synoptics. At the conclusion of this war most scholars agreed in thinking Jn a very late product of a Greek environment. Thereupon, at the beginning of the present century, came the books of Schlatter[9] and Burney[10] and gave reason to doubt the truth of this opinion. A review of the literature which they called forth is given by W. Howard in the first section of his book, The Fourth Gospel.[11] In all these later works, the primary interest of the authors has historical, and there has been no discussion of the parallels between Jn and the synoptics for their own sake. Indeed, some of the authors, such as Burney, have scarcely noticed their existence. But it has been necessary to mention the variety of opinions because almost all those who have discussed the parallels have done so in order to collect material to buttress their historical theories.

To these two literatures - that on the synoptic problem and that on the relation of Jn to the synoptics - must be added a third - that of the commentators, for it is almost impossible to write a commentary on one of the Gospels without mentioning its relations to the others, and some commentators, e.g., W. Allen[12] in his commentary on Mat, have made these relations the principal subject of their study. On the Jewish side the problem of the parallels between the various books of TL was not at first grasped as a single problem - undoubtedly this failure was due to the great mass of the material involved. A second cause was the fact that the material was generally considered, not as a thing in itself, but as a part of the legal tradition of which the great document was the Babylonian Talmud. At all events, the basic synopsis which will give all the parallel passages in parallel columns (not only the passages from those works I have selected as TL, but also the baraitaot of the two Talmuds and the parallel passages from the oldest of the haggadic midrashim) is still a desideratum. How complicated such a synopsis would be, can be imagined from the collection of parallel forms (and these only the ones to be found in the Babylonian Talmud) of a single tradition, printed as an example by Melamed.[13] But the lack of such a synopsis leaves only two possibilities for preliminary research: (1) the collection of parallels without critical study of them - as was done in 'Massoret Hashshas'; (2) the critical study of the parallels to a single book or group of books - as was done by the editors of the various midrashim, by Lieberman in his commentary on Tosefta,[14] Hoffmann and Albeck in their books on the halakic midrashim,[15] and Zuckermandel in his book Tosefta, Mischna u. Boraitha.[16]

Here, of course, it is impossible to attempt an exact answer to the

questions, What are the complete parallels to be found between the
books of TL, or, between the books of the Gospels? It must therefore
suffice to emphasize the fact that, as regards complete parallels, the
relation between one book of the Gospels and another is similar in
many details to the relation between one book and another of TL. To
illustrate this similarity I have chosen one pair of passages from the
Gospels - the sermon on the mount from Mat and the parallel sermon
from Lk - and one pair of passages from TL - Peah 1-3 and Peah T
1. I know, of course, that the relation between Tosefta and the Mishnah changes from tractate to tractate, and that yet other relationships
are to be found between the Mishnah and the midrashim, between
Tosefta and the midrashim, and between one book and another of the
midrashim. I know also that the relationship between the books of the
Gospels changes not only from book to book, and not only from
'source' to 'source,' but also from passage to passage. (Thus, for
example, the relation between Mat and Mk in the passion story is quite
different from that between them in the stories of the Galilean ministry, although, according to the generally accepted theory, the 'source'
of both these sections of Mat is Mk.) Therefore I am sure that the
comparison of the two relatively small pairs of parallels here chosen
will not display all the sorts of parallels of parallelism to be found
between the Gospels and TL. But I think it will display a number of
the more important details, and, should it do so, this will suffice. For
it must be pointed out here, at the beginning, that a comparison of the
relationship between the books of the Gospels with the relationship
between the Mishnah and Tosefta will reveal not only important similarities, but also important differences, and only an examination of all
the material, passage by passage - an examination which would require a synopsis for its undertaking and a work of several volumes
for its completion - would make possible an exact review of these
similarities and differences and an adequate estimation of the evidence
for and against any historical theory as to the nature of the traditions
behind the works studied. Any pretensions to historical significance
thus specifically excluded, I can procede to the comparison of the two
pairs of parallel passages above specified. These are copied out at
length in Appendix C. Their sections there are numbered, and from
here on I shall cite them according to those numbers.
    The striking parallel between 1, 2, and 4 on the one hand, and 32
and 33 on the other, is emphasized by similarity in content - all the
passages contain lists of good or bad characteristics and promises of
pay or punishment - and by similarity of function - all the passages
serve as haggadic introductions to halakic material. But for the purposes of this chapter the interesting thing is that, to a list of blessings,
Mat and the Mishnah add blessings, Lk and Tosefta, curses. 'Blessings' and 'curses' and 'add' are convenient abbreviations, but the relationship can be described abstractly without the use of terms which

imply a development of the text, thus: In Mat and the Mishnah are found long lists of elements similar in one respect, in Lk and Tosefta are found short lists of these same elements together with short lists of elements antithetical to them.

The relationship between Lk 6.20 ('poor') and Mat 5.3 ('poor in spirit'), and between Lk 6.21 ('hungering') and Mat 5.6 ('hungering... after righteousness') is very interesting, and I recall none like it between the books of TL, but the like is often found between a single Gospel and a book of TL (or a law from the Old Testament), e.g., Mat 6.6 'Give not that which is holy to the dogs,' Lk 11.44, 'Woe to you (scribes and Pharisees) for you are like unseen graves, and the men who walk over them do not know (that they have been polluted).' These passages give figurative, moral meanings to the laws about holy things and about unmarked graves: Temurah T 4.11 (556): 'Holy things are not to be redeemed (by substitution of their money value or of an equivalent plus a penalty) in order that they may be fed to dogs.' Zabim T 2.9 (678) 'What is "pollution of the depth"? (Pollution caused by a grave) of which no one anywhere (lit. at the end of the world) knew.' etc.[17]

In 3, Peah T has in the midst of its list a reference to the legally fixed minimum of the peah, which is referred to in Peah (no. 6) after the list. It happens that this is the only instance in these chapters of a change in order between the elements in the Mishnah and those in Tosefta. And even this is not a true change in order, for in spite of the fact that in Peah T the rule appears before the list of curses, yet it immediately follows the list of blessings, and so it does also in the Mishnah. Thinking in terms of the development of the text it would seem likely to guess that the Mishnah added its extra blessings before the rule, and Tosefta its curses after it, but that the position of the rule remained unchanged in both texts. As opposed to this absence of changes of order in the chapters of the Mishnah and Tosefta here cited, the passages cited from the Gospels show many such changes, not only rearrangement of adjacent passages, as of 40 and 41, but also transference over considerable intervening sections, as from 41 to 48. Moreover, whole sections of the Matthaean sermon are found in Lk outside the parallel sermon (e.g., 44 in Lk 12).

In 5, the haggadic introduction of Tosefta is extended by similar material not in the Mishnah. In the same way the introduction in Mat is extended by means of the haggadic material of 34, lacking in Lk.

In 7, the same rule is found in the two passages, and there are only slight verbal differences between them. Such is the relationship between Mat 5.39b and Lk 6.29a, and between Mat 5.42a and Lk 6.30a.

In 10 and 11 is seen a relationship typical of that which exists between Tosefta and the Mishnah. 11 is an explanation of the rule found in 10. But the rule itself is not found in the present text of Tosefta. Therefore the present text of Tosefta presupposes, here, a knowledge of the rule. And since the rule is found in the Mishnah it is a likely guess that the present text of Tosefta presupposes a knowledge of the Mishnah. (This conclusion, however, is not a necessary one, for Tosefta might presuppose a knowledge of some other text, now lost, which also contained the rule.[18] I do not think that a clear case of this sort of relationship is to be found between any passages of the two sermons cited from the Gospels in Appendix C. Whether or not such a relationship is to be found at all between different books of the Gospels, is a much disputed question. W. Howard,[19] for example, thinks that a number of passages of Jn presuppose a knowledge by the reader of complementary passages in the synoptics - or, at least, of the content now found in those passages. But other scholars have maintained that Jn did not know the synoptics at all.[20]

As against this dubious state of affairs, there are many passages in Tosefta which would be quite incomprehensible without a knowledge of the content of the Mishnah (even if they do not presuppose a knowl- of the text of the Mishnah), and there are some passages which re- quire a knowledge even of details of this content, and which have been miscopied by scribes who forgot for a moment such details. For ex- ample: Maaser Sheni T 2.11 (89), where the Erfurt Ms reads, 'R. Jose said, "If, in a box which was used both for profane things and for second tithe, coins should be found, then, if the majority put in it pro- fane things, (the coins are to be considered) profane, and if the ma- jority put in second tithe, second tithe." R. Simon said to him, "And do not peace-offerings contain the breast and the thigh which are pro- hibited to non-Israelites?"' The second sentence is explicable only by the text of the Mishnah (Maaser Sheni 3.2) which reads, 'It is not permitted to purchase produce from the priest's share of the crop with second-tithe money, because one who does so decreases the num- ber of those who can eat the equivalent of the second tithe, but R. Simon permits this. R. Simon said to them, "If the more lenient opin- ion were adopted in the case of peace-offerings, which may be made unfit or profaned by failure to destroy the remnant or by consumption by the unclean, shall we not adopt the more lenient opinion in the case of the priest's share of the crop?" They said to him, "If the more lenient opinion were adopted in the case of peace-offerings, which non- Israelites are permitted to eat, shall we adopt the more lenient opin- ion in the case of the priest's share of the crop, which is forbidden to non-Israelites?"' It is clear that the copyist of the Erfurt MS erred by connecting the words of R. Simon to those of R. Jose, and therefore wrote 'said to him' where he should have written 'said to them,' which, in fact, is found in the Vienna MS and in the printed editions. Such an instance, in which the text of one book is dependent on that of another so closely that neglect of the other is likely to cause error in the copy- ing of the one, is not to be found in the Gospels.

12 contains a digression (on duties in the matter of tithes) found

147

only in the Mishnah. Similarly, for example, 47 contains a digression found only in Mat.

13 contains rules beginning, like the rules in 40-41, with identical words, but afterwards changing, not only in words but also in content, so far that the rules found in one list are quite different from those found in the other. In the beginning of 40-41 the order of the rules is inverted in one of the parallels, a detail not found in 13. In both, the complete or almost complete parallels are found at the beginning and in the middle of the lists, but not at the end. The end of 13 is especially interesting as containing words found in the Mishnah not only in a different place, but in a different meaning. 'If ants nibbled it and if the wind or cattle broke it down' are found here as excuses for division between one field and another, whereas in 16 they appear as conditions which excuse from the duty of leaving a peah. In the same way the words 'and it shall be given you' appear in 45 after 'give,' and in 48 after 'ask,' carrying quite different meanings. In this latter instance, however, it can be supposed that it was only by accident that the two editors of the Gospels used the same words, but as against this supposition it must be remembered that J. Hawkins[21] drew up a considerable list of 'words used with different applications or in different connexions, where the passages containing them are evidently parallel.' The example under discussion is not in Hawkins' list, perhaps because the two passages in which the words are found are not 'evidently parallel'; but the list suffices to prove that the parallels between the Gospels show a number of instances in which the same words are used with different meanings. Moreover, in 23 a single end of a sentence is found attached to two quite different sentences - exactly the use of 'and it shall be given you' in 45 and 48.

The relationship between Mat 5.40 and Lk 6.29 is famous, and I recall no instance in which exactly the same relationship is found between different sayings in TL. However, contradictions between Tosefta and the Mishnah are very frequent. To take an example from Peah: Peah T 2.16 (20) gives all the spikes of grain found in ant-holes to the land-owner, Peah 4.11 divides them - those in the area where the grain is still standing go to the land-owner, those behind the reapers are again divided - the upper go to the poor, the lower to the land-owner. But the curious thing in the relation of these vss. of Mat and Lk is that there is no contradiction as to the general rule, only a reversal in the order of examples.

In 14, 15 and 16 is found a large section of legal material, present in the Mishnah and absent in Tosefta. So Mat twice includes large sections of legal material lacking in Lk, secs. 36-9 and 42. In 17-24 the two texts contain rules for the most part different, but concerning similar subjects - again like 40-41 and the beginning of 45. Thereafter 25-8 contains another legal section found in the Mishnah but lacking in Tosefta, like the passages of Mat mentioned above.

The last of these laws, that found in 28, is interesting because it serves as a transition to a new subject. The question is, What is the smallest area of land on which one is obliged to leave a peah. The Mishnah cites a number of opinions, last among them that of R. Akiba who says that any piece of land, however small, lies under the obligation of peah. Thereafter, in 29-31, appear 3 laws dealing with 'any piece of land, whatsoever' and without any relation to peah. The last two of these laws are found in Tosefta, in spite of the fact that the first of them, and the opinion of R. Akiba which served as a transition to the subject of 'any piece of land,' and the argument in which the opinion of R. Akiba was cited, - all these are lacking in Tosefta; i.e., Tosefta lacks the transition, but contains the material to which the transition leads, in spite of the fact that this material is altogether out of place in the tractate, except as conclusion of the missing transition. In the case of the Gospels, it is possible that such a transition as this was lost from the sermon in Lk 6, but exactly what it contained cannot be determined. One of the most noticeable instances in which one Gospel contains a transition lacking in another is Mat 14.12-13 which parallels Mk 6.29-32. After Herod killed John the Baptist, according to Mat, 'His disciples....buried him and, coming, brought the news to Jesus. And Jesus, hearing, went away.' In Mk this transition is lacking and Jesus' journey is introduced as if without relation to the death of John.

Yet one more detail: In 30 both texts cite the opinion of R. Jose as to the case in which 'a man signs away his possessions to his sons and signs over to his wife any (piece of) land, whatsoever.' There is no contradiction between the two opinions, but that in Tosefta is so worded as to give an impression favorable to the wife, that in the Mishnah so worded as to give an impression favorable to the sons. The best known example of this sort of relationship as found in the Gospels is that of Mk 9.40: 'He who is not against us is for us.' and Mat 12.30 (= Lk 11.23): 'He who is not with me is against me.' One half of another example is found in the sermon on the mount, in Mat 6.22-3, which begins, 'The light of the body is the eye,' and concludes, 'If then the light in you be darkness, how great is the darkness?', whereas Lk 11.34-6, though it begins with the same words, concludes, 'Beware then lest the light in you be darkness. If then your body be all light, having no dark part, it will be all light, as when the lamp with its shining illumines you.'

To sum up, briefly: It has been found that the relations between the complete parallels found between Peah 1-3 and Peah T 1 are very similar to the relations between the complete parallels found between the sermon on the mount in Mat and its equivalent in Lk. This parallelism extends even to many details. However, there are very important differences. The differences in the order of the elements between one Gospel and another are more frequent than those between the

Mishnah and Tosefta. The Gospels do not contain passages in which it is unmistakeably clear that the understanding of one Gospel depends on a knowledge of the content, if not of the text, of another, but the understanding of Tosefta often depends on a knowledge of the Mishnah. From such facts it would be easy to develop a historical theory to the effect that the relation of Tosefta to the Mishnah was closer than that of one Gospel to another because of the different ways in which written sources had been used. But either the demonstration or the refutation of such a theory would require a complete examination of the material.

NOTES

1. These are the conclusions reached by C. Albeck, Untersuchungen über die hal. Midraschim, Berlin, 1927, p. 154.

2. For the material v. Albeck, idem, pp. 21 ff.

3. Tübingen, 1911, p. 5.

4. Rabbinische Wundergeschichten, Berlin, 1933, p. 3.

5. Stuttgart, 1926.

6. pp. 63-5.

7. A. Schweitzer, Geschichte d. Leben-Jesu-Forschung, 4 ed., Tübingen, 1926.

8. P. Wernle, Die synoptische Frage, Leipzig, 1899.

9. A. Schlatter, Sprache und Heimat des vierten Evangelisten, Gutersloh, 1902.

10. C. Burney, The Aramaic Origin of the Fourth Gospel, Oxford, 1922.

11. W. Howard, The Fourth Gospel, London, 1931.

12. The International Critical Commentary, N.Y., 1907.

13. E. Melamed, Halachic Midrashim of the Tannaïm in the Talmud Babli, Jerusalem, 1943, p. 32.

14. S. Liebermann, Tosefeth Rishonim, Jerusalem, 1937-39.

15. D. Hoffmann, Zur Einleitung in die hal. Midraschim, Berlin, 1887. C. Albeck, Untersuchungen etc., cited above n. 1.

16. Frankfurt a.M., 1908-9.

17. The opinion of Strack-Billerbeck in Lk 11.44 ($\mu\nu\eta\mu\varepsilon\tilde{\iota}\alpha \ \overset{\text{\'}}{\alpha}\delta\eta\lambda\alpha$) is certainly wrong. They say: 'Gräber, die als solche nicht für jedermann erkennbar waren und deshalb durch Übergiessen mit Kalktünche oder durch Aufstellen getünchter Steine gekennzeichnet werden mussten.' I think they were led into error by the parallel in Mat 23.27-8. A fine exposition of both passages is found in pp. 352-4 of the article by J. Mann, Rabbinic Studies in the Synoptic Gospels, HUCA, I, 323 ff.

18. On this question see especially the preface by Prof. Lieberman to the photostatic reprint of Zuckermandel's Tosephta, pp. 21 ff.

19. The Fourth Gospel, London, 1931, pp. 149-151. He thinks

Jn 3.24 presupposes Mk 1.14, Jn 6.30 ff. presupposes Mk 14.12-31, and Jn 18.24, 28, 30, 33, 40 presuppose some synoptic form of the passion story, since they refer to details found only in the synoptics.

20. Reviews of the literature on the question of the relation of Jn to the synoptics are found in:

      T. Sigge, Das Johannesevangelium und die Synoptiker, Münster i.W., 1935 (Neutestamentliche Abhandlungen XVI, 2/3 Heft)

      H. Windisch, Johannes und die Synoptiker, Leipzig, 1926 (Untersuchungen zum N.T., Heft 12)

Among the more recent defenders of the theory that Jn was ignorant of the synoptics is P. Gardner-Smith, St. John and the Synoptic Gospels, Cambridge, 1938. Such information as I have on this matter is due to the kindness of Fr. P. Benoit, who found the above books for me.

(Since the composition of this study, Jn's ignorance of the synoptics has also been maintained in a brilliant article by E. Goodenough, John a Primitive Gospel, JBL, 1945, pp. 145 ff.)

21. Horae Synopticae, 2 ed., Oxford, 1909, p. 67. The most striking example in his list is Mat 3.5: 'There went out to him.... all the vicinage of the Jordan.' // Lk 3.3: 'He came into all the vicinage of the Jordan.'

Chapter 8

PARALLELS WITH A FIXED DIFFERENCE

Hitherto parallels have been discussed without any attention - except in a few unusual cases - being paid to the differences between them. But sometimes it is possible to draw up a fairly long list of parallels in all of which the same difference appears, and such a list must be the basis of any theory as to the development or substitution of ideas from one literature to another, and also of any philological account of the change of usage from language to language. This can best be illustrated by a philological example: It has long been known that the use of the passive in Mat is similar to the use of the impersonal in Hebrew, especially in the matter of its use as a respectful circumlocution to avoid the mention of God. (e.g. 'In that measure in which you mete it will be measured to you.' In Hebrew: 'In the measure in which a man measures they measure to him.' where 'they measure' = מודדין, lit. 'measuring,' the m. pl. ppl. Though both of these can be understood as referring to retribution by men, they almost certainly referred primarily to retribution by God.) But in order to prove what is known, it would be necessary to make a list of parallels like the above, each of them containing this fixed difference. In a word, parallels with a fixed difference are the textual basis of all theories of equivalence (as opposed to mere 'similarity').

Here will be discussed only one group of such parallels - those of which the element from TL refers to God and His Law, the element from the Gospels to Jesus and his teachings. So far as I know, parallels of this sort have never hitherto been discussed as a peculiar group, and no student has pointed out the fact that it is common to find a saying which was applied to God in TL applied to Jesus in the Gospels. But R. Charles[1] has already remarked that the Gospels speak of Jesus as the Old Testament speaks of God, and many - though not all - of the individual parallels to be used hereinafter have already been noted by a number of scholars, sometimes with the note that in the Gospels God was replaced by Jesus. Thus, for example, Fiebig, when he notes the famous[2] parallel between Abot 3.2: 'When two sit and speak of the Law the Shekinah rests between them.' and Mat 18.20: 'For where there are two or three gathered together in my name, there am I in the midst of them,' remarks,[3] 'Jesus setzt sich nach diesem Wort an Gottes Stelle.'

But what has always been lacking has been the remark, that the Gospels customarily put in Jesus' mouth, or say of him, what TL puts in the mouth of, or says of, God. Therefore, the novelty of this

152

chapter lies not principally in hitherto unnoted parallels but rather in the emphasis on the fact that <u>the difference noted in these parallels is a fixed difference and one typical of the relationship of the literatures.</u>

I. Jesus = God. Here must first be mentioned the verbal parallels between the Gospels and TL, for the Gospels frequently describe the relationship between Jesus and his disciples in words which might be the Greek translations of those used by TL to describe the relationship of all Israel (or of some Israelites') to God. For example: Mat 10.32-33, Jesus is 'confessed' or 'denied.' (The same words are used in the parallel in Lk 12.8-9, but in Mk 8.38 and Lk 9.26 the word 'deny,' which is equivalent to the Hebrew, is replaced by 'be ashamed of,' to which there is no parallel in the Tannaïtic descriptions of the relationship of Israel to God, but which better describes the feelings of Jesus' disciples in the face of the Greek world.) Mat 11.29-30, Jesus' disciples take his yoke upon them. Jn 14.12-15, His disciples believe in Jesus and pray to him, and he answers for his name's sake; they love him and keep his commandments. Such parallels as these constitute the greater part of the parallels between Jesus and God (as regards their works) to be found between the Gospels and the OT - and hence also between the Gospels and TL.[4] It was of these parallels that Charles wrote (v.s.), and I need not repeat what he has said, though it would be possible to multiply several times the number of his examples, and this especially by means of substitution, for example: Jn 1.11 says of Jesus, 'He came into his own and his own received him not.' Now, according to Jn, those who did not receive Jesus were the Jews; hence it can be concluded that according to Jn the Jews were 'the own,' the 'peculiar people' (τὰ ἴδια = [עם] סגולה) as in the Old Testament and in TL Israel is always the peculiar possession of God.

But apart from these more general usages, there are a number of passages in which the substitution takes place in more nearly complete parallels. Of these one has been mentioned above - Mat 18.20 and its parallel in <u>Abot</u> 3.2. Other parallels to Mat 18.20 are found in <u>Abot</u> 3.6 (and in Mekilta 20.24 and Mekilta of R. Simon ib., parallels only in meaning, without any verbal similarity): 'R. Halafta, a man of Kefar Hannanya, says, "Whence do we know (that, in the case of three who sit and study the Law, the Shekinah is among them?) Because it is said"...."And whence even (in the case of) two?"' etc. Other examples of nearly complete parallels with this fixed difference are the following:

(1) Mat 10.25 (Jesus is speaking to his disciples): 'It is enough for the disciple that he become as his teacher.'
  Sifra 25.23 (God is speaking to Israel): 'You are my servants.' (Sifra comments): 'It is enough for the servant that he be as his master.'

(2) Mat 10.40 (Jesus is speaking to his disciples): 'He who receiveth you receiveth me.' (The parallels in Mat 18.5, Mk 9.37, and Lk 9.48 give three forms of the saying, actually different from this though similar to it.)

Mekilta 18.12 (Mekilta of R. Simon ib., end, bracketed): 'Whoever receives the Sages (lit. the faces of the Sages) is as if he received the Shekinah.' (lit. the faces, etc.) (Most MSS have, 'Whoever receive his companion.')

(3) Mat 13.17 (= Lk 10.24) (Jesus is speaking to his disciples): 'For I tell you truly that many prophets and just men desired to see what you see, and saw not, and to hear what you hear, and heard not.'

Mekilta 15.2: ' "This is my God," R. Eliezer says, "Whence do you (find justification for) saying that a servant girl at the sea saw what Isaiah and Ezekiel did not see? Because it is said" '...

(4) Mat 25.35 and 40 (Jesus is speaking to the just in the last judgment): 'For I hungered and you gave me to eat....I tell you truly, inasmuch as you did to one of the least of these my brothers, you did to me.'

Midrash Tannaïm 15.9, end: 'And so the Holy One, blessed be He, said to Israel, "My children, whenever you feed the poor I count it up for you as if you fed me." '

(5) Jn 5.46 (Jesus is speaking to the Jews): 'For if you had believed Moses you had believed me.'

Mekilta 14.31 (and Mekilta of R. Simon ib.) (spoken of Israel): 'If they believed Moses a fortiori (they believed) the Lord.'

II. The teachings of Jesus = the Law. Here must be mentioned first of all a list of parallels of idiom found within Jn, for Jn cites the words of Jesus with the same formulae with which he cites the Old Testament. This fact was remarked by A. Faure (Die alttestamentlichen Zitate im 4. Evangel. ZNW 21.99 ff.) A similar parallel, but one found between the Gospels and TL, is that between 'I hear....The text says' (שמע הכ.....אני) and 'You have heard....But I say' (ἠκούσατε .... ἐγὼ δὲ λέγω).[5] This parallel is recorded by Abrahams[6] as a discovery of Schechter's. The impression of parallelism is strengthened by the overtone of contradiction which the Tannaïtic expression always has. On the other hand it must be remarked that this expression is found almost only in the midrashim, and that, as was shown above in ch. III, the expression '(and) I say' was also current in TL. Stronger proofs than these for the equation of Jesus' teachings with the Law are found especially in parallels to some verses of the synoptics. Most striking of all is the parallel between Mat 7.24 ff. (= Lk 6.47): 'Therefore, whoever hears these words of mine and does them, will be likened to a wise man who built his house upon a rock.' etc. and Abot 3.17

'Whoever has wisdom greater than his deeds, what is he like? He is like a tree with many leaves and few roots; and the wind comes and uproots it and overturns it on its face, for it is said....But whoever has deeds greater than his wisdom, what is he like? He is like a tree with few leaves and many roots; which, even if all the winds in the world come and blow on it, they cannot move from its place, for it is said'...(Needless to say, 'wisdom' has here its standard rabbinical meaning - knowledge of the Law; and the word 'deeds' means 'practice.')

Of course, those who thought Jesus a Rabbi thought his teaching part of the Law - the oral Law, which lived in the mouths of the Sages - and many parallels show only this idea. So, for example, Mk 4.33: 'And with many such parables he spoke the word to them, as they were able to hear.' Mekilta of R. Simon 19.18 (and Mekilta ib.): ' "Like the smoke of a furnace" Can it possibly mean, really like the smoke of a furnace? The text says....("And the mountain burned with fire." And why does the text say,) "Like smoke"? They let the ear hear what it can hear. (i.e., God speaks to men in terms they can understand.) Similarly....'

I think that here there is nothing more than the notion that, like all other legal teaching, the teaching of Jesus was adapted to the understanding of his listeners. In the Mekilta of R. Simon the reference is to the limits of human understanding, in Mk to the limits of the understanding of listeners from the villages of Galilee, but the underlying idea is identical. And there are even certain passages from which it can be seen that the editors of the Gospels wrote of the words of Jesus as of the words of the Sages (דברי חכמים). Of these passages the clearest is Mk 8.31: 'And he began to teach them that the Son of Man must suffer many things....and be killed and after three days rise again. And he spoke the word openly.' (παρρησία) Cp. Sifre on Deut. 13.7 (and Midrash Tannaïm ib.) ' "Secretly (saying, 'Let us go and serve other gods' ")' This teaches that they speak their words only secretly, and so it says, "In the evening, in twilight" etc. But the words of the Law are spoken only openly.' (בפרהסיא = παρρησία) It is clear that the 'words of the Law' which are 'spoken' are the words of the Sages. Incidentally, the relation of these two passages deserves a little further notice: The fact that Jesus taught openly (παρρησία) is emphasized also in Jn 7.26 'See, he speaks openly, and they say nothing to him.' and in Jn 18.20 (Jesus answers the High Priest): 'I have spoken openly to the world; I have always taught in synagogue and in the Temple where all the Jews assembled, and I have said nothing in secret.' I think this emphasis is explained by the words from Sifre on Deut. cited above, those words being a charge which this emphasis answers.

Further I think the passage in Sifre on Deut. to have been based on the fact that an important part of primitive Christianity was a secret

doctrine which was revealed only to trusted members. Such a doctrine
is suggested by the words put in the mouth of Jesus, speaking to his
disciples[7]: 'To you is given the mystery of the kingdom of God, but to
those outside all things are in parables, that they may surely see and
not perceive.' etc. And Paul himself wrote in I Cor. 2.1-6 'And I,
coming to you, brethren, came not proclaiming the testimony of God
in lofty words or wisdom...that your faith might not be in the wisdom
of men, but in the power of God. But we speak wisdom among the perfect, and a wisdom not of this age...but we speak the wisdom of God in
a mystery.' A similar distinction was recognized by the Tannaïm between material suitable for public teaching and that reserved for
secret teaching, as we learn from Hagigah T 2.1 (233): 'The (passages
of the Old Testament dealing with) forbidden sexual relationships are
not to be expounded to three (at a time,) but may be expounded to two;
and the account of creation not to two, but it may be expounded to a
single hearer; and (Ezekiel's vision of) the chariot may not be expounded to a single hearer unless he be learned in the Law and of good
understanding.'[8] In spite of this the composers of TL thought, as has
been seen, that there was an important difference between the words
of the Law, which were taught openly, and the teachings of the heretics, which were taught secretly. They exploited this difference for
polemical purposes, and their polemic was answered by Mk and Jn,
from whose answers it appears that Mk and Jn thought Jesus' teachings to be 'words of the Law' just as the Jews thought the teachings of
the Sages to be 'words of the Law.'
      But there are other passages which speak of Jesus himself as of
the Law from Sinai, the Law which is the word of God. Only one such
passage is to be found in the synoptics, and even it is dubious, but
comparison with a parallel from TL enables it to be understood in
this sense. Lk 17.22: 'And Jesus said to his disciples, "The days
shall come when you shall desire to see one of the days of the Son of
Man and shall not see it.' // Eduyot T 1.1 (454): 'After the Sages entered the vineyard in Jabneh they said, "The hour will come when a
man will seek for a word from the words of the Law and will not find
(it, and for a word) from the words of the scribes and will not find (it)."'
But as against this single and dubious passage from the synoptics,
there are in Jn a number of very clear passages in which the Gospel
speaks of Jesus as TL speaks of the Law from Sinai.[9] At once the
clearest and the most famous of all is the introduction, Jn 1.1-3: 'In
the beginning was the word and the word was with God and God was
the word. This same was in the beginning with God. All things were
made by him' etc. This parallels Sifre on Deut. 11.10 'The Law, inasmuch as it is more precious than all, was created before all.' and
also Sifre on Deut. 11.22, end: 'Belshazzar, who used for his own
service the implements of the Temple - and they were profane implements - his life was rooted out from this world and from the world to

156

come. He who uses for his own service the implement with which the
world was created, a fortiori his life will be rooted out from this
world and from the world to come.' (The same idea appears in Abot
3.2.)

Especially interesting are such parallels as these in which there
is also a parallel of comparison. Some of the most certain are those
in which the power and teaching of Jesus are compared to water, the
believer and disciple to a well. Thus Jn 4.10-14, 'Jesus answered and
said to her (the Samaritan woman), "If you knew the gift of God, and
who it is who says to you, 'Give me to drink.', you might have asked
him and he might have given you living water....Whoever drinks of this
water will thrist again, but he who drinks of the water which I shall
give him...it will become in him a well of water springing up into
eternal life.' This parallels Sifre on Deut. 11.22 (beginning and middle): 'R. Simon ben Yohai says, "Behold he says, 'Drink water from
your cistern.' (i.e.) Drink of the water you have in the city, and thereafter go about everywhere."....R. Simon ben Menasya says..:"Drink
water from your cistern.' Drink the water of Him who created you
and drink not turbid water nor be drawn after the words of heretics."
R. Akiba says, "Behold he says, 'Drink water from your cistern.' A
cistern from the first cannot produce a drop of water except what was
already in it, so a pupil at first...will contain nothing but what he has
learned. 'And running water from your well'....As a well runs living
water from all its sides, so pupils come and learn from him, and so
it says, 'Your wells will gush forth in the streets'....The words of the
Law were compared to water, as water is life for the world, so the
words of the Law are life for the world." '

The notion that Jesus is life for the world is very common in Jn,
e.g. - to quote the most famous verse in the New Testament - 3.16:
'God so loved the world that he gave his only-begotten Son, that whosoever believeth on him may not perish, but have everlasting life.'
But to return to the matter of water: Jn 7.37-8 reads: 'Jesus stood
and cried saying, "If any thirst let him come to me and drink. He who
believes in me, as the Scripture said, rivers of living water shall flow
from his belly.'[10] The first verse of the Old Testament to which Jn
refers here (by imitation) - Isaiah 55.1 - is expounded also in TL,
where the words of the Law are also compared to water: Mekilta
15.22 and Mekilta of R. Simon ib. (end): ' "And they went three days
in the wilderness and they found no water." The interpreters of things
marked (i.e., symbols? - דורשי רשומות) said, "And they found no
water," (this refers to) the words of the Law which were compared to
water. And whence (do we know) that they were compared to water.
Because it is said, "Ho, whoever thrist, come to the water." ' And
this comparison may perhaps explain the strange passage in Abot
1.11: Abtalyon says, "Sages, be wary in your words, lest you incur
the penalty of exile, and be exiled to a place of bad water, and the

disciples following you drink and die, and the Name of Heaven be thus profaned." '

Along with these passages must be mentioned the hypothesis made by Z. Lauterbach in his article The Ancient Jewish Allegorists,[11] in which he discussed the 'interpreters of things marked' and succeeded in showing that their interpretations were generally allegorical and that several times (e.g., in Mekilta 15.22, the above-cited passage, in which they interpreted 'water' as 'Law'), their interpretations agree with the allegorical interpretations of Philo (who interpreted water as meaning the Divine word.)[12] Moreover, Mekilta 16.31 (and Mekilta of R. Simon, ib.) states, ' "And the house of Israel called its name 'man.' " The interpreters of things marked said, " 'The house of Israel called its name "man." ' " ' Because this piece of exegesis adds nothing whatever to the text, Lauterbach thinks that here was an allegorical interpretation since lost, and supposes that, since Philo saw in manna a symbol of 'the word of God, all-nourishing wisdom,' therefore, 'It is probable that the allegoristic Dorshe Reshumot interpreted the word מן as a רשום , symbol, signifying "the word of God" or "spiritual food." ' In this connection he refers to Mekilta 16.31 where it is said that the manna was like haggada which attracts the heart of a man.[13] But he could have found a much better proof passage in Jn 6.32 ff. 'Therefore Jesus said to them (the Jews), "Truly, truly I tell you, Moses did not give you the bread from heaven, but my father gives you the true bread from heaven, for the bread of God is he who comes down from heaven and gives life to the world...I am the bread of life. He who comes to me will not hunger and he who believes in me will never thirst." ' Need it be repeated that, according to the introduction of Jn, Jesus was the lifegiving word of God? Thus if Lauterbach's hypothesis be correct, Jn, Philo, and the sources of Mekilta, are found in agreement in their interpretation of the word 'manna' as they agreed in their interpretation of the word 'water.' And the theory concerning the interpretation of 'manna' can be strengthened by reference to yet two more passages: Sifre on Numbers 11.6: 'That which the hucksters of the nations of the world sell them passes out from them, but the manna never passes out from them.' (cp. 'He will never hunger' above.) And Mekilta 13.17 'The Blessed-be-He (sic) said, "If I now bring Israel to the (promised) land, at once every man will lay hold of his field and every man of his vineyard, and they will give up (the study of) the Law. But I shall drive them forth in the wilderness forty years, that they may eat manna and drink the water of the well, and the Law will be included in their bodies.' (cp. I Cor. 10.4) But all this is, at best, based on a comparison with what might once have been in Mekilta, and now is not.

More certain is the similarity between Jesus and the Law to be found in the fact that both of them return to the heavens. Of the Law it is said in Sifre on Deut. 32.4: 'A philosopher met the prefect of his province, he said to him, "Let not your mind be moved by the fact that you have burnt the Law, for it returned to the place from which it emerged, its Father's house." ' In Jn 14.2 Jesus says to his disciples, 'In my Father's house are many dwelling-places....I go to prepare a place for you.', and in Jn 16.28 he says, 'I came forth from the Father and have come into the world, again I leave the world and go to the Father.'

I think these passages suffice to show that Jesus appears in the Gospels in a number of places where the parallel passages of TL have God or the Law. So much is fact. A likely inference would be that Jesus occupied in the minds of the authors of the Gospels much the same place as God and the Law occupied in the minds of the authors of TL. But to make such an inference would involve an act of historical faith, for to pass from the observable similarity of words to the hypothetical similarity of ideas which the words may have been meant to express is to pass from the knowable to the unknown.

NOTES

1. R. Charles, Religious Development between the Old and New Testaments, London, 1914, p. 95: 'If to the synoptic conception of Christ to which we have confined ourselves hitherto we add the Johannine and Pauline, the parallel between the relation of Christ to the kingdom in the New Testament and the relation of God to the promised kingdom in the Old Testament becomes still more complete.' To these a third parallel should be added: the relation of God to Israel in TL. cp. the beginning of Mekilta of R. Simon (שכירת עמהם) with the conclusion of Mat.

2. Found both in Strack-Billerbeck on Mat 18.20 and in C. Montefiore, Rabbinic Literature and Gospel Teaching, London, 1930, p. 265.

3. Pirqe 'aboth, Tübingen, 1906, p. 13, n. 3.

4. The most interesting of these is the collection of parallels found for Jn 1.14: 'And the word was made flesh and dwelt among us...full of grace and truth.' Grace and truth come from Ex. 34.6. The Lord dwelt among (ἐσκήνωσεν) Israel in the tabernacle. Full with reference to spiritual qualities is frequent in the Old Testament. (Ezekiel 28.12, wisdom; Eccl. 9.3, evil; Deut. 33.23, the blessing of the Lord; etc.) But to the expression, 'The word was made flesh' - which is the center of Christianity - I remember no parallel.

5. Mat 5.21 ff.

6. Studies in Pharisaism and the Gospels, 1st series, Cambr. 1917, p. 16. He cites Schechter, Studies in Judaism, but does not give the place, and I have not found it in my reading of Schechter.

7. Mat 13.11, Mk 4.11, Lk 8.10.

8. Interesting, the comparison between חכם מבין מדעתו and τέλειος.

9. On the relation between Jn and TL in the matter of meaning see H. Odeberg, The Fourth Gospel, Uppsala, 1929. O. cites many of the parallels here discussed, but does not grasp clearly the notion of a class of parallels with a fixed difference.

10. The corrections of Torrey and of Burney are unnecessary. The notion is found elsewhere both in the Gospels and in TL, and to object that the citation is not found in the Old Testament in these same words merely shows an ignorance of Jn's way of using the Old Testament. (Burney's correction is found on pp. 109 f. of The Aramaic Origin, Torrey's on pp. 108-9 of Our Translated Gospels).

11. JQR, N.S. I. 291 ff. and 503 ff.

12. idem, p. 310.

13. idem, p. 327. The quotation above is from p. 326.

APPENDIX A: The Use of μισθός in the Gospels

Mat 5.11-12: Blessed are you when men shall revile you and persecute you and say everything bad about you falsely, for my sake. Rejoice and be glad, for your pay is great in the heavens. For thus they
persecuted the prophets which were before you.

5.46-7: For if you love those who love you, what pay do you have?
Do not even the tax collectors do the same? And if you greet your
brothers only, what are you doing that is more than usual?

6.1-2: Take care not to do your righteousness (i.e., give alms) before men, in order to be seen by them; and if not, you have no pay with
your Father who is in the heavens. Therefore, when you give alms,
don't have a trumpet blown before you, as the hypocrites do in the
synagogues and in the streets, so that people may praise them. I tell
you truly, they have their pay.

6.5: And when you pray, don't be like the hypocrites, for they love
to pray standing in the synagogues and in the corners of the public
squares, so that they may be seen by everybody. I tell you truly, they
have their pay.

10.40-42: He who receives you receives me, and he who receives
me receives him who sent me. He who receives a prophet because he
is (lit. in the name of) a prophet will get a prophet's pay, and he who
receives a just man because he is a just man will get a just man's pay,
and whoever gives one of these little ones (anything, if) only a cup of
cold water, to drink, because he is a disciple - I tell you truly, he will
not lose his pay.

Mk 9.41 (// Mat 10.42): Whoever gives you a cup of water because
you are Christ's, I tell you truly that he shall by no means lose his
pay.

Lk 6.22-3 (// Mat 5.11-2): Blessed are you when men shall hate you
and when they shall ostracize you and revile (you) and give you a bad
name (lit. cast out your name as bad), because of the Son of Man.
When that happens (lit. in that day), be happy and jump for joy; for see,
your pay is great in heaven. For their fathers treated the prophets
after the same (fashion).

6.32, 35 (// Mat 5.46-7): And if you love those who love you, what
grace have you? For even people who are lax about their religious
observances (lit. the sinners) love those who love them....But love
your enemies and do favours and lend without the hope of getting anything back, and your pay will be great and you will be the children of
the Highest, for He Himself is kind to the unkind and to the wicked.

Jn 4.35-6: Haven't you a saying (lit. Do you not say that), 'Another four months and the harvest comes.'? Behold I tell you, lift up your eyes and see the fields, that they are white for harvest. Already the harvester gets pay and gathers fruit into eternal life, that the sower and the harvester may rejoice together. ('Gathers fruit into eternal life' is an untranslatable Aramaic pun, meaning: (a) he gathers souls into the barn of Johannine salvation; (b) he lays up for himself rewards which will either help him get eternal life, or make it more agreeable once he has it, or both.)

APPENDIX B: The Use of שכר in TL

1. The Eighteen Benedictions, no. 13 (The Palestinian text): Give us (good) pay with those who do Thy will. (Stärk brackets 'good' as an addition from a later period.)

2. ib. (The present form): And give good pay to all those who truly trust in Thy Name, and let our portion be with them forever.

*3. Mekilta 12.6: R. Matteya ben Heresh used to say (in his exegesis of Ezekiel 16), 'The time came for the performance of the oath which the Holy One, blessed be He, swore to Abraham - viz., that he would deliver his descendants - and they had no commandments which they could practise so as to be delivered....The Holy One, blessed be He, gave them two commandments, (those about) the blood of the Passover and the blood of circumcision, which they could practise so as to be delivered....Therefore Scripture put the taking of the Passover victim four days before its slaughter, for pay is not given except on account of practice.'

4. Mekilta 12.13 (again in 12.23): R. Ishmael used to say, 'And is not everything revealed before Him?....Then why does Scripture say, "And I shall see the blood"? (This cannot have its literal meaning), but (must be understood as God's saying, in effect), "As pay for the commandment you are performing, I am revealing myself and having mercy on you." '

5. Mekilta 12.28: 'And they went and did' (The actions are specified individually) to give (assurance of) pay for the going and pay for the doing. (Mekilta of R. Simon: To give them pay of the going as - or, like - pay of the doing. - i.e., as they get paid for the one, so they get paid for the other; or, the pay they get for the one is like the pay they get for the other.)

6. Mekilta 12.39 (again in *14.15 with a different introduction probably attached to it by textual corruption): 'And also they prepared themselves no food for the journey' - (This is written) to make known the virtue of Israel (which was so great) that they did not say to Moses, 'How shall we go to the wilderness when we don't have provisions for the road?' But (instead of saying this) they believed and went after Moses....What pay did they get for that? (Therefore it was said): 'Israel is holy to the Lord.'

*7. Mekilta 13.2 (and, with minor variants, Sifre on Deut. 15.19): (Every first-born male of man and beast) 'Is Mine.' Why was this

163

said, inasmuch as it says (elsewhere), 'Thou shalt devote the male (to the Lord).' (and this implies that it will be His)?....(But this latter clause was put in to tell the reader), 'Devote it in order to receive pay.' (Is that its meaning,) or (does it mean that) if you devoted it, it is devoted, and if (neither you nor anybody else) devoted it, it is not devoted? Scripture says, 'Is Mine' (i.e., is devoted to Me) anyhow, (whether or not somebody has devoted it by a special ceremony). Why, then, does Scripture say, 'Thou shalt devote the male'? (To tell the reader), 'Devote it in order to receive pay.' As a similar example, you may take the text: 'And the priest shall burn (incense) upon it'.... It was already said, 'And Lebanon is not worth burning.' Why, then, does Scripture say, 'And the priest shall burn (incense) upon it'?.... In order to receive pay. As a similar example (take the text), 'The one sheep' (shall be offered)....Why was this said? Was it not already said, 'And its wild animals are not sufficient for a burnt offering'? Then why did Scripture say, 'The one sheep'?....In order to receive pay. As a similar example (take the text), 'And make Me a temple.'... Why was this said? Was it not already said, 'Behold, I fill the heavens'? Then why did Scripture say, 'And make Me a temple'? In order (that those who did what was said) should receive pay for the doing.

*8. Mekilta 13.2: (R. Elazar ben Azaryah) preached on this rule: 'You are standing (before the Lord) to-day, all of you, your young children, your wives,' (for the contractual acceptance of the Law). And how did these young children know to distinguish between good and evil? But (God, when he gave the Law to Moses, prophetically included them in the list of those present, thus indicating that they should be brought), in order to give pay to those who should bring them, and to increase the pay of those who do his will, and to fulfill what was said, 'The Lord desired for the sake of his justice (or, mercy),' etc. (R. Joshua thought this exposition was something new.) (cp. 100, inf.)

9. Mekilta 13.17: The mouth (Pharaoh's) which said, 'Nor, moreover, will I send away Israel' is the same as the mouth which said, 'I will send you away'....What pay did (the Egyptians) get for that? (The commandment,) 'Thou shalt not abominate an Egyptian.' The mouth which said, 'I have never heard of the Lord,' is the mouth which said, 'For the Lord fights for them.'...What pay did they get for that? (The prophesy,) 'Then shall there be an altar to the Lord in the midst of the land of Egypt.'...The mouth which said, 'Who is the Lord that I should obey Him?' is the mouth which said, 'The Lord is the righteous one and I and my people are the wicked.' And what pay did they get for that? (The Lord) gave them a place for burial.

10. Mekilta 14.22: (To make) a comparison, what was the matter (the rivalry of the tribes as to which should first enter the sea) like? (It was like what happened) to a king...who had two sons, one big and one

little. (When) he entered his bedroom at night he said to the little one, 'Get me up with the sun.' and he said to the big one, 'Get me up at nine o'clock.' (Next) day the little one came to get him up with the sun, and the big one wouldn't let him. Since they were standing (and) quarreling (outside his door), their father awoke. He said to them, 'My sons, both of you wanted only to serve me (lit. intended nothing but for my glory), so I also will not unjustly take away your pay.' So the Holy One, blessed be He, said, 'What pay will the children of Benjamin get because they went down into the sea first? The Shekinah will rest (lit. the S's resting, i.e., the destined location of the Temple) in their portion (of the promised land)....And what pay did the tribe of Judah get because they stoned them. Judah was adjudged worthy of the rulership (i.e., produced the royal house).'

*11. Mekilta 14.31: The faith (with) which Israel believed in Him-Who-Spoke-and-the-World-Was was a great thing, since as pay (for the fact) that Israel believed in the Lord the Holy Spirit rested upon them and they sang the song (of Moses)....And so you find that Abraham our father did not inherit this world and the world to come except by virtue of the faith with which he believed in the Lord. For it is said, 'And he believed in the Lord and He reckoned it (as) righteousness on his (part).'

12. Mekilta 15.1: (Continuing the above): R. Nehemya says, 'Anybody who takes upon himself in faith one commandment is worthy that the Holy Spirit should rest upon him, for so we have found in (the case of) our fathers that, as pay for the faith (with) which our fathers believed in the Lord, they were worthy and the Holy Spirit rested upon them and they sang the song.'...And so you find that Israel were not delivered from Egypt except by pay for faith....'It is good to give thanks to the Lord...to declare thy mercy in the morning and thy faithfulness in the nights...for thou hast made me joyful, O Lord, by thy works.'...What caused us to enter into this joy? The pay for that faith which our fathers had (during their life) in this world which is wholly night.... And so you find that the dispersions are gathered only as pay for faith....(So) behold, faith is a great thing in the sight of the Holy One, blessed be He, because as pay for faith the Holy Spirit rested upon them and they sang the song.'

*13. Mekilta 16.13 (end): If the Holy One, blessed be He, thus provided (manna) for those who angered him, a fortiori he will give good pay to the just in the destined future.

*14. Mekilta 16.28: Lest you should say, 'What pay does anyone who keeps the Sabbath get for that?', Scripture says....'He who keeps the Sabbath from profanation also keeps his hand from doing evil.' See, we have learned that everyone who keeps the Sabbath is kept far from transgression.

15. Mekilta 19.2: While I had not yet given you the commandments I advanced you the pay for keeping them (lit. the award of their pay.) For it is said, 'And it came to pass on the sixth day they prepared what (manna) they would bring, and it was double.' And it is written, 'And I shall command my blessing upon you in the sixth year.' etc. Can it be that these (instances are) the only (ones found)? Scripture says, 'And he will give them the lands of the gentiles.' Why? 'In order that they shall keep his statutes and guard his laws.'

*16. Mekilta 19.8: 'And Moses took the words of the people back to the Lord.'...(This was specified) in order to give Moses pay for each individual ascent (of Mt. Sinai) and for each individual descent.

17. Mekilta 19.9: 'And Moses came and told the people': He said to them, 'If you agree to the penalties (for anyone who goes up on Mt. Sinai) gladly, you will receive pay (lit. behold, you are receiving pay), and if not you will receive punishment (lit. as above).' And they agreed to the penalties gladly.

18. Mekilta 20.12: Come and see their pay (that of 2 commandments). It was formerly said, 'Honor the Lord from your wealth.' and over against it is written, 'And your barns shall be full of plenty.' And it said, 'Honor your father and your mother.' and over against it, 'In order that your days may be long.' 'Fear the Lord your God' - 'and to you who fear My Name shall shine forth the sun of righteousness.'... What is said in the case of the Sabbath?... 'Then you will rejoice in the Lord and He will cause you to ride upon the high places of the earth.'

19. Mekilta 20.12 (end): 'Upon the land': On the basis of this they said, 'No human court is charged with the enforcement of any commandment which has its pay stated alongside it.'

20. Mekilta 22.20 (end): Proselytes are dear (to God). For Abraham our father was circumcised only at the age of ninety-nine. For had he been circumcised as a man of twenty or thirty, no one could have become a proselyte except while less than thirty. Accordingly God (lit. the Place) procrastinated with him until he reached 99 years, in order not to lock the door in the face of future proselytes, and to give pay for days and years, and to increase the pay of those who do His will.

21. Mekilta 22.30: 'You shall throw it to the dog'....(This was commanded in order) to teach you that the Holy One, blessed be He, does not unjustly take away the pay of any creature, for it is said, 'And at the children of Israel no dog will stretch his tongue.' The Holy One, blessed be He, said, 'Give him his pay.' And cannot one argue a fortiori: If (matters stand) thus (in the case of) an animal, (in the case of) a man is it not all the more certain that (God) will not unjustly take away his pay?

22. Mekilta of R. Simon 6.2: R. Joshua says, ' "And God spoke unto Moses (saying, 'I am the Lord.')" The Holy One, blessed be He, said to Moses, "I can be trusted to give the pay of Isaac the son of Abraham who gave half a cupful of blood upon the altar." '...R. Judah says.... 'The Holy One, blessed be He, said to him, "I am the Lord of the World, I am full of tender mercies, I can be trusted to give the pay of my children who are held in servitude by the hand of flesh and blood." ' ...R. Joshua ben Karhah says....'The Holy One, blessed be He, said to Moses, "Israel were not worthy that manna should be given them in the desert, but (they deserved) hunger and thirst, nakedness and shame. But what can I do? For I am giving them the pay of Abraham who loved me, (the pay he earned by) what he did in the presence of the ministering angels." '

23. Mekilta of R. Simon 12.16 (end) (also Yom Tob T 2.6 (203)): (There is) a story about Simon the Temanite, (to the effect that once) on the night of a festival, he did not come to the study hall. Next morning R. Judah ben Baba found him (and) said to him, 'Why didn't you come to the study hall last night?' He said to him, '(The opportunity of per-forming) a commandment came to me, and I performed it. An armed body of tax-collectors (or, robbers) entered the city and we feared lest they should trouble the people of the city. We killed them a calf and gave them food and drink and anointed them, in order that they should not trouble the people of the city.' He said to him, 'I shall be surprised if your pay was not consumed by your loss, for see, (the sages) said, "Food is not (to be) prepared, either for gentiles or for dogs, on a holiday." ' (For the equation of gentiles with dogs, see Jesus' reply to the Syrophoenecian woman, Mk 7.27, Mat 15.26.)

24. Mekilta of R. Simon 13.5 (Again in 13.11 (of the first-born) and in
* Sifre on Deut. 17.14 (on the establishment of the monarchy), 18.9 (on the abominations of the gentiles), and 26.1 (firstfruits). Midrash Tannaïm 18.9 and Mekilta Ledebarim 12.29 (printed in Midrash Tan-naïm have statements to the same effect, but adapted to negative com-mandments, the pay being given for not doing.): 'And you shall keep the Passover' - Perform the commandment stated in this matter, for as pay for it you shall enter the land.

25. Mekilta of R. Simon 19.9: Rabbi says...that he (Moses) said to them, (Israel, before he gave them the Law), that pay would be given if they obeyed; and whence (do we learn) that in case they should not obey he declared to them all the penalties? Scripture says...(proof texts).

26. Mekilta of R. Simon 20.1: 'And God spoke (all these words, say-ing)': (He said,) 'I exact penalties according to these rules, and I (am He) who gives pay according to these rules.'

27. Mekilta of R. Simon 20.5 (bracketed): 'For I am the Lord your God': (This) teaches that they (Israel, at Mt. Sinai) saw the aspect (of God) which is going to give the just (their) pay in the destined future.

28. Mekilta of R. Simon 20.11: Why was it said 'For in six days God made the heavens'? Only to (justify the) exaction of penalties from the wicked, because they destroy the world which was six days being created, and to give good pay to the righteous because they maintain the world which was six days being created. (cp. inf. 115)

29. Mekilta of R. Simon 20.20: 'And Moses said to the people'....Formerly (when you sinned) you were sinning in ignorance, now (if you sin you will be) sinning deliberately; formerly you did not know the pay of the just and the plague (which is the) punishment of the wicked in the destined future, now you know the pay of the just, etc.

30. Mekilta of R. Simon 22.26: 'For he (the poor man who is oppressed) will cry unto me and I shall hear, for I am merciful.' (This is to be understood as God's saying,) 'In spite of the fact that I exact penalties according to these rules, I am (also) He who gives pay according to these rules.' R. Simon used to say, 'The people who love money love one another, and the robbers love one another,...Who can becomingly exact penalties from all these? "I," He in whom there is no one of all these characteristics.' (Cp. Mat 5.46-8; Lk 6.32-5)

31. Mekilta of R. Simon 6.3: 'And I appeared to Abraham, Isaac and Jacob as God Most High'....(In the case of) the patriarchs, when the Holy One, blessed be He, revealed himself to them to command them, he did not make conditions with them (as he did later, saying,) 'If you walk in my statutes' and 'If you loathe my statutes.' Why? Because they knew the importance of the pay of the just and the punishment of the wicked and did not need to be warned formally of them. But as for the rest of the prophets, - would that several times he would specify to them the pay of the just and the punishment of the wicked!

*32. Sifra 5.17 (end): R. Akiba says, 'He who eats fat brings a sin offering costing a sela; (if there be) doubt (whether) he ate or didn't eat, he brings a conditional guilt offering costing two sela's. If Scripture thus punished one into whose hand came (sic, but prb., who came into the hands of, i.e., fell into) a suspicion of transgression, how much more will it award pay to him who performs a commandment?' (cp. 34 and 69 below.)

*33. Sifra 5.17 (end): R. Jose says, 'If you want to know the pay of the just in the destined future, go and learn from Adam the primal man (lit. hakkadmoni), who was given only one commandment, (and that one only) a prohibition, and transgressed it. See how many deaths entered into him and into his descendants and into the descendants of his

descendants, to the end of his descendants.' And now which is the
greater characteristic (of God's government)? Is the characteristic
of goodness greater, or the characteristic of punishment? Say, "The
characteristic of goodness." If, the characteristic of punishment being
minor, behold!, so many deaths entered into him and into his descendants and into the descendants of his descendants to the end of all the
generations, (then) he who turns away from (eating) sacrifices offered
without proper intention and sacrifices left over (beyond the time in
which they might legally have been eaten), and he who humbles himself on the Day of Atonement, he, a fortiori, acquires merit for himself and for his descendants and for the descendants of his descendants, to the end of all the generations.' (Cp. Rom. 5)

*34. Sifra 5.17 (end) (Also in Midrash Tannaïm 17.6, and *Makkot 1.7):
R. Akiba says, 'Behold, He says, "By the mouth of two witnesses or
of three." If evidence (given) by two is legally sufficient to establish
fact, why did the Scripture specially mention three? Only to include
the third, to subject him to a more severe (law than would otherwise
be applicable), to make his case analogous with (that of) these (first
two). [Thus, e.g., if three men connive in giving false witness, in
spite of the fact that the testimony of the first two legally established
the fact, and the testimony of the third did not, therefore, legally help
to establish it, nevertheless the third shall be liable to the same
punishment as the others.] If the Scripture thus (decreed that) the unnecessary accomplice of those who commit iniquity should be punished
(as are those who commit iniquity), how much more will it award pay
to (the unnecessary assistant of) those who perform a commandment
as (it does to) those who perform a commandment.' (cp. 32, sup. and
69 inf.)

35. Sifra 7.33: And thus R. Simon used to say, 'See, it says, " 'Who
even among you will (so much as) close the doors,' saith the Lord of
Hosts, 'And I shall not accept with favor an offering from your hand?'"
There are two things serviceable to the body which men do not refuse
to perform (for each other) and for which they do not take pay. For a
man says to his fellow, "Light me this lamp." and "Do me (the favor)
of shutting the door after you." No one refuses to do these things,
and no one takes pay for them. (But God says,) "You have not done
these things for (lit. with) me (without) pay. And is it not a fortiori
(that) if, when you have done for me those things for which men do not
receive pay, you have not gone unrewarded, (then) all the more so (you
will not go unrewarded if you do for me) those things for which men do
receive pay?

36. Sifra 8.29: 'And Moses took the chest and waved it as a wave-
offering before the Lord.' (This) teaches that the Holy One, blessed
be He, does not unjustly take away the pay of any creature. And thus

he says, 'Who even among you will (so much as) close the doors' and 'You shall not see my altar for nothing.' (Cp., beside 35, also 21. The last quotation is ambiguous in Hebrew as in the above translation; in the Bible it means, 'You shall not come to my altar without bringing something.' Here, 'without getting something.')

37. Sifra 10.3: When Aaron knew that his sons were known of God (lit. the Place) he kept silent and received pay for his silence. Hence they said, '(If) anyone accepts (divine punishment) and keeps silent, (that is) a good sign for him.'

*38. Sifra 18.2 (Also 18.5, twice, 14, 15, 19. The first instance in 5, and that in 19, contain only the last clause, the others only the last two clauses. The last clause is found also in *19.37; *22.31, 33; 26.2 and Sifre Zutta 15.41): 'I am the Lord your God.' I am the Lord (of whom it can be said) that 'I spoke and the world was.' I am a judge, I am full of tender mercies, I am a judge to exact penalties and I can be trusted to give pay.

39. Sifra 18.3 (again in 27): 'Why did the Canaanites deserve to dwell in their land forty-seven years (after the punishment of the Egyptians, since they were just as wicked as the Egyptians)?...Only for the sake of pay, because they honored Abraham our father.

40. Sifra 26.9: 'And I shall be free for you.' To make a comparison, what is this like? It is like a king who hired many laborers, and there was there one laborer who worked for him a long while. The laborers came in to get their pay, and that laborer came in with them. The king said to him, 'My son, I shall be free for you (in a moment). These many (laborers) are those who did little work for me, and I am giving them little pay, but as for you, I have a large account to settle with you.' So Israel were asking their pay of God and the gentiles also were asking their pay of God. And God says to Israel, 'My children, I shall be free for you (in a moment). These gentiles did little work for me, and I am giving them little pay, but as for you, I have a large account to settle with you.' Therefore it is said, 'And I shall be free for you.'

*41. Sifre on Numbers 10.29 (middle): And whence (do we learn) that the children of Jonadab ben Rekab are identical with the children of Jethro. (From the fact) that it is said, 'They are the Kenites who came because of the father of the house of Rekab.' What pay did they get for that (i.e., for going to Jabez to learn the Law? They got that pay which is described in the following quotation:) 'And Jeremiah said to the house of the Rekabites, "Thus saith the Lord of Hosts the God of Israel, 'Inasmuch as you have obeyed the commandments of Jonadab your father, Jonadab ben Rekab shall never be without a man to stand before me.'"' R. Joshua says, 'And do gentiles in fact enter the Holy

Place? And is it not (the fact that) no Israelite, (as opposed to Priest), entered the Holy Place? But (what is meant is) that they were sitting in the Sanhedrin and expounding the words of the Law:' But there are some who say (that some) of their daughters were married to priests and (some) of their grandchildren offered sacrifices upon the altar. And see, matters stand a fortiori: If these, who brought themselves near, were brought so (much) nearer by God (lit. the Place), then how much more so (those of) Israel who obey the Law. And so you find in (the case of) Rahab. (etc.)

42. Sifre on Numbers 12.8 (end): 'And he unrolled it (the book given Ezekiel, Ez. 2.10) before me and it was written inside and out.' And do not even persons of no special intelligence and without much education do so (i.e., write on both sides of a scroll)? And why should Scripture say, 'inside and out'? 'Inside' (refers) to this world and 'outside' (refers) to the world to come. 'Inside' is the rest of the wicked and the punishment of the just in this world, and 'outside' is the pay of the just and the punishment of the wicked in the world to come.

*43. Sifre on Numbers 15.41 (middle): 'I am the Lord your God.' Again, why was it said? And was it not said already?...And why did Scripture say again, 'I am the Lord your God'? In order that Israel should not say, 'Why did God (lit. the Place) command us? (Was it) not in order that we should perform and receive pay? (Well, we prefer) not to perform, and not to receive the pay.' As Israel said to Ezekiel (20.1)....'Does not a slave whose master sold him go out of (that master's) authority?' He said to them, 'Yes.' They said to him, 'Since God (lit. the Place) sold us to the nations of the world, we went out of his authority.' He said to them, 'Consider: Does a slave whose master sold him on the condition that he should revert (to the seller's possession) go out of his authority? And that (thought) which arose in your spirit will not come to fulfillment, (that thought) which you (expressed in) saying, "Let us be like the gentiles who are round about us."..."As I live," saith the Lord, "If I shall not reign over you with a strong hand and with an outstretched arm and with outpoured wrath."' 'With a strong hand,' this is the pestilence;...'And with an outstretched arm,' this is the sword;...'And with outpoured wrath,' this is famine. (But God's meaning was,) 'After I bring on you these three punishments, one after another, then, after that, I will reign over your against your will.'

*44. Sifre on Numbers 15.41 (end): R. Nathan says, 'You cannot find any commandment in the Law which does not have beside it (the promise of) the pay to be given (for performing) it. Go and learn from the commandment (to put) tassels (on your garments). There is a story of a certain man who was careful in (his observation of) this

171

commandment about tassels. He heard that there was a prostitute in a seaport city....When he got to the act itself, his four tassels came and appeared to him as four witnesses and struck him on the face. He immediately got out (of bed) and sat on the ground. She also got out and sat on the ground. She said to him, "By the Agape of Rome, I shan't let you rest till you tell me what fault you saw in me." He said to her, "By the (Divine) Service, I saw no fault in you, for there is not in all the world the like of your beauty. But the Lord our God gave us one (comparatively) unimportant commandment, and wrote in it 'I am the Lord your God, I am the Lord your God,' twice: 'I am the Lord your God' - I shall surely give pay; 'I am the Lord your God' - I shall surely exact penalty." She said to him, "By the (Divine) Service, I shall not let you rest till you write me your name and the name of your city and the name of your school in which you learn the Law." And he wrote (them) for her....She thereupon disposed of all her property...and came and stood in the school house of R. Hiyya.' She said to him, "Rabbi, make me a proselyte." He said to her, "Can it be that you have your eyes set on one of the students?" She produced for him the writing which she had with her. He said to him (the student), "Stand up and acquire legal right to your purchase." (i.e., Take her.) "Those same bed-clothes which she spread for you when (that was) forbidden, she shall spread for you when (it will be) permitted. This is her pay in this world, and in the world to come I know not how much." (cp. 51 inf.)

45. **Sifre on Numbers 27.22:** 'And he took Joshua' - he took him by words and taught him the pay, in the world to come, of those who nourish Israel (viz. national leaders).

46. **Sifre Zutta 5.28:** 'And she (the woman suspected of adultery, and proved by ordeal to be innocent) shall be sown seed.' R. Eliezer says, 'The suffering (involved in the trial) was sufficient so that children will be given her (as) her pay, so that if she were (formerly) sterile she will be visited.'...R. Simon says, 'Pay is not given for transgression. But (the text includes this detail because, did it not, one might argue that) as she was formerly, (while under suspicion), forbidden for seed (i.e., forbidden to have intercourse with her husband) she may possibly be so in the future. (Therefore) the Scripture says, "And she shall be sown seed." '

47. **Sifre Zutta 6.26 (end):** Beloved is peace, for (in return for) all (good) actions and meritorious deeds which Abraham our father did, God (lit. the Place) gave him nothing as his pay save peace....And so you find in (the case of) Pinhas that God gave him nothing as his pay save peace....And so you find that the Holy One, blessed be He, gave no pay for the study of the Law save peace....And so you find that God gave no pay to those who do works of charity save peace.

48. Sifre Zutta 10.29 (middle, following the examples of Rahab, the Gibeonites, and Ruth.): See, God (lit. the Place) gives any instrument which does anything in his service its pay. And thus he says, 'And Moses said to Hobab ben Reuel the Midianite, the father-in-law of Moses.' This was his (reward) for everything, that he should be called the father-in-law of the King.

49. Sifre Zutta 10.32: 'And if you will come with us, then that good which the Lord will do with us, we will do to you.' 'That good,' this is the Temple....Another explanation, 'That good,' this is the Law.... Another explanation, 'That good,' this is the pay of the just....He promised him that his sons should have a share in all these.

50. Sifre Zutta 11.31: (With reference to the quail and the manna): Can't one argue a fortiori: If God (lit. the Place) thus had mercy on those who transgress his will in this world, how much the more will he give good pay to the just in the destined future?

51. Sifre Zutta 15.41: Another explanation: In (connection with) the commandment about tassels it is twice said, 'I am the Lord your God': 'I am the Lord your God' - to exact a penalty from anyone who abrogates it and denies it; 'I am the Lord your God' - to give pay to him who fulfills it and admits it.

52. Sifre Zutta 18.31: 'And you (Levites) shall eat it (your share of the tithe) anywhere...for it is pay for you in exchange for your service in the tabernacle. (You are) like men who received their pay, pay for what they did with me in the wilderness.

53. Sifre Zutta 27.1: 'Then came the daughters of Zelofehad, the son of Hefer, the son of Gilead.' See, every pure man who arises in the midst of a wicked generation acquires the right to receive all its pay. Noah arose in the generation of the flood and acquired the right to receive all its pay. Abraham arose in the generation of the division and acquired the right to receive all its pay. Lot arose in the generation of Sodom and acquired the right to receive all its pay. These (above mentioned) arose in the generation of the wilderness and acquired the right to receive all its pay.

54. Sifre Zutta 28.2: R. Judah says, '(The text says), "My sacrifice, My bread"....Does God actually eat and drink? (No, for) the text says, "For my sacrifices made by fire," since they offer (them) for sacrifices made by fire....If so, why was it said, (continuing the above) "The sweet savour which I delight in, you shall take care to offer me at its proper time."? In order to increase the pay of Israel.'

55. Sifre on Deut. 1.1: Why does the text say, 'The words of Kohelet'? It teaches that they were words of rebuke. For it is said, 'And the sun rises and the sun sets...goes to the south and comes around to the

north....All the rivers go to the sea.' (The text) symbolized the wicked by sun and moon and sea which get no pay.

56. Sifre on Deut. 1.6: 'It is great for you, (your) dwelling in this mountain' (an idiom, meaning, 'You have dwelt in this mountain too long.' The commentary deliberately misinterprets): Your dwelling in this mountain is pay for you; your dwelling in this mountain is profit for you; you have taken upon you the Law, you have appointed over you seventy elders, etc.

57. Sifre on Deut. 6.5: 'And you shalt love the Lord your God.' Perform (the commandments) from love. The text distinguished between the man who performs from love and the man who performs from fear; from love - his pay is doubled and redoubled.

58. Sifre on Deut. 6.7: 'And you shall repeat them to your sons,' (so) that they will be ready in your mouth....What (is the) pay for this? 'Peoples shall fall beneath you.' etc.

*59. Sifre on Deut. 11.12 (Here the text is probably corrupt. In the first instance 'in pay of' is found in all MSS but one (Assemani 32), which has 'for the sake of'; in the second instance, 'in pay of' is found in all MSS. Finkelstein has adopted the reading of Assemani 32 in the first instance and has emended the second to the same reading, remarking in his note that there is here no question of pay.): 'A land which the Lord your God looks after.' And does He look after it alone? And does He not look after all the lands?....And why should the text say, 'A land which the Lord your God looks after'? As it were, He does not look after any save it, and for the sake of (or: in pay of) the care (with) which He looks after it, He looks after all the (other) lands along with it. As a like case you might instance....'The keeper of Israel.' And does He keep Israel alone? And does not he keep everything?...And why should the text say, 'The keeper of Israel'? As it were, He does not keep any save Israel, and for the sake of (or: in pay of) the keeping with which He keeps them, He keeps all things along with them.

60. ib.: Another explanation, 'A land which the Lord your God looks after.': This declares that it was given (to Israel) as pay for interpretation (Heb. 'looking-after' sc. of the Biblical text), for it is said, 'And you shall teach them to your sons.' etc.

*61. Sifre on Deut. 11.13: And just as (the text threatens) punishment for (neglect) of the study (of the Law) more than (for the neglect of) the practice, so it appoints pay for the study more than for the practice, for it is said, 'And you shall teach them to your sons, to speak of them.' (And) what does it (go on to) say? 'In order that your days and the days of your sons may be many.' And it says, 'And He will give them the treasures of (the) gentiles, and they shall inherit the toil of nations.'

174

APPENDIX B

62. Sifre on Deut. 11.14: 'And I shall give the rain of your land in its season.'...R. Nathan says, 'In its season,' (i.e.) every Friday night the way they came down in the days of Queen Shelamzu.' And why all this? Rabbi says, 'In order not to give an opening to the peoples of the world to say, "See, the pay of all the commandments (is) only...'I shall give your rains in their seasons.'"' (i.e. - according to Friedmann, ad loc. - they will fall every Friday night in order to prove the miraculous nature of the pay.)

63. Sifre on Deut. 11.29: 'And it shall come to pass, when (the Lord your God) shall bring you (unto the land)': Take upon yourself the commandment stated in the context (to put the blessing on Gerizim and the curse on Ebal) because in pay for it you shall enter the land.

64. Sifre on Deut. 12.20: 'When the Lord your God will enlarge your border.' Perform the commandment stated in the context (to abstain from eating blood), because in pay for it the Lord your God will enlarge your border.

65. Sifre on Deut. 12.29: 'When the Lord your God will cut off the nations.' Perform the commandment stated in the context (to abstain from idolatry), because in pay for it the Lord your God will cut off the nations.

66. Sifre on Deut. 15.4: 'Which the Lord your God giveth thee to take possession of.' As pay for taking possession you shall subdue (the promised land).

*67. Sifre on Deut. 15.10, the second, third and fourth sentences are also in *Peah T 4.17 (24)): 'For because of this thing (giving to the poor) the Lord your God will bless you in all your doings.' If (a man) said he would give and gave, he is given (lit. they give him) pay for saying and pay for doing. If he said he would give and did not find it in his power to give, he is given pay for saying, like pay for doing. If he did not say that he would give, but said to others, 'Give.', he is given pay for that, for it is said, etc....If he did not say that he would give and did not say to others, 'Give,' but was gentle to (the beggar and answered) him with good words, whence (do we learn) that he is given pay for that, the text says, 'For because of this thing' (and thing, in Hebrew, is also word.) (cp. 84 inf.)

68. Sifre on Deut. 18.14 (Midrash Tannaîm as in 24, sup.): 'For these nations whom you disinherit.' Perform the commandment stated in the context (to abstain from withcraft) because in pay for it you disinherit these nations.

*69. Sifre on Deut. 23.8: 'Do not abominate an Egyptian.' Why? 'Because you were a sojourner in the land of Egypt.' R. Elazar b. Azaryah said, 'The Egyptians did not receive Israel save for their own sake, and (nevertheless) God (lit. the Place) appointed pay for them.

175

Can't one argue a fortiori: If one who did not intend to perform a virtuous action and (nevertheless) did so is rewarded by the Scripture as if he performed a virtuous action, he who intends to perform a virtuous action (and does so), a fortiori. (cp. 32 and 34 sup.)

70. Sifre on Deut. 23.21: 'Upon the land whither you are going to inherit it.' As pay for going you will inherit.

*71. Sifre on Deut. 25.3 (end. Also *Makkot 3.15): R. Simon the son of Rabbi says.... 'If, (in the case of) blood, from which a man's soul revolts, the man who abstains from it gets good pay, (then in the case of) theft and forbidden sexual relations, which a man's soul delights in and values highly, it is a fortiori that the man who abstains from them will acquire merit for himself and for his descendants to the end of all generations.

*72. ib. (Also in*Makkot 3.15 in the name of R. Simon): Rabbi says.... Anyone who sits still and does not commit transgression is given pay as one who performs a commandment.

*73. Sifre on Deut. 25.15: '(Have a full and just weight (in your scales))...in order that your days may be long.' This is one of the commandments in the law which has beside it the award of its pay. And do not matters stand a fortiori: If for a dried fig which is worth only a hundredth of a cent the Law gave length of days, how much more so for the other commandments which involve financial loss?

74. Sifre on Deut. 26.9: 'And He brought us to this place.' As pay for our coming to this place He gave us this land.

75. Sifre on Deut. 32.1 (between the middle and the end): And can't one argue a fortiori: If these (the heavens, the sun, the earth, the sea, etc.) which were not made for pay and not for penalty, (which) if they be found innocent do not receive pay, and if they sin do not receive punishment, and (which are not restrained from sin by) consideration for their sons and for their daughters (because they don't have any), - (if these) did not change from their appointed ways; (then) you, who if you be found innocent do receive pay, and if you have sinned do receive punishment, and (who should be restrained from sin by) consideration for your sons and your daughters (to whom the punishment or reward you deserve will be extended) - a fortiori it is necessary that you should not change from your appointed ways (lit. your characters).

*76. Sifre on Deut. 32.4: Another explanation: 'The Rock,' i.e., the Mighty, 'His work is perfect.' i.e., the work of the inhabitants of the world is complete before Him (i.e., He sees the whole course of human existence as finished [tam, cognate with tamim above translated perfect] and the individuals as already in their final condition) - the

award of the pay of the just and the award of the punishment of the
wicked. These, in this world, got nothing of what was theirs, and
those, in this world, got nothing of what was theirs,...When will these
and those (alike) get (their due)?...To-morrow, when He sits on the
seat of judgment....A God of faithfulness: As to the confirmed saint
he gives in the world to come the pay for (any) commandment which
the latter performed in this world, so, in this world, he gives the confirmed sinner the pay for (any comparatively) unimportant commandment which he performed; and as, in the world to come, he exacts
from the confirmed sinner the penalty for (any) transgression which
he committed in this world, so, in this world, he exacts from the confirmed saint the penalty for (any comparatively) unimportant transgression which he committed in this world. (cp. 89 inf.)

77. Sifre on Deut. 32.9 (end): (Another explanation: 'Jacob is the lot'
- i.e., in Hebrew, 'rope' - 'of his inheritance'....) As a typical rope
is of three strands, so Jacob was third among the patriarchs and received the pay of all of them.

*78. Sifre on Deut. 32.47: 'For it (the word of the Lord) is not a vain
thing for you.': There is not an empty word in the Law, (a word) such
that if you will investigate it (you will find) that it does not imply the
award of pay (here also, profit) in this world and the principal's remaining intact for the individual (and due to be given him in) the world
to come.

79. Sifre on Deut. 33.6: 'Let Reuben live,' in (virtue of his part in)
the affair of Joseph, 'And let him not die,' in (virtue of) the affair of
Bilhah. R. Hananya b. Gamliel says, 'Merit is never exchanged for
guilt, nor guilt for merit, except that of Reuben and that of David'....
And the Sages say, 'Merit is never exchanged for guilt, nor guilt for
merit, but pay is given for the (performance of) commandments and
men are punished for the transgressions (they have committed). And
why does Scripture say, "Let Reuben live and let him not die."? Because Reuben repented.'

80. Sifre on Deut. 33.21: 'And he shall come the heads of a people':....
(This) teaches that Moses is destined to enter (the world to come) at
the head of every single company (of saints) - at the head of the company of authorities on the Bible, at the head of the company of authorities on the traditional Law, at the head of the company of authorities
on the study (of the Law); and he receives pay with every single one.

81. Midrash Tannaïm 3.25: Why did Moses put himself to such trouble
to enter the land of Israel? Was it, perhaps, to eat of its fruits?....
(No), but Moses spoke thus, 'Master of the world, there are many commandments which Thou hast given Israel by me and which are not to
be performed except in the land of Israel....I shall go in with them (the

Israelites) and with them I shall perform the commandments in order
that I shall receive pay in the destined future.' The Holy One, blessed
be He, said to him, 'Do not distress yourself about this matter, for I
(shall) declare in writing, by the prophets, that (whenever) even a single individual from Israel does and performs one of all the commandments which I have given by you, you have a share with him (in the
reward which will be given) in the destined future.

82. Midrash Tannaïm 11.31 (and Sifre on Deut. 17.14): 'And you shall
take possession of it (the promised land) and you shall dwell in it.'
As pay for taking possession of it you shall dwell (in it).

83. Mekilta Ledebarim, 12.19: 'Take heed that you hear' etc. Why
was this said, since it says, 'And you shall hear, O Israel, and take
care to do.'? (From this latter text) can be deduced only that one receives pay for taking care. And whence (can it be deduced that pay is
given) also for hearing? The text says, 'Take care that you hear.'
Whence, for doing? The text says, 'And you shall take care and you
shall do.' Whence, for studying? The text says, 'And you shall learn
them.'... Whence, for teaching? The text says, 'And you shall teach
them to your sons.' etc.

84. Midrash Tannaïm 16.20: 'Justice, justice shalt thou pursue.' (The
interpretation puns on zedek, justice, and zedakah, almsgiving.)....
See, he who did not have it in his power to give alms, but who was
asked to go and entreat others to give alms, and went...is given credit
as if he gave from his own (goods), for it is said, 'Justice, justice
shalt thou pursue.' (This means,) 'Pursue after almsgiving and after
the returning of kindnesses.' What pay does one get for that? 'He
who pursues almsgiving and mercy will find life, righteousness (also
zedakah) and glory.' (cp. 67, sup.)

85. Midrash Tannaïm 23.23: 'And if you cease to vow, that will be no
sin on your part.' Why was this said? Because (had it not been) I
should have said, 'Since a man gets pay for them (his vows) when he
performs them, if he should sit still and not make (them) he will get
punishment for (not making) them. The text says, 'And if you cease'
etc....And see, matters stand a fortiori: If (in the case of) things for
which a man gets pay, he does not get punishment for (neglecting)
them should he sit still and not do them, (then in the case of) things
for which he gets punishment, it follows that, should he sit still and
not do them, he will get, for (not doing) them, pay and something over.

86. Midrash Tannaïm 25.15: 'In order that your days may be long.'
This is one of the commandments in the Law which has its pay (stated)
alongside it. Abba Hannin (says) in the name of R. Eliezer, 'No (human) court is charged with the enforcement of any commandment
which has its pay (stated) alongside it.' (cp. 19 and 73 sup.)

87. Midrash Tannaïm 31.14 (middle): Moses answered and said before the Holy One, blessed be He, 'It is written in Thy Law, "You shall give (a workman) his pay in the day (on which he does the work)." I, who have served Israel forty years in the desert, have (received) no pay. I (stand) before Thee, O Master of the world, like (one of those who danced before) a bride....And the young men were dancing before her. When they reached the bridechamber others came and drove away the first and entered with her. And the last were sitting with her eating and drinking, and the first went away in disappointment....(So) also I, if I do not enter the land of Israel - see, I am weary and go away in disappointment, with no pay.' The Holy One, blessed be He, said to him, 'As you live, I am giving you all your pay, complete, in the destined future, more than all Israel.' (Apart from the many striking parallels of thought between this and the Gospels, there is one interesting parallel in a detail of the literary form: The situations compared are similar, but their component parts are not accurately correlated. Moses says, 'I am like a bride,' when he means 'I am like one of the young men who danced before a bride.' So in the parables of the Gospels. 'The Kingdom is like a man seeking pearls'; actually it is like one of the pearls.)

88. ib.: He (Moses) said before Him, 'Master of the world, (is it) as pay for the trouble which I have taken with Israel that Thou sayest to me, "You shall not pass over."?'....The Holy One, blessed be He, said to him, 'I have created my world as a series of archai. Was it because Abraham sinned that he departed from the world? (No,) but because the arche of Isaac came pressing on....And now the arche of Joshua presses on.'

89. Midrash Tannaïm 32.34: The just have not received anything of their (due)...and the wicked have not received anything of their (due)... When (are) these and those (alike) going to get their pay. To-morrow. (cp. 76, sup.)

90. Midrash Tannaïm 32.35: 'Vengeance is mine and repaying.' 'And I shall repay' is not written, but 'and repaying.' The Holy One, blessed be He, said, 'I have already repaid the nations of the world the pay of (any comparatively) unimportant commandment which they performed before me in this world.'

91. Midrash Tannaïm 33.7: When Reuben saw that Judah arose and confessed (his sin), he also arose and confessed his sin....What pay did they get for that? The land was given to them alone.

92. Berakot T 4.16-18 (10-11): There is a story about R. Tarefon (to the effect that) he was sitting in the shade of a dove-cote on a Sabbath (with his disciples around him)....He said to them, 'I shall ask a question.' They said to him, 'Teach us, Rabbenu.' He said to them, 'Why did Judah deserve the kingdom (i.e., deserve to produce the royal

house)?' They said to him, 'Because he confessed in (the affair of) Tamar.'...He said to them, 'Is pay, then, given for transgression? But why did Judah deserve the kingdom?' (They said to him), 'Because he delivered his brother from death.'...He said to them, 'The delivery was sufficient to atone for the sale, but why did Judah deserve the kingdom' (They said to him,) 'Because of humility (because he offered to stay in Egypt as Joseph's prisoner in place of Benjamin).' ...He said to them, 'And was he not a guarantor (of Benjamin's return)?...But why did Judah deserve the kingdom? Because he hallowed the Name of God (lit. the Place) at the (Red) Sea (by going down into it first.)'

93. Berakot T 7.13 (16): He who says the blessing (in circumcision) says, 'Who hallowed (His) beloved from the womb, placed a law in his flesh, sealed his offspring with the sign of the holy Covenant; therefore as pay for this, O living God, our portion, our rock, command to deliver our beloved flesh for the sake of His commandment which He put on our flesh; blessed be He who maketh the Covenant.'

94. Hallah T 2.10 (99): All these 24 gifts of the priesthood (i.e., perquisites of the priests) were given to Aaron and to his sons with general (laws) and with (laws about) particular (details) and a covenant of salt, so that (men) should be found guilty (if they transgressed) the general and found guilty (if they transgressed) the particular, and so that pay should be given for (the observance of) the general and pay should be given for (the observance of) the particular.

95. Sukkah T 4.28 (200): No bad neighbors received pay except Jeshbab who was the neighbor of Bilga and received pay (the right to serve in the Temple.)

96. Yebamot T 4.4 (244): A cistern near a water-course may be filled by the first(-comer) for himself. If the second got ahead of him and filled it, see, he is alert and is paid. If a man acted promptly and diverted a water-course over the cistern of his neighbor, see, he is alert and is paid. In the case of a debtor and an inheritor, one of whom anticipated (the other) and laid hold of the moveables (of the estate), see, he is alert and is paid.

97. Yebamot T 4.8 (245): There is (the man who is) alert and is paid, (or) alert and loses (by it), lazy and is paid, lazy and loses by it. (The man who is) lazy and is paid (is he who is lazy on) the eve of Sabbath and Sabbath and the night following the Sabbath, in the period preparatory to the seventh year and the seventh year and the period following the seventh year, in the minor days of a festival and (in) everything in which there is (the likelihood of committing) an act at which people shake their heads as wrong. See, this man is lazy and is paid.

APPENDIX B

98. <u>Ketubot T</u> 8.2-3 (270): He who has control of the property of his wife and plans to divorce her, if he anticipated (the divorce) and detached anything from the land [things physically attached to the land being the wife's estate which must be returned on divorce, and moveables belonging to the husband], see, he is alert and is paid. He who has control of the property of captives and who heard of them that they were slowly coming (back from captivity), if he anticipated (their return) and detached anything from the land, see, he is alert and is paid.

*99. <u>Sotah T</u> 7.9 (307): There is a story about R. Johannan ben Barokah and R. Elazar Hisma, (to the effect) that they came from Jabneh to Lydda and paid a visit on R. Joshua in Pakiin. He said to them.... 'Whose Sabbath was it (to preach)?' It was R. Elazar ben Azaryah's Sabbath. He said to them, 'And what did he preach about?' (He preached on the text,) 'Assemble the people, the men and the women and the children.' (He said,) 'If the men come to learn (and) the women come to hear, why do the children come? In order to receive pay for those who bring them.' (sic. cp. 8, sup.)

100. <u>Sotah T</u> 7.21 (309): Another explanation (of Prov. 24.27): 'Prepare your work without,' these are the laws; 'and make it fit for yourself in the field,' this is doing good; 'and build your house afterwards.' interpret and receive pay. (The text is much expanded in the Vienna MS and in the earlier printed editions.)

101. <u>Sanhedrin T</u> 11.6 (431): (The case of) the dissolute and rebellious son (as outlined in Dt. 21.18f.) never arose and never will arise. And why was it written? To say, 'Interpret and receive pay.' (Also in 14.1 (436), about the city to be destroyed for apostacy, and in <u>Negaïm T</u> 6.1 (625), about the house to be destroyed for leprosy.)

102. <u>Sanhedrin T</u> 13.6 (435): R. Menahem the son of R. Jose says, '("And the Lord said, 'My spirit) will not judge (man forever.'") God (<u>lit.</u> the Place) said, "I do not judge at the time when I give good pay to the just, but the spirit of the wicked is harder on them than anything (else), for it is said, 'Their spirit shall eat them as fire.'"' (i.e., God's rewarding the just is not intended as a punishment - judgment - of the wicked, but their envious disposition makes it one.)

*103 <u>Hullin T</u> 10.16 (512): R. Jacob says, 'There is no commandment in the Law which does not have its pay alongside it and the resurrection of the dead written in it. (Consider, for example,) that it is said, "You shall surely let the mother go (if you find a mother bird sitting on a nest) (...that it may be well you and that you may prolong your days.") A man went up to the top of a tree (and found a nest and let the mother go) and fell and died, or to the top of a building and fell and died. Where is the good he was to receive and the length of his days? Hence say, "That it may be well with you," in the good world, "and that you may prolong your days," in a long world.'

104. Shebiit 9.9: If a man have produce raised in the seventh year (and therefore not to be eaten) which fell to him by inheritance or was given him as a gift, R. Eliezer says, 'Let it be given to those who will eat it,' and the Sages say, 'The sinner is not to profit; but let it be sold to those who will eat it and let the proceeds be divided among everybody.'

105. Hallah 2.7: The measure of the hallah (the priest's share of a batch of dough) is one (part) from twenty-four....The baker who bakes for sale in the market and likewise the woman who bakes for sale in the market (are required to give only) one (part) from forty-eight. If a woman's dough was made impure by accident or by force (against her will, she gives) one from forty-eight. If she deliberately made it impure (she gives) one from twenty-four, so that the sinner will not profit.

106. Kiddushin 4.14 (The first sentence of this is also in Kiddushin T 5.16 (343): R. Nehorai says, 'I am letting go all the arts which are in the world and am teaching my son only the Law, of which a man eats the profits (or, pay) in this world, and the principal remains intact for (him in) the world to come. None of the rest of the arts are like this. (With them) when a man falls into the hands of sickness or old age or punishment and is not able to work at his trade, see, he dies from hunger; but the Law is not so, on the contrary it guards him from all evil in his youth and gives him a future and hope in his old age.'

*107. Abot 2.1: Rabbi says,...'Be (as) careful about a (comparatively) unimportant commandment as about an important one, for you do not know the pay for (the performance of) commandments. And calculate the loss (involved in the performance) of a commandment as against its pay, and the pay of a transgression as against its loss.'
(Jastrow's translation: 'an easy commandment' and 'a difficult commandment (requiring self-denial)' (i.e. to observe) derives, I think, from the theological reflection that, since all commandments are alike expressions of the will of God, all transgressions are alike - and, therefore, equally - wicked as flouting His will. This may or may not be correct, but the translation based on it is discredited, to my mind, both by the parallel use of the same adjectives (קלה and חמורה) for transgressions (to suggest that an עברה חמורה was a transgression 'requiring self-denial' would not be plausible) and by the general common sense of TL which is tolerant of paradoxical theology, but usually bases its moral teaching on plain Scripture and everyday experience. (For the use of the adjectives to describe transgressions, v. no. 76, sup.))

108. <u>Abot</u> 2.2: Rabban Gamliel the son of R. Judah the Nasi says....
'Let all those who work with the congregation work with them for the
glory of God (<u>lit.</u> for the name of the Heavens); 'for the merit of their
ancestors aids them and their righteousness endures forever. And as
for you, I assign you much pay, as if you (yourselves) had acted.'

*109. <u>Abot</u> 2.14: R. Elazar says, 'Be anxious to learn the Law,...and
know before whom you work, and your employer can be trusted to
give you the pay for your work.' (The MS evidence for this conclusion is bad. Taylor, <u>Sayings of the Jewish Fathers</u>, Cambridge, 1877,
reads, 'And know before whom thou toilest and who is the Master of
thy work.' and numbers the verse 18 instead of 14.)

*110. <u>Abot</u> 2.15: R. Tarefon says, 'The day is short and the work is
plentiful and the workers are lazy and the pay is great and the householder is urgent.'

*111. <u>Abot</u> 2.16: He used to say....'If you have learned much Law you
are given much pay, and your employer can be trusted to give you the
pay for your work.' And, 'Know the pay of the just in the destined
future.'

*112. <u>Abot</u> 3.2 (This text is also dubious. Taylor, <u>op. cit.</u>, no. 3.4,
gives another version containing no reference to pay.): R. Hannanya
ben Teradyon says,...'Whence (do we learn) that, even (in the case of)
one who is sitting and studying the Law, the Holy One, blessed be He,
appoints him pay? (From the fact) that it is said, "He sits alone and
will keep silence for he put upon him." '

*113. <u>Abot</u> 4.2: Ben Azzai says, 'Run (to perform) an unimportant
commandment (as you would an important one), and flee from transgression, for (the performance of) a commandment brings after it
(the performance of) a commandment, and a transgression brings
after it a transgression, for the pay for (performance of) a commandment is a commandment and the pay for a transgression is a transgression.'

114. <u>Abot</u> 4.10: R. Meir says....'If you have worked at the Law (He)
has much pay to give you.'

115. <u>Abot</u> 5.1: The world was created with ten utterances. And why
should Scripture say so? And could it not have been created with one
utterance? But (it was created with ten) to (justify God's) exacting
punishment from the wicked who destroy the world which was created
with ten utterances, and (His) giving good pay to the just who establish
the world which was created with ten utterances. (cp. sup. 28)

116. <u>Abot</u> 5.2: There were ten generations from Noah to Abraham, to
show how patient God is, for all the generations were angering him
progressively, until Abraham came and took upon himself the pay of
them all.

117. <u>Abot</u> 5.11-14: There are four types of temperament: Easy to anger and easy to reconcile - his pay is consumed by his loss; hard to anger and hard to reconcile - his loss is obliterated by his pay.... There are four types of student: Quick to learn and quick to forget - his pay is consumed by his loss; slow to learn and slow to forget - his loss is obliterated by his pay....There are four types of those who go to the study hall: He who goes and does nothing - he has pay for going; he who works (when he goes) but does not go (often) - he has pay for working. (Taylor - numbering these 17-20 - rejects the words from the last semi-colon to the end of the sentence.)

APPENDIX C[1]

Peah[2]

1   **I.1 These (are) things which have no (legally fixed) limit:** the peah and the first-fruits and the visiting (of the temple) and returning kindnesses and study of the Law.

2   These (are) things (of) which a man eats the fruits in this world and the principal remains for him for the world to come: Honoring father and mother and returning kindnesses and bringing peace between a man and his fellow, and study of the Law is the equivalent of them all.

3   (See 6)

4

5

Peah T.[3]

I.1 Things which have no (legally fixed) limit: The peah and the first-fruits and the visiting (of the temple) and returning a kindness and study of the Law.

Peah has a (legally fixed) limit from below and does not have a (legally fixed) limit from above. (But if) one makes all his field a peah it is not a peah.

.2 For these things they exact penalties from the (average) man in this world and the principal remains for him in the world to come: For idolatry and for incest and for bloodshed, and for slander as the equivalent of them all.

Merit has a principal and has fruits, for it is said....
3. Transgression has a principal and does not have fruits, for it is said....How, (maintaining this, can) I establish (the text), 'And they shall eat of the fruit of their way, of their plans shall they be satiate.'? But a transgression which bears fruits _has_ fruits and (one) which does not bear fruits has no fruits.
4. A good thought is conjoined by God (lit. the Place) to practice, an evil thought is not conjoined by God (lit. the Place) to practice, for it is

185

Peah	Peah T
	said....Behold! How, (maintaining this, can) I establish, etc.

6   .2 They do not give less for peah than (one part) from sixty, and (this) in spite of the fact that they said, 'Peah has no (legally fixed) limit.' Everything (is) according to the size of the field and according to the number of the poor and according to the greatness of the poverty (or yield, sc. of the field, or humility, sc. of the giver).[4]

                cp. 3.

7   .3 They give peah from the beginning of the field and from its middle. R. Simon says, 'And provided only that he will give in the end according to the (legally fixed minimal) limit.' R. Judah says, 'If he left one stalk (at the end) he can join (what he left in other parts of the field) to it as peah, and if not he gives (what he gives in other parts of the field) only as abandoned property.'

                .5 A man gives peah from the beginning of the field and in the middle and in the end. If he gave, whether in the beginning or in the end, he satisfied (his obligation). R. Simon says, 'If he gave, whether in the beginning or in the end, see, this is peah; and, (nevertheless), it is necessary that he should give in the end according to the (legally fixed minimal) limit.' R. Judah says, 'If he left one stalk (at the end) he can joint (what he left in other parts of the field) to it (and so is) giving as peah, and if not he gives (what he gives in other parts of the field) only as abandoned property.'

8   R. Judah said, 'With what (reference are these) things said? With (reference to) an instance in which one gave the peah and wishes to add (to it). If one did not give...

9   R. Simon said, 'Because of four things the Law said a man shall not give peah except in the end of his field, because of robbery of the poor and because of the loss of time of the poor and because of appearances and because of cheats. Because of robbery of the poor: How?...

186

Peah	Peah T

10 .4 They stated a rule in (regard to) peah: 'Everything which is good and is kept watch over and grows from the ground and is harvested (all) at once and is taken in for storage, is liable to peah.' And grain and peas are in (the class defined by) this rule.

.5 And among the trees the sumach and the carobs and walnuts and the almonds and the grapevines and the pomegranates and the olives and the palms are liable to peah.

11

.7 Truck, in spite of the fact that it is harvested (all) at once, is not taken in for storage; and figs, in spite of the fact that they are taken in for storage, nevertheless they are not harvested (all) at once. R. Jose bar Judah says, 'Juicy dates are free from peah, for the first does not wait for the last.' (i.e., the first rots before the last ripens, so they cannot be harvested all at once.) R. Elazar bar Zadok says, 'Jujubes are liable to peah.' Others say also white figs and puffy figs.

12 .6 A man may give (an area of his field) as peah and (be) free from (the duty of paying) tithes (on that area), at any time until (the produce) is heaped up (to be tithed)....If a priest or Levite bought (the content of) the threshing floor, the tithes are theirs (provided they made the purchase) before (the produce) be heaped up. He who dedicates (his harvest) and (then) redeems (it) is liable for the tithes (if he redeemed it) before the assessor (of tithes) heaped it up.

Peah	Peah T
13 **II.1** And these (things) limit (fields, etc.) for (the purpose of) peah (so that if two parts of a property be separated by one of these things a separate peah must be given for each part): a ravine and a pool and a private road and a public road and a private path fixed in summer and in the rainy season and a cistern and fallow land and a different crop. 'And one who cuts for fodder limits (the field).' (These are) the words of R. Meir, and the Sages say, 'He does not limit (it) unless he plough.' **.2** (If there be) a channel of water (so broad) that (the produce on either side) cannot be cut at the same time, R. Judah says (this) limits (the field.) And (as for) all hills which can be hoed with a hoe, in spite of the fact that oxen cannot get over (them) with a plough, one gives a single peah for all. cp. 16 (.7)	**.8** These (things) limit (fields, etc.) for (the purpose of) peah (so that if two parts of a property be separated by one of these things a separate peah must be given for each part): a ravine and a pool and a private road and a public road and a private path fixed in summer and in the rainy season, a cistern and fallow land and a different crop. And one who cuts for fodder and three furrows' (space) of opening (i.e., of unplanted land.) And, (if there be) a channel of water (so broad) that (the produce on either side) cannot be cut at the same time, R. Judah says, if (the reaper has to) stand in the middle and cut first on one side and then on the other, (this) limits (the field), and if not it does not limit (it). (If) <u>hagab</u> locusts ate an area, (or if) <u>gobai</u> locusts ate it, and (if) ants nibbled it, and if the wind or cattle broke it (down), everybody admits that if he plough (the wasted area) (that) limits (the field), and if not it does not limit (it).
14 **.3** All (these things) are limits for sown crops, and nothing is a limit for trees but a fence, and if the branches of the trees touch (across the fence, then even) this does not serve as a limit, but (the owner) gives one peah for all. **.4** And for carob trees (he gives one peah for) all which can be seen one from another. Rabban	

188

APPENDIX C

Peah	Peah T
Gamliel said, 'My father's household were accustomed...	

15   .5 If a man sow his field with one kind (of seed), then in spite of the fact that he makes two threshing floors...
.6 (There is) a story (to the effect that) R. Simon of Mizpah...

16   .7 A field which Samaritans reaped, robbers reaped, ants nibbled, the wind or cattle broke down, is free (from peah). (If the owner) reaped half of it and robbers (later) reaped (the remaining) half of it, it is free, for the liability to peah (went) with the standing grain.
.8 (If) robbers reaped half of it and (the owner later) reaped (the remaining) half of it, he gives peah from what he reaped. (If) he reaped half of it and sold half of it, the purchaser gives peah for the whole. (If) he reaped half of it and dedicated half of it, whoever redeems it from the assessor gives peah for the whole.

17
.9 (If) he cut half of it and sold what was cut (or) cut half of it and dedicated what was cut, he gives (peah) from the remainder for the whole.

18
(If he planted on) terraces ten handbreadths high, he gives a peah from each one. If the ends of the rows ran together he gives a peah from one for the whole (planting).

cp. 19.

19   III.1 (In the case of) beds of grain between olive trees, the house of Shammai say, 'A peah from each one.'; the house of Hillel say, 'From one for the whole.' And it is admitted that if the ends of the rows ran together he gives a peah from one for the whole.

cp. 18.

Peah	Peah T
20	He who follows the rows (of the garden bed, to pick out only a few vegetables) is liable when he begins and when he stops.
21 .2 He who cleans out patches of his field and leaves some green stalks, R. Akiba says...And the Sages say... .3 He who takes out bunches of green onions for the market and leaves dry ones for the storehouse, gives a peah for these by themselves and for those by themselves; and so in (the case of) peas and so in (the case of) a vineyard.	
22	.10 If (a man) had four or five grapevines and (was) picking the grapes (as he needed them) and taking them (straight) into his house, he is free from the duty of leaving grapes which he happens to drop or which he did not at first notice, but he is bound to leave the gleanings. If he left, (to vintage time, a small crop which he had not taken for table use) he gives (peah etc.) from what is left for what he left.
23 One who thins out (vegetables) gives (a peah) from what is left for what he left; and if he takes (all) from one place he gives from what is left for all (the original planting).	And one who thins out (vegetables) gives (a peah) from what is left for what he left. R. Judah said, 'With what (reference are these) things said? With (reference to) one who thins out to (take the thinnings to) market. But in (the case of) one who thins out (and keeps the thinnings for food) inside his own household, he gives from what is left for the whole (original planting).'
24	.11 If a man cut (produce as he needed it) and brought it (straight) into his house, even (though in this way he gradually denuded) all his field, (he would be) free from the

APPENDIX C

Peah	Peah T
	(requirement to leave) gleanings, a 'forgotten' sheaf, and peah, but liable for the tithes.
25 .4 Onions kept for seed are liable to peah, but R. Jose declares (them) free.	
26 As for beds of onions between (other) vegetables, R. Jose says ....And the Sages say....	
27 .5 Brothers who divided (a property) give two peot....	
28 .6 R. Eliezer says, 'A (piece of) land (sufficient for sowing) a quarter (kab of seed) is liable to peah. R. Joshua says... R. Tarefon says... R. Judah ben Beterah says... R. Akiba says, 'Any (piece of) land whatsoever is liable to peah and to firstfruits and (is sufficient to satisfy the requirement) for writing a prozbul and for the acquisition, together with itself, of moveable property'...	
29 .7 (In the case of a man who) lying sick, signs away his property, (if) he left (for himself) any (piece of) land whatsoever, his gift is a (valid) gift...	
30 (If) a man signs away his property to his sons and signs over to his wife any (piece of) land whatsoever, she has lost her dowery. R. Jose says, 'If she agreed to (it), in spite of the fact that he did not sign (it) over to her, she lost her dowery.'	.12 (If) a man signs away his property to his sons and retain for his wife any (piece of) land whatsoever, she has lost her dowery. R. Jose said, 'With what (reference are these) things said? With (reference to) an instance in which she agreed to (it) as (an equivalent for her) dowery. But (if) she did not agree to (it) as (an equivalent for her) dowery, what he gave he gave (validly) and (beside that) she may collect her dowery from the rest of the property.'

191

Peah

31 .8 (If) a man sign away his property to his slave, (the slave) is (thereby) freed. (If) he left (for himself) any (piece of) land whatsoever, (the slave) is not freed. R. Simon says, 'He is always freed unless (the master) say, "Behold, all my property is given to so-and-so my slave except for one ten-thousandth part of it." '

Peah T

.13 (If) a man sign away his property to his slave, (the slave) is thereby freed. If he left (for himself) any (piece of) land whatsoever, (the slave) is not freed. R. Simon says,[5] 'He is always freed unless (the master) say, "I have given all my property to so-and-so my slave except for one ten-thousandth part of it." (Such a statement) says nothing at all. (But if he said,) "Except for such-and-such a city," "Except for such-and-such a field," in spite of the fact that he have nothing but that field or that city, the servant acquired the right to possessions (and so) acquired himself as a free man.' And when they said (these) things before R. Jose he said, 'Every man shall kiss his lips who answers rightly.'

Mat

32 5.3 Blessed are the poor in spirit, for theirs is the kingdom of Heaven.
.4 Blessed are the mourners, for they shall be comforted.
.5 Blessed are the meek, for they shall inherit the earth.
.6 Blessed are those who hunger and thirst after righteousness, for they shall be filled.

.7 Blessed are the merciful, for they shall receive mercy.
.8 Blessed are the pure in heart, for they shall see God.
.9 Blessed are the peacemakers, for they shall be called the children of God.
.10 Blessed are those persecuted because of righteousness, for theirs is the kingdom of Heaven.

Lk

6.20 Blessed are the poor, for yours is the kingdom of God.

see 21b

.21 Blessed are those who hunger now, for you shall be filled.

.21b Blessed are those who weep now, for you shall laugh.

APPENDIX C

<u>Mat</u>

.11 Blessed are you when you shall⁶ be reviled and persecuted and everything bad shall be said against you falsely for my sake.

.12 Rejoice and be glad, for your pay is great in the heavens; for thus they persecuted the prophets before you.

<u>Lk</u>

.22 Blessed are you when men shall hate you and when they shall ostracize you and revile you and cast out your name as bad, for the sake of the Son of Man.
.23 Rejoice in that day and jump for joy, for behold, your pay is great in heaven, for their fathers acted in these same (ways) towards the prophets.

33

.24 But woe to you, the rich, for you have your consolation.
.25 Woe to you, who are filled now, for you shall hunger; woe (to you) who laugh now, for you shall mourn and weep.
.26 Woe, when all men speak you well, for their fathers acted in this same way towards the prophets.

34 .13 You are the salt of the earth..
.14 You are the light of the world...

35 .17 Do not think that I came to destroy the Law...

36 .21 You have heard that it was said...
.22 But I say to you...(murder)

37 .27 You have heard that it was said...
.28 But I say to you...(adultery)

38 .31 And it was said...
.32 But I say to you...(divorce)

39 .33 Again you have heard that it was said...
.34 But I say to you...(oaths)

40 .38 You have heard that it was said, 'An eye for an eye'...
.39 But I say to you not to resist evil.
.39b But whoever strikes you on the right cheek, turn him the other also.

see .29

Mat	Lk

Mat

.40 And to one who wishes to go to law with you and take your shirt, give your coat also.

.41 And whoever compels you to carry his burden a mile, go with him two.

.42 Give to the one who asks you, and do not turn away the man who wants to borrow from you.

41 .43 You have heard that it was said, 'You shall love your neighbor and hate your enemy.'

.44 But I say to you, 'Love your enemies and pray for those who persecute you.'

see .39

see .40

see .42

see 7.12

.45 In order that you may become children of your father in the heavens, for he makes his sun rise on the evil and the good and sends rain on the just and the unjust.

.46 For if you love those who love you, what pay have you? Do not even the tax-collectors do the same?

.47 And if you greet your brothers only what do you do more (than usual)? Do not even the gentiles do the same?

Lk

see .29

see .30

.27 But I say to you, to those who hear, 'Love your enemies, do good to those who hate you,

.28 bless those who curse you, pray for those who outrage you.

.29 To one who strikes you on the cheek, turn the other also; and to him who takes your coat, do not deny your shirt also.

.30 Give to everyone who asks you, and do not ask your property back from the one who takes it.

.31 And as you wish that men should treat you, so treat them.'

see .35, end.

.32 And if you love those who love you, what sort of grace is there for you;[7] for even the tax-collectors love those who love them.

.33 And if you do good to those who who do good to you, what sort of grace is there for you? Even those who are lax about their religious observances (lit. the sinners) do the same.

.34 And if you lend (to those) from whom you hope to receive, what sort of grace is there for you? Even the lax (v.s.) lend to the lax in order that they may receive in turn the like (favors).[8]

Mat	Lk
	.35 But love your enemies and do good and lend hoping for nothing in return, and your pay will be great and you will be children of the Highest, for He Himself is good to the thankless and wicked.
.48 Be you, then, perfect, as your heavenly Father is perfect.	.36 Become merciful, as your Father is merciful.
42 6.1 Take care not to give alms publically, so as to be seen... .2 When, therefore, you give alms.. .5 And when you pray... .16 And when you fast...	
43 .19 Lay not up for yourselves treasures on earth... .24 You cannot serve God and mammon.	
44 .25 Therefore I tell you, 'Take no thought for your life...nor for your body... .34 Sufficient unto the day is the evil thereof.'	
45 7.1 Judge not, that you be not judged. .2 For by what judgment you judge, you shall be judged.	.37 And judge not, and you shall not be judged.
	.37b And do not condemn, and you shall not be condemned. Release and you shall be released. .38 Give and it shall be given you... .38b For in what measure you mete it shall be measured back to you. .39 And he told them a parable, 'Can one blind man lead another? Will not both fall into a ditch? .40 A pupil is not above his teacher. Fully trained, each will be as his teacher.
See .7 .2b And in what measure you mete it shall be measured to you.	
46 .3 Why do you see the straw in your brother's eye? And do you not notice the beam in your eye? .4 Or how will you say to your brother, 'Let me take the straw out of your eye.' and see, the beam is in your eye?	.41 Why do you see the straw in your brother's eye? And do you not notice the beam in your own eye? .42 How can you say to your brother, 'Brother, let me take out the straw which is in your eye.' not seeing, yourself, the beam in your eye?

Mat	Lk
.5 Hypocrite! Take first, from your eye, the beam and then you will see clearly to take the straw from the eye of your brother.	Hypocrite! Take first the beam from your eye, and then you will see clearly to take out the straw which is in your brother's eye.

47 .6 Give not that which is holy to the dogs...

48 .7 Ask, and it shall be given you; seek, and you shall find; knock, and it shall be opened to you.
.8 For everyone who asks, gets...
.9 Or what man among you, whose son asks for bread, will give him a stone?
.11...If, then, you, being wicked, know how to give good gifts to your children, how much more so your Father in heaven...?
.12 Therefore, all such things as you may wish that men might do to you - you also do thus to them, for this is the law and the prophets.

see .38

see .41

49 .13 Enter through the narrow gate, for broad is the gate and easy the road which leads to destruction....

50 .15 Beware of false prophets....

51 .16 From their fruits you shall know them. Are grapes gathered[9] from thorns, or figs from thistles?
.17 Thus every good tree gives good fruits and the rotten tree gives bad fruits.
.18 A good tree cannot bear bad fruits, nor a rotten tree bear good fruits.
.20 So, then, from their fruits you shall know them.
see .16

see .44

.43 For there is no fine tree giving rotten fruit, nor rotten tree giving fine fruit.
.44 For every tree is known from its own fruit. For figs are not gathered from thorns, nor is the grape plucked from the briar.
.45 The good man, from the good treasure of his heart, brings forth good...

APPENDIX C

Mat	Lk
52 .21 Not everyone who says to me, 'Lord, Lord.' shall enter into the kingdom of Heaven, but he who does the will of my Father... .22 Many will say to me in that day, 'Lord, Lord, did we not prophesy in thy name?'...	.46 And why do you call me, 'Lord, Lord,' and not do what I say?
53 .24 Therefore, whoever hears these words of mine and does them, will be likened to a wise man who built his house on bedrock.[10] .25 And the rain came down and the rivers came and the winds blew and attacked that house and it did not fall, for it was founded on bedrock.	.47 I shall show you what anyone coming to me and hearing my words and doing them is like: .48 He is like a man building a house, who dug and went deep and put a foundation on bedrock. And when there was a flood, the river ran against that house and was not able to shake it because it was well built.
.26 And everyone hearing these words of mine and not doing them shall be likened to a foolish man who built his house on the sand. .27 And the rain came down and the rivers came and the winds blew and struck that house and it fell, and its fall was great.	.49 But one hearing and not doing is like a man building a house on dirt without a foundation, (a house) which the river ran against and, straightway, it fell, and the break-up of that house was great.

NOTES

1. To illustrate the verbal similarities of the texts it has been necessary to make the translations in this appendix considerably more literal - and therefore less like English - than those in other parts of the book.

2. Peah means a corner, end, border or fringe, and in this connection especially the corner or end of the field left unharvested as a portion for the poor. v. Lev. 19.9, 27; 23.22.

3. In comparing this translation with the text of Tosefta, note the corrections of the latter printed by Zuckermandel p. 103, which I have generally followed. Both in Tosefta and in the Mishnah, I have not hesitated to abbreviate material which did not seem to me of interest for the purpose of this chapter.

4. The text of the Mishnah has 'humility,' slight emendations give 'poverty' and 'yield.'

5. Lieberman, in Tosefeth Rishonim, ad loc. prefers the reading of the previous printed editions: 'R. Simon says, "He who says, 'All my property

is given to so-and-so my slave except for one ten-thousandth part of it.'
has said nothing at all."' (i.e., his words are not legally actionable.)

6. Mat has the Rabbinic impersonal plural, Lk has supplied a subject. I
therefore translate Mat by the passive, which is the normal equivalent of
the Semitic construction, and translate literally the Lucan emendation.

7. Here Lk has the Semitic 'What x is there for you?', meaning 'What x
have you?', whereas Mat has the Gk. verb 'have.' I have translated Lk
literally, at the risk of misleading the reader, to emphasize the difference.

8. Or, 'the like (amounts),' but I rather think the irreligious expected
interest.

9. Another Rabbinic impersonal pl., this time Lk has it too.

10. τὴν πέτραν. But this is dubious, for τὴν γῆν in Lk 49 clearly means (just any) dirt.

WORKS REFERRED TO

Abrahams, I., Studies in Pharisaism, Cambridge, 1st Series 1917, 2nd Series 1924. (Refs. in) Ch. II, n. 77; III, n. 1, n. 6; VIII, n. 6.

Albeck, C., Untersuchungen über die hal. Midraschim, Berlin, 1927 (Veröffentl. der Ak. f.d. Wiss. d. Jdts., Talm. Sektion, Bd. III). Ch. V, n. 17, n. 18, n. 20; VII, n. 1, n. 2, n. 15.

   Untersuchungen über die Redaktion der Mischna, Berlin, 1923 (Voröffentl. der Ak. f.d. Wiss. d. Jdts., Talm. Sektion, Bd. II). Ch. III, n. 60; V, n. 2, n. 35.

Allen, W., The Book of Sayings, in 'Studies in the Synoptic Problem' ed. W. Sanday, Oxford, 1911, pp. 234 ff. Ch. IV, n. 8.

   A Critical and Exegetical Commentary on...Matthew, N. Y., 1907 (ICC). Ch. II, n. 100; VII, n. 12.

   The Gospel according to St. Mark, N.Y., 1915. Ch. II, n. 100.

Aptowitzer, V., The Rewarding and Punishing of Animals and Inanimate Objects, HUCA, III. 117 ff. Ch. III, n. 58.

Bartlett, V., The Sources of St. Luke's Gospel, in 'Studies in the Synoptic Problem,' ed. W. Sanday, Oxford, 1911, pp. 315 ff. Ch. V, n. 13.

Belser, J., Das Evangelium des hl. Johannes, Freiburg i.B., 1905. Ch. III, n. 38.

ben Iehuda, E., Thesaurus totius hebraitatis, Berlin-Jerusalem, 1911 ff. Ch. II, n. 14.

Black, M., An Aramaic Approach to the Gospels and Acts, Oxford, 1946. Ch. 2, n. 4.

Blau, L., Observations sur l'histoire du culte juif, REJ, 73.138 ff. Ch. 1, n. 9.

Bonsirven, J., Le Judaïsme Palestinien, Paris, 2 v., 1934-5. Ch. III, n. 55.

Bultmann, R., Die Geschichte der synoptischen Tradition, Göttingen, 1921. Ch. IV, n. 24.

Burney, C., The Aramaic Origin of the Fourth Gospel, Oxford, 1922. Ch. II, n. 4, n. 9, n. 10, n. 11; III, n. 51; VII, n. 10; VIII, n. 10.

199

TANNAITIC PARALLELS TO THE GOSPELS

Burney, C., The Poetry of Our Lord, Oxford, 1925. Ch. IV, n. 5.

Caspari, W., _____, ZNW, 21.122 ff. Ch. I, n. 20.

Chajes, H., Markus-Studien, Berlin, 1899. Ch. I, n. 20; II, n. 14.

Charles, R., Religious Development between the Old and New Testaments, London, 1914. Ch. VIII, n. 1.

Colwell, E., The Greek of the Fourth Gospel, Chicago, 1931. Ch. II, n. 4.

Dalman, G., Gramm, d. jüd.-pal. Aramäisch, ed. 2, Leipzig, 1905. Ch. 1, n. 46.

       Jesus-Jeschua, Leipzig, 1922. Ch. II, n. 4.

       Die Worte Jesu, I, ed. 2, Leipzig, 1930. Ch. II, n. 4; III, n. 1.

Danby, H., tr., The Mishna, Oxford, 1933. Ch. II, n. 73.

Daube, D., ἐξουσία in Mk. 1.22 and 27, JTS, 39.45 ff. Ch. II, n. 96.

Deissmann, A., Licht vom Osten, 4 ed., Tübingen, 1923. Ch. II, n. 112.

Delitzsch, F., Sifre Habberit Hehadashah, Berlin, 1877. Ch. I, n. 52, n. 54.

Delling, G., ἀρχαῖος, in 'Theologisches Wörterbuch zum Neuen Testament,' ed. G. Kittel, vol. I, Stuttgart, 1933. Ch. II, n. 93.

Dibelius, M., From Tradition to Gospel, tr. B. Woolf (from the 2 ed. of Die Formgeschichte des Evangeliums) London, 1934. Ch. II, n. 85, III, n. 27; IV, n. 15, n. 19, n. 28; V. n. 16.

Diodati, D., De Christo Graece loquente, Neapoli, 1767. Ch. II, n. 4.

Easton, B., The Gospel before the Gospels, New York, 1928. Ch. IV, n. 1.

The Eighteen Benedictions, cited according to Stärk, W., q.v.

The Excavations at Dura-Europos, Preliminary Report of the Ninth Season, Part I, New Haven, 1944. Ch. I, n. 26.

Faure, A., Die alttestamentlichen Zitate im 4. Evangel. ZNW, 21.99 ff. Ch. VIII, in text, before n. 5.

Feigin, S., The Oriental Language of the Gospels, JNES, 2.187 ff. Ch. V, n. 6.

Feibig, P., Altjüdische Gleichnisse u. die Gleichnisse Jesu, Tübingen, 1904. Ch. II, n. 67; III, n. 37; IV, n. 4, n. 7, n. 8.

WORKS REFERRED TO

Feibig, P., <u>Der Erzählungsstil der Evangelien</u>, Leipzig, 1925. Ch. IV, n. 5.

<u>Das Griechisch der Mischna</u>, ZNW, 9.297 ff., Ch. I, n. 34, n. 41.

<u>Jesu Bergpredigt</u>, Göttingen, 1924. Ch. II, n. 67, n. 75; III, n. 1.

<u>Jüdische Wundergeschichten des neutestamentlichen Zeitalters</u>, Tübingen, 1911. Ch. IV, n. 12; VII, n. 3.

<u>Pirque 'aboth</u>, Tübingen, 1906. Ch. I, n. 13; II, n. 67; IV, n. 7, n. 10; VIII, n. 3.

<u>Rabbinische Wundergeschichten</u>, Berlin, 1933. Ch. VII, n. 4.

Finkelstein, L., ed., <u>Siphre zu Deuteronomium</u>, Breslau, 1935-8. See index.

Forbes, J., <u>The Symmetrical Structure of Scripture</u>, Edinburgh, 1854, Ch. IV, n. 5.

Gardner-Smith, P., <u>St. John and the Synoptic Gospels</u>, Cambridge, 1938, Ch. VII, n. 20.

Geden, v.s. Moulton & Geden.

Godet, F., <u>Commentaire sur l'évangile de St. Jean</u>, 4 ed., Neuchatel, N.D. (1902-5). Ch. III, n. 38.

Goodenough, E., <u>John a Primitive Gospel</u>, JBL, 1945.145 ff. Ch. VII, n. 20.

<u>The Gospels</u> are cited according to <u>Novum Testamentum Graece</u>, q.v.

Grätz, H., <u>Geschichte der Juden</u>, 5 ed., ed. M. Brann, Leipzig, 1905, Ch. I, n. 10.

Guignebert, C., <u>La vie cachée de Jésus</u>, Paris, 1921. Ch. I, n. 20.

Hatch and Redpath, <u>A Concordance to the Septuagint</u>, Oxford, 1897-1906. passim.

Hawkins, J., <u>Horae Synopticae</u>, 2. ed., Oxford, 1909. Ch. I, n. 56; VII, n. 21.

Herford, T., <u>The Pharisees</u>, London, 1924. Ch. II, n. 86.

Hoffmann, D., <u>Zur Einleitung in die hal. Midraschim</u>, Berlin, 1887. Ch. V, n. 19, n. 20; VII, n. 15.

<u>Die erste Mischna</u>, Berlin, 1881. Ch. V, n. 2.

Hoffmann, D., ed., Mechilta de-Rabbi Simon b. Jochai, Frankfurt a.M., 1905. See index.

ed., Midrasch Tannaïm, Berlin, 1908-9. See index.

Horovitz, H., ed., Siphre ad Numeros adjecto Siphre Zutta (Corpus Tannaiticum III 3.1) Leipzig, 1917. See index.

Horovitz and Rabin, eds., Mechilta d'Rabbi Ismael, Frankfurt a.M., 1931. See index.

Howard, W., The Fourth Gospel, London, 1931. Ch. VII, n. 11, n. 19.

Howard, see also Moulton and Howard.

Jastrow, M., A Dictionary of the Targumin (etc.), N.Y., 1926. passim.

Jebb, J., Sacred Literature, London, 1820. Ch. IV, n. 5.

Johannessohn, M. Der Gebrauch der Präpositionen in der Septuaginta, Berlin, 1926. Ch. II, n. 46, n. 102.

Kasowski, C. J. (also Kassowski, H. Y.), Thesaurus Thosephthae, vols. I-III, Jerusalem, 1932-42, passim.

Ozar Leshon Hammishnah, 2 v., Jerusalem, N.D., passim.

Kittel, G., Die Probleme des palästinischen Spätjudentums u. das Urchristentum, Stuttgart, 1926. Introduction. Ch. II, n. 96; III, n. 1; VII, n. 5, n. 6.

ed., Theologisches Wörterbuch zum NT. See under Delling and under Stauffer.

Klausner, J., Jesus of Nazareth, tr. Danby, N.Y., 1925. Ch. II, n. 78.

Klein, G., Zur Erläuterung der Evangelien aus Talmud u. Midrasch, ZNW, 5.144 ff. Ch. V, n. 6, n. 7, n. 8.

Krauss, S., Griechische u. lateinische Lehnwörter, Berlin, 2 v., 1898-9. Ch. I, n. 22, n. 25, n. 37.

Kümmel, W., Jesus u. der jüd. Traditionsgedanke, ZNW, 33.105 ff., Ch. II, n. 87, n. 90.

Lagrange, M.-J., L'évangile selon St. Marc, 4 ed., Paris, 1929, Ch. II, n. 100.

L'évangile selon St. Matthieu, 3 ed., Paris, 1927, Ch. II, n. 100.

Lake, K., Montefiore's 'Judaism and St. Paul,' HTR, 9.242 ff. Ch. III, n. 32.

a Lapide, C., Commentaria in quatuor evangelia, ed. A. Padovani, 2 ed., Augustae Taurinorum, N.D., Ch. II, n. 100; III, n. 38.

Lauterbach, Z., The Ancient Jewish Allegorists, JQR, NS I.291 ff. and 503 ff. Ch. VIII, n. 11, n. 12, n. 13.

Levertoff, P., Midrash Sifre on Numbers, London, N.D. (1926). Ch. II, n. 105; IV, n. 9.

Lévi, I., Le prosélytisme juif, REJ, 50.1 ff, 51.1 ff. Ch. IV, n. 40.

   Le sacrifice d'Isaac et la mort de Jésus, REJ, 64.161 ff. Ch. III, n. 5.

Liddell & Scott, A Greek-English Lexicon, ed. Jones & McKenzie, 2 v., Oxford, N.D., passim.

Lieberman, S. (also Liebermann), Greek in Jewish Palestine, N.Y., 1942. Ch. VI, n. 4.

   Review of Finkelstein's 'Siphre zu Deut.', in Kiryat Sefer, 14.323 ff. Ch. I, n. 22.

   Supplement to the Tosephta (printed as a preface in the reprint of the Tosephta), Jerusalem, 1937. Ch. VII, n. 18.

   Tosefeth Rishonim, Jerusalem, 2 v., 1937-39. Ch. VII, n. 14; Appendix C, n. 5.

Mann, J., Rabbinic Studies in the Synoptic Gospels, HUCA, I.323 ff. Ch. VII, n. 17.

Marmorstein, A., Les Rabbins et les Evangiles, REJ, 92.31 ff. Ch. V, n. 14, n. 15.

Mekilta, v.s. Horovitz & Rabin, Mechilta.

Mekilta of R. Simon, v.s. Hoffmann, D., Mechilta

Melamed, E., Halachic Midrashim of the Tannaïm in the Talmud Babli, Jerusalem, 1943. Ch. V, n. 18, n. 20; VII, n. 13.

The Mishnah is cited sometimes according to the Shoken ed., Jerusalem, 1937 (anastatic reprint of the Stettin ed. of 1862-3), sometimes according to the fourth Horeb ed., New York and Berlin, N.D. See the index.

Montefiore, C., Rabbinic Literature and Gospel Teachings, London, 1930, Ch. III, n. 1.

Moore, G., Christian Writers on Judaism, HTR, 14.197 ff., Ch. III, n. 30.

   Conjectanea Talmudica, JAOS, 26.315 ff. Ch. II, n. 103.

   Judaism in the First Christian Centuries, Cambridge, 3 v., 1927-30. Ch. III, n. 31.

Moulton and Geden, A Concordance to the Greek Testament, 2nd ed., N.Y. 1900. passim.

Moulton and Howard, A Grammar of New Testament Greek, 2nd ed., Edinburgh, 2 v., 1906-29, Ch. II, n. 5, n. 111.

Nestle, v.s. Novum Testamentum Graece

Newman, L., Parallelism in Amos, (Part I of Studies in Biblical Parallelism, Univ. of Cal. Pubs. in Sem. Philol. I.2-3 Berkeley, 1918. Ch. IV, n. 5.

Norden, E., Agnostos Theos, Berlin, 1913. Ch. IV, n. 20, n. 21, n. 22.

Novum Testamentum Graece, ed. Nestle & Nestle, ed. 14, Stuttgart, 1930. See index.

Odeberg, H., The Fourth Gospel, Uppsala, 1929. Ch. VIII, n. 9.

Plummer, A., An Exegetical Commentary on...Matthew, London, 1909. Ch. II, n. 102.

de-Rossi, G., Della lingua propria di Cristo, Parma, 1772. Ch. II, n. 4.

Rostovtzeff, M., The Social and Economic History of the Roman Empire, Oxford, 1926. Ch. III, n. 20.

Russell, B., An Inquiry into Meaning and Truth, New York, 1940. Ch. III, n. 3.

Sanday, W., ed. Studies in the Synoptic Problem, see under Allen and under Bartlett.

Schechter, S., Studies in Judaism, N.Y., 1896. Ch. III, n. 61; VIII, n. 6.

Schlatter, A., Sprache u. Heimat des vierten Evangelisten, Gütersloh, 1902. Ch. II, n. 4, n. 65, n. 66, n. 69, n. 79, n. 81, n. 83; IV, n. 7, n. 8; VII, n. 9.

Schmidt, K., Der Rahmen der Geschichte Jesu, Berlin, 1919. Ch. IV, n. 11.

Schulthess, F., Das Problem der Sprache Jesu, Zürich, 1917, Ch. II, n. 4.

Zur Sprache der Evangelien, Anhang. ZNW, 21.241 ff. Ch. I, n. 21.

Schweitzer, A., Geschichte der Leben-Jesu-Forschung, 4 ed., Tübingen, 1926, Ch. IV, n. 25, n. 26; V, n. 1; VII, n. 7.

Segal, M., A Grammar of Mishnaic Hebrew, Oxford, 1927. Ch. II, n. 14.

WORKS REFERRED TO

The Septuagint is cited sometimes according to Swete, q.v., sometimes according to Hatch and Redpath, q.v.

Sifra, v.s. Weiss.

Sifre on Deuteronomy, v.s. Finkelstein, Siphre zu Deut.

Sifre on Numbers, v.s. Horovitz, Siphre ad Numeros adjecto Siphre Zutta.

Sifre Zutta, v.s. Horovitz, Siphre ad Numeros adjecto Siphre Zutta.

Sigge, T. Das Johannesevangelium und die Synoptiker, Münster i.W., 1935. (Neutestamentliche Abhandlungen, XVI, 2/3 Heft). Ch. VII, n. 20.

Smythe, H., A Greek Grammar for Colleges, N.Y., n.d. Ch. IV, n. 6.

Soiron, T., Die Logia Jesu, Münster i.W., 1916 (Neutestamentliche Abhandlungen, VI, 4 Heft). Ch. IV, n. 27; V, n. 3, n. 4, n. 5.

Spitta, F., Das Johannes-Evangelium, Göttingen, 1910. Ch. III, n. 38.

Stärk, W., Altjüdische Liturgische Gebete, Bonn, 1910. See index under the names of the prayers.

Stauffer, E., ἐγώ , in 'Theologisches Wörterbuch zum NT,' ed. G. Kittel, vol. II, Stuttgart, 1935. Ch. II, n. 88, n. 89, n. 96.

Strack, H., Einleitung in Talmud u. Midrasch, (Unveränd. Abdr. d. 5....Aufl. der Einl. i.d. Talmud) München, 1921. Ch. III, n. 1.

Strack and Billerbeck, Kommentar zum Neuen Testament aus Talmud u. Midrasch, München, 1922-8. passim.

Studies in the Synoptic Problem, see under Allen and under Bartlett.

Swete, H., ed., The Old Testament in Greek, Cambridge, 1887-94, passim.

Taylor, C., Sayings of the Jewish Fathers, Cambridge, 1877. Appendix B, nos. 109, 112, 117.

Taylor, V., The Formation of the Gospel Tradition, London, 1933. Ch. IV, n. 2, n. 18; V, n. 38.

Thayer, J., A Greek-English Lexicon of the New Testament, corr. ed., N.Y., 1896. Ch. I, n. 43.

Theologisches Wörterbuch zum NT. See under Delling and under Stauffer.

Tosefta, v.s. Zuckermandel, Tosephta.

Torrey, C., The Four Gospels, N.Y., 1933. Ch. I, n. 12, n. 20, n. 21; II, n. 4, n. 61; III, n. 41.

Torrey, C., The Name 'Iscariot,' HTR, 36.51 ff. Ch. I, n. 18.

Our Translated Gospels, N.Y., 1936. Ch. II, n. 4, n. 61, n. 110, n. 113, n. 114, n. 115, n. 117, n. 118, n. 120; III, n. 41; VIII, n. 10.

The Translations Made from the Original Aramaic Gospels in, 'Studies in the History of Religions pres. to C. H. Toy' N.Y., 1912. Ch. II, n. 6, n. 7, n. 109.

Völter, D., Boanerges, ZNW, 17.212 ff., Ch. I, n. 20.

Weiss, I., ed., Sifra, Vienna, 1862. See index.

Wellhausen, J., Einleitung in die drei ersten Evangelien, 2 ed., Berlin, 1911. Ch. I, n. 16; II, n. 8, n. 104.

Wernle, P. Die synoptische Frage, Leipzig, 1899. Ch. VII, n. 8.

Windisch, H., Johannes u. die Synoptiker, Leipzig, 1926. (Untersuchungen zum NT, Heft 12). Ch. VII, n. 20.

Zeitlin, S., Les 'dix-huit mesures,' REJ, 68.22 ff. Ch. V, n. 39.

Zuckermandel, M., Tosefta, Mischna u. Boraitha, Frankfurt a.M., 2 v., 1908-9, Ch. VII, n. 16.

ed., Tosephta, ed. 2, Jerusalem, 1937. See index.

Zunz, L., Die gottesdienstlichen Vorträge der Juden, 2 ed., ed. N. Brüll, Frankfurt a.M., 1892. Ch. IV, n. 37, n. 40.

PASSAGES DISCUSSED

Note: Passages containing translations are starred.
Material cited in the notes is referred to by the number of the note.
Thus 3.6 means chapter 3, note 6, in the notes.
Material cited in the text is referred to by the number of the note which the citation precedes. Thus 3 b n 6 means chapter 3 before note 6, in the text.
Material in appendix B is referred to by the numbers given the passages there cited, Gospel sermons outlined in ch. 4 are referred to by the letters assigned them in that chapter. Thus B 4 means passage no. 4 of appendix B, and 4 B means the sermon numbered B in ch. 4. A and C standing alone refer to the appendices.
Three detailed discussions (in ch. 3, of the material in appendices A and B, in ch. 4, of the sermons there outlined, and in ch. 7, of the material in appendix C) have not been indexed.

I. Rabbinic material

Alenu 6 b n 5

Kaddish 6 b n 5*

The Mishnah
as a whole - 7 b n 17
Abodah Zarah
as a whole I.60
Abot
1.11 - 8 b n 11*
1.12-14 - 5 b n 36
1.13-14 - 5 b n 25
2.1 - B 107*
2.2 - B 108*
2.3 - 4.7
2.9 - 2.67, 3 b n 11
2.14 - B 109*
2.15 - B 110*
2.16 - B 111*
3.2 - B 112*, 8 b n 3*
3.6 - 8 b n 5*
3.11 - 3 b n 12
3.17 - 8 b n 7*
4.2 - B 113*
4.10 - B 114*
4.11 - 1.9
4.12 - 4 b n 9

5.1 - B 115*
5.2 - B 116*
5.11-14 - B 117*
5.18 - 3 b n 12*
5.19 - 2 b n 65, 3 b n 25, 3.44
Baba Mezia
6.6 - 2 b n 65
Bekorot
5.4 - 6.7
Berakot
2.5-7 - 5 b n 25*
4.2 - 2 b n 65
9 end - 2 b n 85
Bezah
2.6 - 2.15
Demai
as a whole - 1.60
2.2 - 6 b n 5*
5.3 - 2.98
Eduyot
1.3 - 5.28
1.5 - 5.25*
2.2 - 5.28
2.3 - 5.28
2.4-10 - 5.29
2.8 - 5.31*
3.10 - 2.15

TANNAITIC PARALLELS TO THE GOSPELS

Eduyot (contd)
5.6 - 5.27, 28
7. - 5.28
7.7 - 4 b n 15
8. - 5.28

Erubin
2.6 - 5 b n 24*
4.8 - 3.54
5.1 - 3.54
9.3 - 3.59

Gittin
as a whole - 1.60
5.5 - 5 b n 33
6.5 - 2.94

Hagigah
1.8 - 2 b n 65

Hallah
2.7 - B 105*

Kelim
as a whole - 1.60
5.10 - 4 b n 15
8.2 - 2.31
25.9 - 2.31
26.2 - 4 b n 7
28.6 - ib.

Ketubot
9.6 - 3.59
10.5 - 3.54

Kiddushin
4.14 - B 106*, 6 b n 5*

Kilayim
2.2 - 2.73*

Kinnim
as a whole - 1.60
3.3 - 2.98

Maaser Sheni
3.2 - 7 b n 21*

Makkot
1.7 - B 34
3.15 - B 71, 72

Middot
as a whole - 1.60

Nazir
7.3 - 2.73*

Nedarim
8.1 - 3.59
9.6 - 2.94
9.10 - 5 b n 25*
11.12 - 2.94

Negaim
8.10 - 3.54

Niddah
10.6 - 2.94

Peah
1-3 appendix C*
1.1 - 3 b n 52*
4.11 - 7 end

Sanhedrin
7.4 - 2 b n 65
10.1 - 3 b n 12*, b n 31, b n 32

Shabbat
as a whole - 1 b n 34
1.3 - 2.73*
1.4-5 - 5 b n 39
5.4 - 4 b n 1*
10.4 - 2.73*

Shebiit
9.9 - B 104*
10.3 - 2.92*

Shebuot
3.5 - 3.59
8.3 - 2 b n 119*
8.6 - 2 b n 119

Sotah
as a whole - 1.60
1.4 - 2.15
1.7 - 6 b n 2*, b n 5*
5.2-5 - 5 b n 35, b n 39
8.1 - 4 b n 38*
9.9 - 2.92*

Taanit
2.1 - 4 b n 38*
3.8 - 2.18; 4 b n 14

Tebul Yom
4.5 - 2.94

Teharot
3.7 - 2.98

Terumot
2.1 - 2.73*

Yadayim
4.1-4 - 5 b n 39

Yoma
as a whole - 1.60
4.1 - 4 b n 15
6.2 - 4.3
6.8 - 4 b n 15*
8.9 - 4 b n 37

Zebahim
1.3 - 5 b n 39

PASSAGES DISCUSSED

209

TANNAITIC PARALLELS TO THE GOSPELS

Midrash Tannaïm (contd)
22.17 - 5.33
23.23 - 6 b n 4; B 85*
25.15 - B 86*
31.14 - B 87*, 88*
32.6 - 2 b n 62*
32.34 - B 89*
32.35 - B 90*
33.7 - B 91*

Mekilta to Dt. (in Midrash Tannaïm)
11.28 - 3 b n 11
12.9 - B 83*
12.29 - B 24
13.17 - 3 b n 11

Sifra
as a whole - 7 b n 1
1.2 - 2.82
2.1 - 2.82
4.2 - 5 b n 39*
4.4 - 2.82
4.22 - 2.82
5.1 - 2.82
5.17 - B 32*, 33*, 34 *
5.23 - 2.82
7.33 - 5 b n 25, B 35*
8.29 - B 36*
10.3 - B 37*
14.3 - 2.82
14.21 - 2 b n 96*
15.2 - 2.82
15.3 - 2.82
15.10 - 2.82
15.13 - 2.82
15.33 - 2.94
18.2 - B 38*
18.3 - B 39*
18.5,14,15,19 - B 38
18.27 - B 39
19.18 - 6 b n 5*
19.37 - B 38
22.27 - 2.82, 98
22.31,33 - B 38
25.9 - 2.98
25.23 - 8 b n 5*
26.2 - B 38
26.3 - 2.98
26.9 - 3 b n 15*; B 40*
27.28 - 2 b n 116*

Shemoneh Esreh v.s.
The Eighteen Benedictions

Sifre on Deuteronomy
as a whole - 7 b n 1
1.1 - B 55*
1.6 - B 56*
1.9 - 2.116
3.23 - 4 b n 41*
6.4 - 2 b n 95*; 5 b n 34
6.5 - 4.40; B 57*
6.7 - B 58*
11.10 - 8 b n 10*
11.12 - B 59*, 60*
11.13 - 4 b n 44*; B 61*
11.14 - B 62*
11.16 - 3 b n 11
11.22 - 3 b n 11, b n 12; 5 b n 24;
    8 b n 10*
11.26,28 - 3 b n 11
11.29 - B 63*
12.5 - 6 b n 5*
12.20 - B 64*
12.23f - 2.81,82
12.29 - B 65*
13.18 - 6 b n 5*
15.4 - B 66*
15.10 - B 67*
15.19 - B 7
17.14 - B 24, 82
18.9 - B 24
18.14 - B 68*
19.17 - 4.8
21.18 - 1.22
22.17 - 5.33
23.8 - B 69*
23.21 - B 70*
23.23 - 6 b n 4*
25.3 - B 71*, 72*
25.15 - B 73*
26.1 - B 24
26.9 - B 74*
29.9 - 2.101*
32.1 - B 75*
32.2 - 5 b n 25*
32.4 - 4 b n 15; 8 end*; B 76*
32.9 - B 77*
32.36 - 3 b n 12
32.38 - 3 b n 12*
32.47 - B 78*

Sifre on Deuteronomy (cont)
32.48-50 - 2.116
33.6 - B 79*
33.21 - B 80*

Sifre on Numbers
as a whole - 7 b n 1
6.26 - 4.40, b n 41*
9.8 - 4 b n 9; 6 b n 2*
10.29 - 6 b n 5*; B 41*
11.6 - 8 end*
11.21-2 - 2 b n 95*; 5 b n 35
12.8 - B 42*
12.15 - 6 b n 2, b n 5
15.31 - 2.2; 3 b n 11
15.36 - 6 b n 2
15.41 - B 43*, 44*
18.20 - 3 b n 12
27.5 - 6 b n 2
27.22 - B 45*
28.26 - 4 b n 16*

Sifre Zutta
as a whole - 7 b n 1
5.28 - B 46*
6.26 - B 47*
10.29 - B 48*
10.32 - B 49*
11.31 - B 50*
15.30f - 3 b n 11
15.41 - B 38, 51*
18.31 - B 52*
27.1 - B 53*
28.2 - B 54*

The Eighteen Benedictions
.13 (Palestinian text) - B 1*
.13 (Present text) - B 2*

Tosefta
as a whole - 7 b n 1
Abodah Zarah T
2.5-7 (462) - 1 b n 23*
7.2 (471) - 2.94
Baba Batra T
1.3 (398) - 2 b n 65
Bekorot T
6.15 (541) - 2 b n 96*
Berakot T
3.7 (6) - 6 b n 5

3.20 (8) - 4 b n 14
4.16-18 (10-11) - 5 b n 39*, B 92*
7.13 (16) - B 93*
Bikkurim T
1.2 (100) - 2 b n 96*
Demai T
3.4 (49) - 2.94
Eduyot T
1.1 (454) - 8 b n 9*
1.3 (455) - 5.28
1.4 (455) - 5.26
1.7 (455) - 5.32*
1.8 (455)-1.15 (456) - 5.29,30,31
1.14 (456) - 5 b n 33*
2.9 (458) - 5.27
3.1 (459) - 5.28, 2 b n 97*
Gittin T
1.1 (323) - 2.94
6.9 (329) - 2.98
Hagigah T
2.1 (233) - 8 b n 8*
3.2-3 (236) - 2.106
Hallah T
2.10 (99) - B 94*
Hullin T
2.17 (503) - 6 b n 4
2.22 (503) - 1 b n 19; 3.64; 4 b n 14*
10.16 (512) - B 103*
Kelim T, Baba Kamma
1.6 (569) - 2 b n 76
        Baba Mezia
2.14 (580) - 2.65
Ketubot T
8.2-3 (270) - B 98*
Kiddushin T
5.16 (343) - B 106
5.15 (343) - 6 b n 5
Maaser Sheni T
2.11 (89) - 7 b n 21*
4.12 (94) - 2.98
5.1 (95) - 2.98
Mikwaot T
1.2 (652) - 2.98
3.4 (655) - 2 b n 96*
6.3 (658) - 2.98
Moed Katan T
2.15 ff. (231) - 5 b n 25
Negaim T
6.1 (625) - B 101

TANNAITIC PARALLELS TO THE GOSPELS

Niddah T
1.6 (641) - 2.98
Oholot T
16.1 (613) - 2.98
16.10 (614) - 2.98
Parah T
3.8 (632) - 3 b n 17
Peah T
1 - Appendix C *
2.16 (20) - 7 end
4.17 (24) - B 67
4.18 ff. (24) - 6 b n 3
Pesahim T
1.27–28 (157) - 4 b n 16*; 5 b n 39*
4.2 (162) - 5 b n 39*
4.3 (163) - 1.31
Sanhedrin T
6.6 (424) - 4 b n 14
8.3 (427) - 4.13
11.6 (431) - B 101*
12.9 ff (433) - 3 b n 12
13.5 (434) - 3 b n 11
13.6 (435) - B 102* ·
14.1 (436) - B 101
Shabbat T
1.16 ff (111) - 5 b n 39
6.6 (117) - 2 b n 103*
10.1 f (123) - 1 b n 13
10.13 (124) - 1 b n 13
15.16 (134) - 6 b n 5 *

Shebuot T
3.4 (449) - 3 b n 12*
Sotah T
3.1 (295) - 6 b n 2, b n 5
5.12-6.11 (302-6) - 5 b n 34, b n 35
6.6-11 (304-6) - 2.95
7.9 (307) - B 99*
7.21 (309) - B 100*
13.8 (319) - 4 b n 14*
Sukkah T
4.28 (200) - B 95*
Taanit T
1.8 (215) - 4 b n 38*
Temurah T
4.11 (556) - 7 b n 17*
Terumot T
8.17 (40) - 2.98
Yadayim T
16-18 (683) - 5 b n 39
Yebamot T
4.4 (244) - B 96*
4.8 (245) - B 97*
Yom Hakkippurim T
2.4 (183) - 4 b n 16
5.11 (191) - 3 b n 12
Yom Tob T
2.6 (203) - B 23
Zabim T
2.9 (678) - 7 b n 17*

II. New Testament Material

Acts
1.18 - 3 b n 62*
2.40 - 4.23
3.20 - 4.23
9.11 - 3.65
9.15 - 3 b n 58*
10.14 - 2 b n 106
10.28 - 2 b n 106
10.42 - 4.23
11.8 - 2 b n 106
17.23 ff - 4 b n 22*
17.30–31 - 4 b n 23*
19.13 - 4.14

Gospels

Jn
as a whole - 2 b n 13; 7 b n 1, b n 20;
    8 b n 5
1. - 2 b n 11
1.1-3 - 8 b n 10*
1.11 - 8 b n 5*
1.14 - 2 b n 113; 4.8; 8.4 *
1.38-9 - 2.68 *
1.45-7 - 2.65*, 67, 68 *
3.2 - 2.70 *
3.7 - 2.80 *

Mat (contd)

5.5 - 2 b n 64*
5.6 - 2 b n 62*
5.11-12 - A*
5.19 - 2 b n 75*
5.21-44 - 3.21; 8.5
5.22 - 1 b n 21
5.32 - 2 b n 93
5.34 - 6 b n 4*
5.46-8 - A*, B 30
6.1-2 - A*
6.5 - A*
6.9f - 6 b n 5*
6.13ff - 6 b n 5*
6.19ff - 6 b n 3
6.22-3 - 7 end *
6.24 - 6.6
6.25ff - 4 b n 38
6.26 - 6 b n 5*
6.30-34 - 6 b n 5*
7.2 - 6 b n 1*, b n 5*
7.1-6 - 4.30
7.7 - 6 b n 5*
7.7-11 - 4.31
7.11 - 6 b n 5*
7.13-14 - 3 b n 11
7.15 - 4.32
7.21ff - 4 b n 43
7.24 - 8 b n 7*
7.28 - 2.97*
8.12 - 3.9*
9.16 - 4 b n 7
10 - 4 b n 26
10.4 - 1 b n 11
10.5-42 - 4 D*
10.25 - 8 b n 5*
10.32-3 - 8 b n 4
10.40-42 - 8 b n 5*; A*
11. - 4 b n 24
11.11 - 4 b n 9
11.24 - 3 b n 11
11.29-30 - 8 b n 4
12. - 4 b n 24
12.30 - 7 end *
13. - 4 b n 24
13.11 - 8.7
13.12 - 6 b n 2
13.17 - 8 b n 5*
13.24-42 - 3 b n 8
13.42,50 - 3.9 *

14.12-13 - 7 end *
15.6 - 2 b n 92*
15.26 - B 23
16.17 - 4 b n 8
16.18 - 2 b n 103*
16.22-3 - 2 b n 100
16.24 - 2 b n 102
17.25 - 2.22*
18.5 - 8 b n 5
18.6f - 2 b n 65
18.20 - 8 b n 3*; 8.2
18.28 - 6 b n 7*
19.16-17 - 2 b n 113*
19.27-9 - 2 b n 65; 3 b n 24*, 43
19.30 - 3 b n 22
20.1 - 3.22
20.1-15 - 3 b n 13*; 6 b n 2
20.14 - 2 b n 65
20.16 - 3 b n 18*
20.28 - 3.5
21.5 - 2 b n 46
21.31-2 - 3 b n 27*
22.13 - 3.9*
22.38 - 6 b n 5*
22.40 - 2 b n 65
23.2-39 - 4 F*
23.27 f - 7.17
24.4-25.46 - 4 G*
24.13 - 4.35
24.42 - 4 b n 38
24.51 - 3.9*
25.13 - 4 b n 38
25.29 - 6 b n 2
25.30 - 3.9*
25.31-46 - 3 b n 8
25.35-40 - 8 b n 5*
25.41-2 - 3 b n 9*
26.6-13 - 4.38
26.25 - 2.76
26.28 - 3.5
26.64 - 2.2,76
26.70 - 2 b n 117*
27.11 - 2.76
28.1 - 2 b n 103

Mk

as a whole - 7 b n 1
1. - 2 b n 11
1.2 - 4.3
1.14 - 7.19

214